PRAISE FOR *BIG TECH IN FINANCE*

'A deep dive into the fast-changing frontier of money from blockchain and Big Tech to Web3.'

Ronit Ghose, Global Head, Future of Finance, Citi

'Essential reading for anyone who thinks they understand the ongoing transformation of the orthodox geopolitical landscape. A brilliant examination of the fact that what matters is who owns banks, not tanks. The ownership of data, including your identity, who controls marketing and fulfilment for SME e-commerce, who designs the prevailing digital token of exchange and how it facilitates global payments, will determine whether central banks and financial-services incumbents or fintech and Big Tech insurgents will control our destinies.'

Bob Wigley, Chairman, UK Finance

'This wide-ranging book is a must-read for builders and operators looking to tame the disruption happening in the financial industry. From exploring the role of centralized technology companies to understanding the infrastructure of decentralized blockchains, readers will learn about the most important levers of tomorrow's economic landscape.'

Lex Sokolin, Chief Cryptoeconomist, ConsenSys and founder of the *Fintech Blueprint* newsletter

'*Big Tech in Finance* is a must-read for anyone interested in the impact of digital on the finance industry. The book provides a comprehensive overview of how Big Tech companies and new technologies such as distributed ledgers are transforming the landscape, and how these trends are converging. The author's ability to break down complex concepts into clear and concise chapters makes this book accessible to readers with varying levels of expertise. Overall, it offers very valuable insights into the future of digital finance by explaining its history.'

Huy Nguyen Trieu, Co-founder of CFTE (Centre for Finance, Technology and Entrepreneurship)

'Many of us working in financial services innovation can clearly see that Big Tech is circling the banking and finance industry. In this book Igor Pejic describes why Big Tech is interested and what they will probably do next. What is more interesting is what should be done about it – banning them would deprive us of the innovation and improvement they will bring. Big Tech needs to be monitored and regulated. It is time that regulators and governments worldwide realise that they need to up their game to address a fast-changing industry. A necessary book that is also fun. Don't miss it.'

Alessandro Hatami, Founder, Pacemakers.io and co-author of *Reinventing Banking and Finance*

'Provides a comprehensive and insightful analysis of the impact that Big Tech has on the finance industry. It is required reading for anyone interested in understanding the motivations, risks and opportunities associated with Big Tech's foray into finance and how to navigate the ever-changing world of blockchain technology.'

Karl Zettl, Co-Founder and CEO, Iknaio Cryptoasset Analytics

'Blockchain technology has the potential to revolutionize society for the better, and those institutions embracing this technology will thrive in a society where data is controlled by the user. Igor Pejic succinctly describes how the world is changing, what the impact will be on the financial services industry and how the future of money will change geopolitics. A vital read if you want to understand the future of finance.'

Mark van Rijmenam, strategic futurist, author and speaker

'This is a book that should make anyone interested in the future of our economy sit up and take notice. The world of the 2020s will be defined by the clash of the titans of tech and finance, and it will be a new wave of technologies – like blockchain – that will determine the winner. Igor Pejic's sharp and thoughtful book gives an up-to-the-minute view of what will drive the economy of the next ten years, and what is at stake for everyone today!'

Laura Stojcevic

Big Tech in Finance

How to prevail in the age of blockchain, digital currencies and Web3

Igor Pejic

KoganPage

First published in Great Britain and the United States in 2023 by Kogan Page Limited

2nd Floor, 45 Gee Street
London
EC1V 3RS
United Kingdom

8 W 38th Street, Suite 902
New York, NY 10018
USA

4737/23 Ansari Road
Daryaganj
New Delhi 110002
India

www.koganpage.com

Kogan Page books are printed on paper from sustainable forests.

ISBNs
Hardback 978 1 3986 0898 6
Paperback 978 1 3986 0896 2
Ebook 978 1 3986 0897 9

British Library Cataloguing-in-Publication Data
A CIP record for this book is available from the British Library.

Library of Congress Cataloging-in-Publication Data
Names: Pejic, Igor, author.
Title: Big tech in finance : how to prevail in the age of blockchain, digital currencies and the metaverse / Igor Pejic.
Description: London, United Kingdom ; New York, NY : Kogan Page, 2023. | Includes bibliographical references and index.
Identifiers: LCCN 2023003592 (print) | LCCN 2023003593 (ebook) | ISBN 9781398608962 (paperback) | ISBN 9781398608986 (hardback) | ISBN 9781398608979 (ebook)
Subjects: LCSH: Finance–Technological innovations. | Financial institutions–Effect of technological innovations on. | Digital currency. | Blockchains (Databases) | Metaverse.
Classification: LCC HG4515.5 .B45 20234 (print) | LCC HG4515.5 (ebook) | DDC 332.0285–dc23/eng/20230202
LC record available at https://lccn.loc.gov/2023003592
LC ebook record available at https://lccn.loc.gov/2023003593

Typeset by Integra Software Services, Pondicherry
Print production managed by Jellyfish
Printed and bound by CPI Group (UK) Ltd, Croydon, CR0 4YY

CONTENTS

ABOUT THE AUTHOR

Igor Pejic is a leading expert on tech-driven shifts in banking and finance. He is the author of *Blockchain Babel* (Kogan Page, 2019), finalist of the 2016 Bracken Bower Prize and winner of the Independent Press Award 2020 (technology category). *Blockchain Babel* was also a *Financial Times* book of the month.

Igor Pejic is the publisher of the valued industry newsletter *The New Frontier*. His articles and interviews regularly appear in the media, including the *New York Times*, *American Banker*, Bloomberg and PwC's *strategy+business*.

A worldwide keynote speaker and expert panelist, he talks at large conferences as well as at private industry events and academic lectures. He has created online courses, white papers and bespoke analytic research about the long-term strategic impact of new tech.

He has held different management positions in banking and payments, currently at one of the largest banking groups in Europe. Before that, he worked as a management consultant advising *Fortune* 100 companies, as a business journalist, and as a lecturer at the University of Vienna.

For more information visit www.igorpejic.net.

Introduction

Like millions of people around the world Armando Aguilar invested his money in real estate. His logic was tried and tested: a finite amount of land meets an ever-increasing demand. There was one peculiarity, though, that made Aguilar feel not simply like a canny investor, but a pioneer: the land he purchased was not composed of soil and rocks, but of bits and bytes and pixels. It was not located in the US or the UK but in the Sandbox, a virtual reality existing only as an entry on a digital ledger. Such deals are harbingers of a new world, and they are getting more frequent among investors as well as businesses. 'I never thought corporations would jump onto the bandwagon so quickly. And still, none of the reports they publish capture the whole value and breadth of the digital economy. Our lives are moving online, that's undeniable. And somebody will monetize it, that's inevitable' (Aguilar, 2022).

Investments like these are not only fascinating because of the underlying assets, but because of the way they are executed. Aguilar bought the land without a bank, without a notary, and even without a government-issued fiat currency. Plus, should he ever need cash, he can drop his asset into an autonomous protocol that will lock his land up as collateral and the loan will be in his account in minutes. No bureaucracy, no credit checks, no banking fees. It is a new world and a new arena that will shape the future of finance. Yet this is only the peak of the iceberg.

The global monetary and financial system is currently being rewired at a scale and pace never seen before. Central banks are struggling to keep their money-printing monopoly. Commercial banks have the customer relationship routinely snapped away by Big Tech. And autonomous organizations composed of much code and no people are handling ever more complex (and risky) financial transactions.

For years the five tech juggernauts – Alphabet, Amazon, Meta, Apple and Microsoft – have been working hard to break into finance. It is a mega industry, but more importantly it is home to the most valuable type of customer data. Time and again technological breakthroughs are playing into the hands of Big Tech. First the triumph of the smartphone turned them into gatekeepers, handing them a unique position in the very heart of money: payments. Then APIs (application programming interfaces) triggered a land rush on financial services. APIs are like glue that lets two computer programs speak to each other. For tech companies APIs meant they could build banking apps and easily link them to the backend machines of licensed banks. But their ambition is larger than ruling the frontend: capture everything but the banking licence itself.

Building killer applications and working their way along the value chain is just the opening gambit. While projects such as Apple or Google Pay were confined to one layer, the invention of blockchain technology lets Big Tech compete on the level of assets, settlements, gateways and applications. In *Blockchain Babel* (2019), I warned that distributed ledger technology would let Big Tech break into banking. Four years later that prediction has turned into reality. Yet the scale and pace at which it has happened surpassed my wildest imaginings. Amazon's cloud powers the vast majority of cryptocurrencies. Google's capital fuels the rise of blockchain unicorns. And Facebook attempted to issue a global mega-currency to displace the US dollar as the world's hegemon. While the latter was quashed by lawmakers, the company, now rebranded as Meta, did not flinch; its next attempt, called Meta Pay, is already in the making.

This book tells the story of how a handful of mavericks invented cryptocurrencies to eliminate centralized institutions but in doing so handed Big Tech a tool for the largest power grab in the history of finance. I will show how the tech tycoons lunged at the opportunity and what strategies they are pursuing. We will see how blockchain, a technology antithetical to Big Tech's worldview, is finding its way into its investment portfolios, its product and strategy departments, its mobile applications and all the way into the number one priority projects.

A pivotal question of the book will be whether Big Tech's entry onto the banking stage is a blessing or a curse. Under the banner of usability and financial inclusion, data giants are rewriting the rules of our financial system. But regardless of how you feel about them biting banks' balance sheets, you should take notice. Their grab for our money might threaten the monetary sovereignty of states, stifle the free market and completely kill data privacy. The problem is, it might also boost innovation, slash consumer costs, and set the stage for an autonomous economy. Which is it going to be?

Things get even more intricate. The battle waged over the future of money is also critical to the geopolitical clash between the US and China. For decades the US has run the global financial system thanks to a powerful dollar and pioneering institutions such as SWIFT. Today, however, China intends to challenge this order by a combination of betting big on blockchain and its tech titans. A digital yuan, issued with the help of Tencent and WeChat, is supposed to give the currency a foothold across the Chinese techno-sphere and beyond. Hence, tech behemoths' involvement with finance is not only a question of financial stability, competition, innovation, privacy and all the other things, but of vital geopolitical significance. Whether they can do more harm or good is still up for debate.

While regulators are struggling to find the right balance between promise and peril, central and commercial banks are countering with their own centralized blockchains. Herds of unicorns are pushing the technology's potential to its limit. The battlefield is a Wild West in which gold diggers, robber barons and sheriffs vie to dominate tomorrow's autonomous economy. The companies with the best chances to succeed will be those that build what I have dubbed the 'super money engine', a hub that can handle all types of on- and off-chain assets, execute smart contracts, and run complex decentralized apps.

Instead of the frontier drawing to a close, more new battlegrounds are emerging. The stakes are raised. I will discuss how smart contracts heave automation to a new level, how the combinatorial nature of decentralized finance (DeFi) does the same with systemic risks and how money in the metaverse might turn out to be an early laboratory in which decisive proxy wars will be fought between Big Tech, Big Banking and Big Government.

For this book I have interviewed leaders from each affected group, all with vivid stories and sharp minds. I spoke to the early monetary economist who inspired the cryptographers behind bitcoin, as well as to the US's leading voice against tech monopolies, who felt Big Tech's grip on his own career and those of his employees. I spoke to regulators, bank managers and tech executives who shared their aspirations and anxieties off-record. And I spoke to entrepreneurs and investors who have earned and lost millions, and are back on the hunt for the next big thing in the future of finance.

Despite their unique angles and starkly opposing visions, all interviewees agreed on one thing: Big Tech is about to rewire the global monetary and financial system at a scale and pace never seen before. Whether you are a commercial or central bank, challenger company, lawmaker or regulator, it is time to act on it. *Big Tech in Finance* is a springboard to do exactly that.

In this book banks and businesses will learn about the strategies Big Tech has been using and will be using to enter the financial world and what impact this has on their market. They will understand how to counter this trend or possibly even benefit from it, especially by understanding what they have to do on the major battlefield, i.e. payments. In the end, readers will have the insights to build a top-level strategy around the most decisive technology of the coming decades: blockchain. They will identify the major actor groups and dynamics on each important tech layer, recognize how to make platform principles work in their favour and learn which coming areas they should branch out into early in order to succeed in tomorrow's hybrid market in which the off-chain world merges with the on-chain one.

Reference

Aguilar, A (2022) Personal interview, 19 August

1

Finance as Big Tech's El Dorado

The high-tech era

In 2011 the famous venture capitalist Marc Andreessen declared to the world that it was being eaten by software (Andreessen, 2011). And it was. Legions of programmers kept biting industry after industry. Uber and herds of other unicorns fed on inefficiencies in distribution as well as legacy systems. And consumers around the world enjoyed the free leftovers. Have any of us recently paid for navigation or bought a dictionary? And when was the last time you visited a travel agent to find the best flight deal? The revolution that Andreessen described, however, had already started with innovative breakthroughs some 30 years earlier. Following a series of watershed moments, the internet officially went live in 1983. For the first time computer networks could communicate with every other computer on the planet thanks to a novel protocol called Transfer Control Protocol/Internetwork Protocol (TCP/IP).

Yet the networked age was really kicked off in 1995 when Netscape went public and triggered the dot-com boom. The company was behind *Navigator*, a web browser that commanded 70 per cent of the market (Campbell, 2020). One of the two founders was the 24-year-old Marc Andreessen.

The public gold-rush mood around the initial public offering (IPO) was palpable. The cyberspace had so far been visited only by tech-savvy pioneers, but most people had heard stories about it. And for the first time the promises of the web could be turned into massive fortunes; at least that was what investors believed. After all, Netscape had yet to turn a profit. And investors believed it so hard, they were ready to put their money into the brainchild of a just-out-of-college graduate who dressed as if he were going to a frat party rather than to a boardroom. Andreessen also fired up his brand with provocative metaphors, for example by likening his competitor Microsoft to the Godfather. Eventually, he became the first web superstar (Campbell, 2020).

The *Wall Street Journal* back then swooned that it took Netscape only a minute to become as valuable as the 43-year-old General Dynamics Corp (Baker, 1995). Despite the euphoria, no one could have imagined the way technology companies would reshape the world in the coming decades.

Following the shakeout in 2000 during the burst of the dot-com bubble, a legion of survivors and newcomers rose to build the digital economy we take for granted today. The new age needed databases and hardware, so early computing giants such as IBM and Oracle regained strength by building the invisible infrastructure of our daily lives. Software experts such as Adobe and social media grandees like Twitter made our work easier and our personal lives richer. PayPal enabled us to shop safely online and thus fuelled the rise of e-commerce.

All of these tech companies are still around. They have survived a market competition far more brutal than what was known in the offline world. Netscape, on the other hand, didn't make it. It fell prey to the intense competition and the winner-takes-all mechanisms of the digital age. Microsoft's Internet Explorer eventually won the browser wars and Netscape was acquired by AOL before the end of the millennium (Campbell, 2020).

Tier-two tech vs Big Tech

PayPal, IBM, Oracle – these are all corporates with market valuations well in excess of $100bn (CompaniesMarketCap.com, 2022). Yet as impressive as they are, those technology experts can best be described as tier-two tech, because the digital age has also given birth to a cohort of the most powerful companies in the history of business, collectively called Big Tech.

Big Tech is sometimes also referred to as the Big Five. The term is based on the five US companies that make up this group: Alphabet (Google's parent company), Amazon, Meta Platforms (Facebook's parent company), Apple and Microsoft. On a global scale China's Tencent and Alibaba complete the roster.

It is hard to do these companies justice in a couple of sentences, so I will let the most impressive figures speak. Of the world's largest 10 companies, seven are tech giants. Of the largest seven, six are tech giants (Wallach, 2021). The pace with which they have reached this dominance is equally striking; in 2008 only Microsoft and Google made the list (Johnston, 2018). In 2022 Apple became the first US company ever to surpass a corporate valuation of $3 trillion (Leswing, 2022). It is more worth than Germany's 30 largest public corporations traded at the DAX *combined* (*The Economist*, 2021a).

Also, whereas corporate behemoths of the past focused on certain territories and one industry, e.g. AT&T on telecommunications and Walmart on retailing, Big Tech knows no such restrictions. The Big Five are capturing industry after industry. And even where they are not competing directly, they are part of the value chain. The three largest computer clouds today are Microsoft's cloud business, Amazon's AWS and Google Cloud Platform. Six out of ten companies using hosted software depend on those three tech behemoths (*The Economist*, 2021b).

Not even in the times of Rockefeller and Carnegie was there a comparable concentration of power and wealth, neither in the hands of corporations, nor their founders. Not to mention the global reach. This massive consolidation was made possible by technologies that enabled blitzscaling – exponential corporations. As Azeem Azhar (2021) explains, they have benefited from the first exponential age. In today's times, high-tech innovation is hitting the world at a speed so staggering, neither institutions nor competitors can keep up. Network effects and platform economics do the rest.

And most importantly, the digital economy runs on a different resource than steam or electricity: it runs on data. And data is prone to what Jim Collins (2001) described as the 'flywheel effect'. Very simply put, the more data you have, the better services you can offer because you know the customers' preferences. This in turn brings you more customers and thus additional data, which in turn improves your product, and so on. Whatever part of the flywheel you feed, it will accelerate your business.

The Big Tech worldview

The resulting super-growth of Big Tech has also fed sky-high expectations that go beyond dividends and swelling share prices. Politicians and societies aren't modest either with their demands. In their eyes, platforms such as Facebook or Google's YouTube should eliminate information asymmetries all over the world by giving everybody access to information. Yet at the same time, according to those people, they should eliminate hate speech, cooperate with law enforcement and fight fake news. And do all this in all languages of the world.

But Big Tech itself has sparked their image of omnipotence. Looking for an inspiring purpose, founders have never shied away from setting world-changing goals. With his space program Blue Origin, Amazon's founder Jeff Bezos wants to colonize space to preserve planet earth and turn humankind into an interplanetary species. In fact, Bezos has been obsessed with space flight since high school (*Wired*, 1999). Google's self-proclaimed mission is nothing less than to organize the entire 'world's information and make it universally accessible and useful' (Google, no date). And Jack Ma, the founder of Alibaba, claims that he is not at the head of a regular company, but an entire economy that by 2036 will connect billions of users on which 100 million businesses depend (Skinner, 2018).

Their optimism stems from their techno-centrism. More importantly though, Big Tech runs on an *application*-centric worldview in particular. Because the data flywheel spins fastest on the application layer, Big Tech was able to grow exponentially. The success spiral for pure hardware and infrastructure companies is not moving even remotely as quickly.

This fixation on the application layer also explains the fascination with artificial intelligence (AI). It is the very crown of what you can do with the troves of data you collect (Gilder, 2018). In the eyes of many futurists, AI is the most powerful tool in history that will turn humans into God-like creators of intelligent life. Tech evangelists such as Yuval Harari ascribe a religious certainty to the progress of software development. Books like his *Homo Deus* (2018) are enjoying huge popularity; they postulate human omnipotence, if only we deploy AI correctly.

Never mind the misnomer that AI couldn't be farther from human-like intelligence. While advances in AI sub-disciplines like machine learning, predictive analytics or optical character recognition helped with process industrialization, we are not one step closer to machine consciousness, creativity and free will than we were in the 1950s, when the term AI was coined. The latter would have been needed if we were to talk about *real* intelligence.

The digital wave that started rolling with Netscape in 1995 is still washing through the world. The Covid-19 pandemic has made it painfully clear that there is still so much catching up to do in terms of digitalization. The Big Five saw a 40 per cent rise in revenue and a 90 per cent hike in profitability within one full year of the pandemic. Big companies were doing well in general, but the market was tilted even more towards Big Tech. Whereas their combined value made up 17.5 per cent of the S&P 500 in January 2020, it had climbed to 22 per cent in October 2021 (*The Economist*, 2021b).

Cracks in the digital paradigm

Yet, as I have written elsewhere (Pejic, 2021), first signs are appearing that the age of concentrated big data has overreached its zenith. The most worrying trend is IT security. We all know the horror stories about computer bugs and hacks that have exposed personal and critical data of millions of customers. Even worse than credit card details and passwords are tax data and medical conditions. And the research of Nicole Perlroth (2021), a *New York Times* cybersecurity reporter, paints an even grimmer picture. Thanks to zero-day software bugs, there is almost no device that hackers cannot infiltrate unnoticed.

The costs of cybersecurity are exploding and still cannot keep up with the threat. On top, the pandemic has led to a sevenfold increase in phishing attacks (Aiyer, Caso and Sorel, 2022). IT experts try to patch systems and retrofit security into them. Data security is treated as an additional layer, rather than an architectural design. But just like with our DNA, such critical functions cannot be added retrospectively. They need to be part of the initial design, the initial architecture. And security was not part of the web's DNA. It was built to openly share information, not value.

Is the new frontier antithetical to tech juggernauts?

As our lives have almost completely moved online, sharing information is not enough. We are increasingly sending money and value and these transactions become part of our daily lives.

With Netscape's mega-IPO, Marc Andreessen was at the forefront of the digital age in 1995. Today, he is among those pushing a new frontier. Through his venture capitalism firm Andreessen Horowitz he has invested a fortune into blockchain companies such as Coinbase, Compound and Uniswap. In 2021 his firm even launched a crypto-fund worth $2.2 billion (Rooney, 2021).

The initial core idea of blockchain was antithetical to Big Tech, but those who believe that one guard of giants will simply be swapped with another will be disappointed. As this book argues, rather the opposite will happen. Andreessen himself is the best illustration. Despite his unwavering belief in blockchain technology, he sits on the board of Facebook's parent company Meta (Meta Investor Relations, no date). Indeed, the interest he has taken in the metaverse points very clearly in one direction: Big Tech and blockchain will merge. And the moment of truth will happen in the financial services industry.

More than just a city of gold

Each of the Big Five followed the same motto to grow to the behemoths they are now: capture dominance in your core business, protect it by all means and spread your tentacles to other industries. This means that they have first reached hegemony in search, e-commerce, hardware, software and social media respectively. Then they snapped up existing and upcoming rivals. When reaching a certain scale, start-ups frequently talk about the 'kill zone', in which they are either acquired or lose in the market. Most challengers opt for the former, which can be highly lucrative (as Instagram can tell you). Facebook dished out the highest price per employee ever for the young platform: $77 million (Thompson, 2012).

Once the battles in their core business were won, they reached for other industries. Those were usually bordering existing business fields and their major competences gave them a competitive edge.

To glimpse into the future, look at Big Tech's acquisition strategy

Today Big Tech controls mega-industries such as communication, entertainment and retailing. Those are big revenue drivers, but equally important is their strategic significance: they deliver data at crucial points in people's lives such as when their attention is captured (social media), when they actively take interest in a topic (search) or when they purchase items (e-commerce).

After 16 months of intense investigations about the state of the digital economy and aggregating 1.3 million documents, a US Congressional Committee issued a report (Judiciary Antitrust Subcommittee, 2020) that lay bare the sheer scale of Google, Amazon, Facebook and Apple. Much can be learned, especially from the acquisitions that almost always gave away the next steps of the giants.

Google acquired Motorola Mobility as part of their effort to gain a grip over today's most-used device – the smartphone. It had entered navigation because it understood the synergy with the smartphone and realized how much location data would be worth when combined with other information. Recently, it is acquiring many AI companies, the very technology that can best process its greatest resource: data. Amazon acquired the film database IMDB in 1998, long before it built its streaming service Amazon Prime. Apple acquired the music service SoundJamMP, a move that hinted at the launch of iTunes one year later.

The finance industry is more akin to the Holy Grail

The list could fill dozens of pages, but the principle is always the same. To see where Big Tech is heading, a look at recent acquisitions will take you a long way.

There is, however, one industry that can be considered Big Tech's ultimate target, an industry that has spurred their imagination more than any other: financial services. It is among the largest economic sectors by and of itself. The global financial market will reach $22.5 trillion in 2021, with a compound annual growth rate of 9.9 per cent (GlobeNewswire, 2021). In short, finance is an El Dorado, full of gold in the form of revenue and a guarantee that Big Tech's balance sheets will continue to swell the way they have in past years.

But actually, finance is more to Big Tech than riches beyond measure: it is its Holy Grail, that equips its finder with miraculous powers. Financial services make money and almost all other value flow through the world. It is the lifeblood of the economy. Whether it is the movement of money, the issuance of loans or insuring risky ventures – everything happening in finance causes a wave or at least a ripple everywhere else.

Sometimes banking innovation poses a risk, as in the late 2000s when risky investment products triggered the global financial meltdown. But for the most part of human history, it has been fuelling economic expansion. Whether it was the invention of coins and bills, double-entry bookkeeping, stock exchanges, bonds or the gold standard – if it weren't for those genius breakthroughs, we wouldn't be discussing Big Tech. There would be no tech at all.

Most people know Sir Isaac Newton as the brilliant physicist and father of our understanding of gravity. Few know that he was also the master of the Royal Mint and thus effectively the most influential central banker of his time. In this position he revolutionized the monetary system as much as he had revolutionized physics. How? Isaac Newton launched the world economy onto the gold standard, which meant that he fixed the value of the British pound to the gold in circulation. Henceforth enterprises could assume reliable exchange rates and stable interest rates, which allowed them to put their money behind more ambitious, riskier and long-term projects around the world.

The gold standard is not in use anymore – President Richard Nixon abandoned it in 1971 – but without Isaac Newton's groundbreaking switch at that time, commerce, capitalism and explorations would have never taken off the way they did.

This episode shows that entering financial services also means taking a seat behind the steering wheel of the world economy. Getting into finance is profitable and grants power, yet there is another reason why Big Tech is obsessed with getting a foot into it. Becoming a lord of finance means you know who is sending money to whom, when, for what and how much. It tells you how much money people own, for what they are willing to take loans and what things they hold so dear that they are willing to dish out insurance premiums. In short, finance is not just feeding the data flywheel, it is turbocharging it. Amazon has been setting itself apart from the other tech giants because its data was closest to the purchase decision of the customer and thus more valuable than 'just' the information about what people are interested in. Now imagine how valuable it would be to know the real flows of value – not only on your platform, but in the entire customer's life.

Isn't techfin just fintech backwards?

Tech's involvement in the finance sector is almost as old as computing. Banks were among the first to realize the enormous potential of bits and bytes. They spent lavishly on big iron, i.e. the large mainframe computers that were used for mission-critical processing of large quantities of data. Many of the core banking systems built in that era were so powerful and so fundamental to banks' operations that they are still around. IT has become so important to finance that swapping a core banking system is routinely likened to exchanging a jet engine 35,000 feet above the ground.

But as we have seen in the last section, tech titans' appetites have grown. While B2B giants such as IBM didn't mind tinkering in the shadows and earning handsome profits, this is no option for Google or Apple. To keep the data flywheel spinning, they must offer financial services themselves. This has been clear to Western Big Tech for a long time, but their efforts finally went wild with the rise of the smartphone and the introduction of Google Pay in 2011.

The first steps into finance were taken outside of Silicon Valley

Yet the real trailblazer came from across the Pacific: Alibaba. In 2003 the Chinese e-commerce giant Alibaba launched Taobao, a platform on which third-party retailers could sell goods directly to Alibaba's customers. The US equivalent is Amazon's marketplace. Yet it was still the early days of e-commerce and trust in the sellers was even lower than in the US. So, to enable trade Alibaba took the money customers paid in escrow. This means Alibaba controlled the money paid by the buyer and only once it had confirmation that the good was delivered without damage did it release the funds to the seller. The system was nothing high-tech. On the contrary, employees were sending around orders via fax. But it worked. Taobao's sales grew and eventually in 2014 Alipay was spun out to handle the volume more systematically (Skinner, 2018).

Today Alipay is just one of Alibaba's many financial services that are pooled together in the Ant Group. Hence, it is no coincidence that it was the founder of Alibaba, Jack Ma, who stuck a label on Big Tech's finance projects: *Techfin* (Soo, 2016).

He was speaking at the China conference in 2016 and wanted to specifically distance tech titans' efforts from the buzzy fintech world. Ma sounded a philanthropic tone, claiming that his major motive to go into finance was financial inclusion. At first glance his argument seems sound. There are 1.7 billion unbanked people on earth without even access to the most basic financial services such as safely storing the few assets they own or taking a loan to start a small business (World Bank Group, 2017). Moreover, Alipay grew to what it is today largely thanks to bringing rural parts of the population into the financial system. Financial inclusion as the goal might still have been credible when Alipay was expanding to financially underdeveloped regions. In 2019, however, Alipay was also rolled out in the UK, not exactly a country suffering from a shortage of credit cards and banks.

Key characteristics of techfin

Putting aside the question of altruism, Jack Ma hit the nail on the head when it comes to the difference between fintech and techfin. In his view (quoted in Soo, 2016) fintechs do nothing more than improve the current financial system. They make it more efficient by using new technology, having less overhead and a more distinct focus. But essentially, they are in the business of making money with money.

Techfin is fundamentally different. It wants to completely overhaul finance. This is mostly a legitimate line you can draw, yet for many blockchain start-ups it could be said too that they target a new model of finance. Hence, it is more accurate to say that while fintech uses technology to improve finance, techfin uses finance to improve technology. In that regard Alibaba is a techfin archetype. Alipay was launched to facilitate e-commerce, not to make a profit. It is an adjacent service with the goal to make the platform more attractive.

This means that Big Tech has a completely different business model than fintech challengers, making them extremely dangerous for banking incumbents. If you are a finance colossus and a young upstart attacks your core business by offering lower fees, it is easy to outprice them on that particular service. You might have to swallow some losses, but you could fend them off. It is a game you know and dominate to perfection. So how do you handle a data giant that offers the same services as you, but makes them permanently free because its revenue comes from e-commerce or advertising?

Why techfin cooperation is tricky

Another thing worrying banks about techfins is the marketing model. Fintechs are start-ups. The number of their customers is negligible, and regardless of how well-funded they are, competing directly with banking incumbents is doomed. Hence, it is not surprising that more than three-quarters of fintech founders list cooperation with an established institution as the major strategic goal (Capgemini, LinkedIn and Efma, 2018). Getting to the large customer pools of retail banks is a sure way to exponential growth. So fintechs either get snapped up by big banks, or they integrate with them. Thanks to innovation such as application programming interfaces (API), technical compatibility has become rather easy today. But what fintechs are definitively not doing is making banks obsolete.

Data giants, on the other hand, have been global marketing machines. Despite running hardly any TV or radio campaigns, everybody in the world knows their brands. Even more, they are the world's dominant advertising players. Google and Facebook hold a digital ad duopoly, capturing far more than 50 per cent of ad dollars spent. Their closest rivals are other tech giants such as Amazon, Tencent and Alibaba (Cramer-Flood, 2021). Steve Jobs is the centre of many business school case studies because of his marketing genius. Apple products enjoy a cult-like following long after the death of the charismatic founder. Big Tech's marketing savvy has resulted in hitherto unseen user bases. As an example, Facebook has 2.9 billion active users (Statista, 2022). So, when Big Tech offers financial services, there is no need to run TV campaigns or buy ads in newspapers. Their heft lies in their highly active users.

Techfins and their obsession with payments

The last defining difference between fintech and techfin is the types of financial services they go after. While each fintech initially goes for a small and defined segment, fintech as a group is scattered. Most of their services fall either into payments, asset management, investing or financing. Some challengers also work on other use cases such as insurance or comparison platforms. In other words, there are plenty of loose screws in the banking world they can tighten. Techfins are much more specialized. As we will see in the coming chapters, payments has traditionally been at the heart of Big Tech's finance initiatives. And while some are starting to spread their tentacles to other finance domains, almost all of them start with monetary transfers.

Besides merging technology and finance, fintechs have little in common with Big Tech. Table 1.1 summarizes the five dimensions along which they can be distinguished.

TABLE 1.1 Fintech vs techfin characteristics

	Fintech	Techfin
Challengers	Start-ups	IT giants
Core business	Financial services	Technology
Business model	Fees and other traditional revenue streams	Platform improvement, data generation
Focus	Clear use cases in different financial segments	Predominantly payment
Market leverage	Partnerships	Own users

Facebook and WeChat want you to exchange more than cat pictures

Jack Ma might have been the first one to use the term *techfin*, but Ant Financial is definitively not the only company practising it. Its closest follower is in China itself: WeChatPay. With 550 million active users, it lags behind Alipay by 100 million (Curry, 2022) – not exactly an insurmountable gap considering the size of the Chinese market. WeChatPay is a central function of the WeChat messaging app and thus part of the powerful Tencent conglomerate that dominates Chinese social media, entertainment and gaming.

WeChat is a so-called 'super app'. It is not called that because it captures more than a billion users – though it does – but because it offers a one-stop-shop for them. Users can book a flight or hotel, pay at the store, chat with friends, send them money, play games or manage their wealth, all without ever leaving the app.

Super apps not only boast popular native features, but thanks to the mini-program capability, they can integrate third-party apps into the platform. This means that programmers don't need to build according to the specifications of the operating system and they don't need to build separate versions for Android and iOS either. Apps like WeChat are not just putting an additional home screen on the operating system but rewriting the rules and capturing the dominance of the smartphone.

Alipay is obviously another super app. And there are more. Line is a mega app from Japan that has even captured the market abroad in countries such as Thailand and Taiwan. Within one app, the user has access to messaging services, video on demand, manga cartoons, cab hailing, shopping, as well as the highly popular LinePay feature that lets you pay via QR code. The principle is similar to its Chinese counterparts.

Today super apps are known primarily in Asia. Facebook provides the best example that the concept hasn't been able to get a foothold in the US. It has separate apps for the social network and for its messenger, two extremely linked functionalities. Some shy super app attempts have been made though. Think Uber Eats. Or even better, PayPal. Besides the classic payments, it has added functionalities such as savings or buy-now-pay-later (BNPL) to its app. It is an attempt at diversification, but those are all still financial services. Overall, app integration in the Western world is in a fledgling state.

Why super apps have not spread to Europe and the US

Many market characteristics have prevented the rise of super apps so far in the US and Europe. First, a highly competitive and diversified ecosystem. China is a mobile-first country; users in the West come from a desktop world. On the big screens competition was so intense that often the only way to succeed was specialization. Mobile apps were just an add-on or extension.

Second, regulators see themselves as guardians of the free market and thus monopoly busters. This scrutiny has deterred large mergers. China, by contrast, has fostered state champions that leverage the market's scale and are easier to control.

Third, Europeans and Americans are sceptical towards governments and data centralization. (Data) privacy is regarded as a foundational value, and this concern is finding its way into harsh regulation such as the EU's General Data Privacy Regulation (GDPR). China is taking the opposite route. There is no inbred scepticism towards governmental authorities, as shown by the Social Credit System (Chen, 2018). It is a massive undertaking that grades the

Chinese on how good a citizen they are in the eyes of the Communist party. The two data giants have naturally been enablers of this system. Both Alibaba and Tencent have launched their own social credit systems. Citizens with a high score don't have to pay deposits for house rentals and can rent bikes for free via the platforms. Elicited data was by default shared with Alipay (Niewenhuis, 2018). For China's tech juggernauts this social credit program is like a mixture of a credit bureau and a loyalty scheme.

Fourth, and very importantly, those super apps can take off only if there is a shared payment platform holding those 'mini-programs' together. If there is no way of easily transferring value, say from your banking account to a ride-hailing service or from a messaging thread to your wealth management fund, then what is the added value of having another layer on top of your smartphone? It can't be to simply have one instead of two logins. Also, in the US and Europe, sharing data between apps or mini-programs is legally tricky, but if you provide the transaction services, data must inevitably go through your hands to deliver the service. In the US and in Europe, super apps will be trickier to pull off due to considerable cultural differences that shape the way we think about money. In most Western countries money is regarded as a private and isolated affair. You don't gift money to grownups, you don't talk about your salary and in most contexts you don't split a restaurant bill. Chinese culture has a much more social attitude towards money. People give monetary gifts to each other all the time. It is not unusual, for example, for a couple to gift each other a red envelope (Hongbao) with cash for their anniversary. You do it for the Chinese New Year, births, weddings and any other celebratory occasion. In fact, when WeChat launched a digital version of the red envelope, users went wild and bestowed WeChat Pay with the largest market catch-up in history, for the first time challenging Alipay's market dominance (Chen, 2018).

Payment features

Still some Western tech titans aspire to build super apps as well. Just like WeChat, Facebook has launched Facebook Pay as one of its first features beyond social media. Users add the payment details in their Facebook, WhatsApp or Instagram app – all part of Facebook's empire – and they can shop online, transfer value to friends or donate to charities. Since Facebook struck a deal with Shopify (Shopify, 2020) the company has also built a bridge to territory outside of the Facebook ecosystem. Shopify offers e-commerce payment modules for more than 1 million online retailers. Merchants using its module can thus offer Facebook and Instagram pay options within their native apps.

Facebook Pay is prototypical for the host of payment apps sweeping the market. It does not build its own payment system, but it wraps itself around existing payment providers such as PayPal and credit and debit card issuers.

As is typical for techfin, the customer can use the features completely for free. The goal is to flood the platform with customers, and even more importantly, to turn users into heavy users. Because every transaction produces more data and makes profiles more valuable for advertisers.

Though not part of the Big Five club, Uber illustrates the payment platform lock-in just as well. Since 2019 Uber Money has given customers 5 per cent cashback for everything they spend in the Uber universe, say by ordering at Uber Eats or using their ride-hailing service (Hazlehurst, 2019). The other side of the double-sided platform, Uber drivers, benefit even more. Thanks to the Uber direct debit account, they get earnings right after the drive instead of having to wait for the weekly payout. The credit card is offered by a traditional bank (Barclays). A neo-bank (Green Dot) powers the account and debit card. Unsurprisingly, all services are free of charge.

Of all tech companies, however, two are uniquely placed to capture the payment interface: Google and Apple.

Google and Apple let their mobile muscles play

I remember sitting through numerous partnership pitches some 10 years ago. Back then I was heading the marketing department of a large credit card company. Entrepreneurs enthusiastically showcased what they believed to be the future of payments. One founder had developed SIM card-based watches linked to a bank account. Another waved a plush giraffe in front of me, explaining that he had equipped it with a payment chip and that from now on I could leave my physical wallet at home. And yet another had stuck a contactless sticker on the back of his phone and proudly proclaimed that the days of Google and Apple were numbered.

It is easy to giggle at those ideas today, but consider that many of those presentations were before Apple Pay was even released and when credit cards in many markets were still working with magnetic stripes, not with chips. And all of those entrepreneurs and R&D visionaries had been tinkering with these prototypes for years before their big pitch. There was no such thing as Host Card Emulation back then, nor could you find a contactless terminal anywhere. Some of them were brilliant people, but the time and market were not ripe yet. They perfectly understood the value of the data generated at the payment terminal. What they didn't understand, though, was that Google and Apple had already won the mobile payments war before even releasing a single payment product.

Powerful gatekeepers

Google and Apple had both made an early bet on the proliferation and impact of smartphones on our daily lives. Since the invention of the iPhone, Apple had made a fortune on smartphone hardware. It was these devices that propelled it to become the most valued company in history. Yet the hegemony that Apple and Google reached with their mobile operating systems, Android and iOS respectively, has been at least equally decisive. It uniquely placed them to launch wallets, meaning that customers could store digital representations of their credit cards on their phones. Thanks to the introduction of NFC antennas (near field communication), it became possible to tap the phone to any contactless terminal and mimic a plastic card. This happened on a larger scale around the time the iPhone 6 was released. Mobile payments did more than digitalize cards; this had already happened the moment you could type in your card credentials at a webstore to make a purchase. What mobile payment really did was to provide a link from a digital ecosystem to the physical POS world. It is not so much different to what Chinese tech titans did with QR codes.

For the wallet providers, mobile payment was a cash machine. Banks and other card issuers had to pay Apple and Google a fee every time their own customers used their own cards. As the *Financial Times* reported back then, Apple charged banks 0.15 per cent in the US and somewhat less in the UK (Arnold, Felsted and Thomas, 2015). Depending on how much data you were willing to let Apple access, you could pay a bit more or less. Either way, it is a significant amount in the margin-thin payment business. As a comparison, in the EU interchange fees are capped at 0.2 per cent for debit cards or 0.3 per cent for credit cards in the consumer business. The UK has similar prices (Visa, 2020). In the US it can be 10 times that amount (Adyen, 2021), which explains why US banks were less price sensitive.

Unlike Apple, Google struggled to mainstream mobile payment. The project started as Google Wallet, turned into Android Pay, before it finally morphed into Google Pay. Even in 2021 it lagged behind Apple Pay, and even trailed Starbucks Pay in the US (eMarketer, 2021). That does not mean it has raised the white flag yet. It is still diversifying its features, for example by adding a peer-to-peer (or P2P) cross-border paying service (Trivedi, 2021b).

Apple was far more ruthless in wielding its gatekeeper power. Access to the NFC chip was granted to Apple Pay only. This effectively barred others such as banks or retailers from using the iPhone's technical capacities for payments. They were thus forced to provide any payment service out of Apple's wallet, feeding the company with data and fees. In an effort dubbed 'Lex Apple Pay', German legislators forced Apple in 2020 to grant others direct access to the NFC chip. The Colossus from Cupertino was found to be misusing its position to evade competition (Franck and Linardatos, 2021). This episode already foreshadows the critical role regulators will play as Big Tech elbows its way into banking.

Payment is the foundation of every real super app

For a long time, mobile payment failed to gain a foothold in the US and Europe. The existing card-based systems had been working reliably for decades and covered even rural areas. There was no real incentive to switch to smartphone payment. I myself (2019) have written about the difficult start mobile phones had. Yet the number of people tapping their phones onto contactless terminals has been shooting up since the outbreak of the Covid-19 pandemic. Not only has the virus jump-started digitalization, but the fear of germs on bills and coins made people pivot away from cash. Credit cards obviously gained traction, but so did smartphones.

At the height of the pandemic in 2021, 56 per cent of all Germans had used mobile payment, up from only 10 per cent in 2016 (Postbank, 2021). In the US, in-store mobile payments rose by 29 per cent in the course of 2020, and the pandemic even made the average annual spending per user go up (eMarketer, 2021).

Payment is not only a window into finance, it is the battlefield on which Big Tech fights its proxy war. Have you noticed that data giants hardly attack each other within their core businesses? Yes, here and there you find some friction, as when Apple decided to tweak its privacy policy, which in turn hurt Facebook's ad revenues. But you wouldn't see Apple launch its own social network. Facebook wouldn't build a search engine, and Amazon wouldn't issue a mobile operating system. Technically and financially, they could venture into each other's domains, but they prefer a cold peace.

Payment, on the other hand, is up for grabs for each of them. And as we have seen from Asia's super apps, it is foundational to every effort of building an ecosystem. Other companies are realizing that too. PayPal, the first real fintech, is straightforward about its goals. It says it wants to build both of its major brands – PayPal and Venmo – into financial super apps. It has continuously been expanding the possibilities of what you can do with your money within the app. Payment via QR codes and BNPL offerings are just some of the latest additions (Trivedi, 2021a).

Other heavyweights are joining the race too. Though its core business is neither in finance nor technology, Walmart has built its own fintech start-up called One. Its major concern: Amazon and its first steps into the offline world. The Beast of Bentonville, as Walmart is known, is as candid about its goals as PayPal: it wants a financial super app where customers can spend, save and lend (Nassauer, 2022).

In a nutshell, while for a long time it was a given that whoever ruled the operating systems also ruled mobile payments, the explosion of new competitors and aspiring super apps speaks a new truth. And those who turn out at the top of mobile finance will be the best candidates to run powerful ecosystems like Alipay and WeChat.

Amazon wants to be your banker

In March 2019 a hitherto unknown Chinese name made headlines in the United States. The *Wall Street Journal* (Xie, 2019) reported that Yu'e Bao had become the world's largest money market fund, with 588 million 'investors' parking their cash in it, 114 million of whom had used the service for the first time within the last year. Though Yu'e Bao feels like a mutual fund, that was not the initial idea behind it. In reality, it is a micro savings tool, bearing some interest. Mostly, it is used by rural Chinese people who don't have (easy) access to bank accounts. They can deposit as little as one yuan. Yu'e Bao then invests the money and passes most of the yield to customers, which makes it more profitable than keeping money at bank deposits. The company behind it: Alibaba.

Launched in 2013, Yu'e Bao has become an indispensable pillar of Jack Ma's finance empire. Payment is a window into financial services, the opening gambit. But there is a thick line between facilitating the transfer of money and actually taking custody of other people's money. Since Alibaba had crossed this line, it decided to go full in. In 2015 China allowed private companies to obtain banking licences. Alibaba-backed Mybank was among the first to receive such a licence. Ever since, it has served farmers and other SMEs (IFC, 2020). Even more intriguing is the powerful by-product that came with the launch: the Ali Finance Cloud. Foreign cloud services such as those offered by Amazon were forbidden in mainland China, so Alibaba decided to build the cloud in-house. It didn't stop there: it sold cloud services to other banks and fintechs.

Alibaba's financial services grab was also reflected in its organizational structure. In 2014 Alipay was rebranded as Ant Financial (now Ant Group) to manage all financial products. Among its portfolio are Mybank, Yu'e Bao and Alipay. Furthermore, the Ant Group has splurged on financial apps abroad. In 2015 it invested $680 million in India's Paytm. It acquired Korea's Kakao and bid for MoneyGram in the US, which was eventually blocked in 2018, citing national security concerns (Skinner, 2018).

Ruling e-commerce payments

The reason I am going into such detail with Alipay and the Ant Group is that they are the best example of Big Tech being obsessed with capturing all types of finance, not just payment. The Western equivalent of Alibaba is Amazon. I am not referring to both of them being e-commerce supertankers. I mean their ambition with regard to financial services.

Amazon's financial flagship is obviously Amazon Pay. Google and Apple may be ruling the interface of mobile phones and the brick-and-mortar store, but when it comes to the ever-expanding e-commerce sector, Amazon reigns supreme. Whether you are shopping on amazon.com, its virtual assistant Alexa or even beyond the borders of the Amazon empire – Amazon Pay is the way to go. Despite sustained speculation it would also introduce a bank account (e.g. Glazer, Hoffman and Stevens, 2018), it has not. The question is 'why should it?' Customers can already load money onto their Amazon account in the form of vouchers. And why wake sleeping regulators to impose banking rules?

It is fascinating to see Amazon's market power. Imagine giving your fiercest competitor a place at the checkout, the most valuable spot in a consumer journey, and paying handily for it. Yet this is exactly what many other web shops are doing. They hand over the customer relationship and transactional data. And the fees paid to Amazon are everything but marginal. On top of a \$0.30 fixed fee, a processing fee of 2.9 per cent domestically or 3.9 per cent for cross-border payments is added (Bilotta and Romano, 2019). Amazon, in turn, touts partners with a checkout that is up to 70 per cent faster and a conversion up to 5 per cent higher. Another impressive figure their research arrived at is that 91 per cent of all customers who have used Amazon's payment method would do so again (Amazon, 2022). For many online retailers this seems to justify the trade-off. After all, Amazon Pay has already reached a market share of 22 per cent in the US online payments market, in spite of being neither a credit card company nor a fintech (CBInsights, 2022).

Amazon is strongarming payment giants as well. In the UK it threatened to block all Visa credit cards should the company go ahead with increasing its payment fees, a harsh warning shot for possible upcoming price hikes in the US. In Singapore it delivered on its threats and levied a 0.5 per cent surcharge for purchases with Visa cards (Adams, 2021).

The tech titan also wants to expand this power into the offline world and has introduced services such as Amazon Cash. Customers can charge their Amazon Pay balance by handing cash to participating retailers such as Walgreens or Gamestop. The process is simple and free. You generate a QR code via the Amazon account, the retailer scans it and the amount is credited to the account within minutes.

Reaching for credits and loans

Unlike other members of the Big Five, Amazon has also dared to dive directly into the world of credit. Amazon lending for customers is provided in cooperation with credit cards from Chase bank. This is still nothing special as it is tied to a payment instrument. Apple is doing the same with Goldman Sachs. But Amazon is also lending money to SMEs. This is significant for two reasons: first, it is a premiere that data giants charge forward into the B2B world. Second, lending is more strictly regulated and requires much highly specific expertise in how you deal with default risk. Strategically, however, the move fits perfectly into the techfin model. Amazon serves two sides of its platform, the buyers and the sellers, so it needs to make its ecosystem more attractive for both. In this concrete case, if a third-party seller is paralyzed by liquidity shortages, they cannot offer their goods on Amazon's website, resulting in less product variety for customers. Hence, the entire platform would lose attractiveness. Since Amazon does not have a banking licence, it has to cooperate with traditional banks such as Goldman Sachs in the US or ING in Germany.

So, Amazon is not just stretching its hand through the cracked window of finance, it is standing in the lobby. Alibaba's MyBank, on the other hand, is already in the living room. It does not require cooperation with a traditional bank. On the contrary, it claims to be 1,000 times more efficient than traditional banks. The loan process is faster, cheaper and fully automatized. And the core advantage: using its network and data-driven assets, MyBank's corporate debtors default much more rarely than those of traditional banks. The ratio of non-performing loans (NPLs) is below 1 per cent. Many of those customers would never get a loan at another bank as they don't have collateral. MyBank has the big advantage that it can mine Alibaba's data. By looking at the past performance of the retailer, for instance their selling history and reviews, they are able to make an automatic credit decision (Bilotta and Romano, 2019).

This is the very nightmare of bankers because it nullifies their core competencies. The major question becomes who can spin the data flywheel faster. At the moment it seems that battle goes to Big Tech. The Ant Group is the best example of this model. It can monitor all the transactions of its 450 million-strong user base in real time. The system can handle 120,000 transactions per second or up to 10 billion per day, outperforming the capacity of long-serving payments giants such as Visa or Mastercard. By volume, Alipay is already the world's largest payment processor. And it is continuously merging new tech such as machine learning, cloud and microservices to mine these troves of data for correlations (Skinner, 2018).

We often hear about this kind of data mining but what does the benefit actually look like? An illustrative example is how data scientists at Ant Financial noticed that women paying for smartphone screen repairs were also very likely to buy skinny jeans. They hypothesized that these two variables were connected as smartphones more easily slipped out of skinny jeans. As a result, women purchasing such jeans were also offered screen protection insurance. In sum, this targeting has been extremely successful. Of the five financial services offered by Ant Financial, 80 per cent of customers use at least three of them (Azhar, 2021).

Baffling Big Tech's game plan

Operating systems, super apps, wallets – this is Big Tech's arsenal in the war for finance hegemony in the 21st century. Banking is being digitalized and thus moving onto their turf. Yes, it will be the most difficult industry to swallow, but they don't have to change their gameplan. Accelerate the data flywheel and wait for the shakeout, then take the profitable parts and leave the regulated plumbing to banks. The scenario might have been inevitable had it not been for a handful of renegades that couldn't be farther away from banks' boardrooms or Big Tech's campuses. Hidden far from the eye of the public, they were building a machine that would completely rewrite the rules of both finance and tech.

KEY TAKEAWAYS

- Big Tech has been working relentlessly to break into finance for more than a decade. For one, because finance is one of the largest industries, but above all because it is turbocharging the data flywheel. Getting their hands on banking data gives tech titans an unprecedented advantage in all other sectors where they are competing.
- Techfins, as Big Tech finance initiatives are called, are fundamentally different to fintechs. Fintechs use technology to improve finance; techfins use finance to improve technology. As such they are not enablers with which banks can partner, but immensely dangerous competitors. Partnerships with tech titans might be inescapable but should be entered into with special care.

- Payment is Big Tech's focal point as it yields the most valuable data and does not require a banking licence. Yet Chinese tech giants and Amazon in particular have transcended this area and venture into deeper banking turf (e.g. lending).

References

Adams, J (2021) Amazon's U.K. Visa ban could foreshadow larger fight in U.S., American Banker, 17 November, www.americanbanker.com/news/amazons-u-k-visa-ban-could-foreshadow-larger-fight-in-u-s (archived at https://perma.cc/53AE-9K6B)

Adyen (2021) Interchange fees explained, 2 November, www.adyen.com/blog/interchange-fees-explained#:~:text=How%20much%20are%20interchange%20fees,They%20are%20also%20regularly%20adjusted (archived at https://perma.cc/M49V-X9CQ)

Aiyer, B, Caso, J and Sorel, M (2022) The unsolved opportunities for cybersecurity providers, McKinsey & Company, 5 January, www.mckinsey.com/business-functions/risk-and-resilience/our-insights/the-unsolved-opportunities-®17 for-cybersecurity-providers?cid=exp-pde-pro-mip-mck-oth-2201 (archived at https://perma.cc/C58N-3J8S)

Amazon (2022) Common business questions about Amazon Pay, 3 February, https://pay.amazon.co.uk/blog/Common-business-questions-about-Amazon-Pay (archived at https://perma.cc/PP53-ZSYL)

Andreessen, M (2011) Why software is eating the world, *Wall Street Journal*, 20 August, www.wsj.com/articles/SB10001424053111903480904576512250915629460 (archived at https://perma.cc/D773-NUM2)

Arnold, M, Felsted, A and Thomas, D (2015) UK banks put squeeze on Apple Pay fees, *Financial Times*, 14 July, www.ft.com/content/02287f44-2a3d-11e5-8613-e7aedbb7bdb7 (archived at https://perma.cc/2F27-JE8H)

Azhar, A (2021) *The Exponential Age: How accelerating technology is transforming business, politics and society*, Diversion Books, New York

Baker, M (1995) Technology investors fall head over heels for their new love, *Wall Street Journal*, 10 August, https://the1995blog.files.wordpress.com/2015/03/netscape-ipo_wsj.jpeg (archived at https://perma.cc/4D3F-K55J)

Bilotta, N and Romano, S (2019) Tech giants in banking: The implications of a new market power, IAI Papers, 13 June, www.iai.it/sites/default/files/iaip1913.pdf (archived at https://perma.cc/4BEX-78W5)

Campbell, J (2020) Memorable moment in an exceptional year: The Netscape IPO of 1995, The 1995 blog, 7 August, https://1995blog.com/2020/08/07/memorable-moment-in-an-exceptional-year-the-netscape-ipo-of-1995/ (archived at https://perma.cc/J7SG-4PXN)

Capgemini, LinkedIn and Efma (2018) World Fintech Report 2018, 27 February, www.capgemini.com/wp-content/uploads/2018/02/world-fintech-report-wftr-2018.pdf (archived at https://perma.cc/82TA-2PHN)

CBInsights (2022) Everything you need to know about what Amazon is doing in financial services, 15 March, www.cbinsights.com/research/report/amazon-across-financial-services-fintech/ (archived at https://perma.cc/8XL3-CHM6)

Chen, C (2018) Why China's 'super-apps' will never succeed in the US, Prototypr.io, 20 May, https://blog.prototypr.io/why-chinas-super-apps-will-never-succeed-in-the-us-64c686c8c5d6 (archived at https://perma.cc/KG8N-K2UC)

Collins, J (2001) *Good to Great: Why some companies make the leap and others don't*, HarperCollins, New York

CompaniesMarketCap.com (2022) Largest companies by market cap, https://companiesmarketcap.com/tech/largest-tech-companies-by-market-cap/ (archived at https://perma.cc/XTL3-SWNC)

Cramer-Flood, E (2021) Duopoly still rules the global digital ad market, but Alibaba and Amazon are on the prowl, eMarketer, 10 May, www.emarketer.com/content/duopoly-still-rules-global-digital-ad-market-alibaba-amazon-on-prowl (archived at https://perma.cc/TGQ2-YB6B)

Curry, D (2022) Mobile payments app revenue and usage statistics (2022), BusinessofApps, 25 October, www.businessofapps.com/data/mobile-payments-app-market/ (archived at https://perma.cc/U99C-R72D)

eMarketer (2021) US payment users will surpass 100 million this year, 30 March, www.emarketer.com/content/us-payment-users-will-surpass-100-million-this-year?ecid=NL1016 (archived at https://perma.cc/SA4L-JE9H)

Franck, J-U and Linardatos, D (2021) Germany's 'Lex Apple Pay': Payment services regulation overtakes competition enforcement, *Journal of European Competition Law & Practice*, 2 February, https://academic.oup.com/jeclap/article-abstract/12/2/68/5905712?redirectedFrom=fulltext (archived at https://perma.cc/QP6C-5UGT)

Gilder, G (2018) *Life after Google: The fall of big data and the rise of the blockchain economy*, Regnery Gateway, Washington, DC

Glazer, E, Hoffman, L and Stevens, L (2018) Next up for Amazon: checking accounts, *Wall Street Journal*, 5 March, www.wsj.com/articles/are-you-ready-for-an-amazon-branded-checking-account-1520251200 (archived at https://perma.cc/KSJ7-NQBH)

GlobeNewswire (2021) Financial Services Global Market Report 2021: Covid-19 impact and recovery to 2030, 31 March, www.globenewswire.com/news-release/2021/03/31/2202641/0/en/Financial-Services-Global-Market-Report-2021-COVID-19-Impact-And-Recovery-To-2030.html (archived at https://perma.cc/8M6A-83FT)

Google (no date) Our approach to Search, www.google.com/search/howsearchworks/mission/ (archived at https://perma.cc/435Q-TXDK)

Harari, Y (2018) *Homo Deus: A brief history of tomorrow*, Harper Perennial, New York

Hazlehurst, P (2019) Introducing Uber Money, 28 October, www.uber.com/newsroom/introducing-uber-money/ (archived at https://perma.cc/3XX7-B5P8)

IFC – International Finance Corporation World Bank (2020) MyBank: MYBank's gender-driven approach to lending, August, www.ifc.org/wps/wcm/connect/3e0cfba8-12c9-42fe-943b-e99f4a36de73/202008_D2E_MyBank.pdf?MOD=AJPERES&CVID=nfvyYCR (archived at https://perma.cc/JP9D-RHE2)

Johnston, S (2018) Largest companies 2008 vs. 2018, a lot has changed, Milford Asset, 31 January, https://milfordasset.com/insights/largest-companies-2008-vs-2018-lot-changed (archived at https://perma.cc/QP43-ML39)

Judiciary Antitrust Subcommittee (2020) Investigation of competition in digital markets: Majority staff report and recommendations, Subcommittee on Antitrust, Commercial and Administrative Law of the Committee on the Judiciary, 6 October, https://judiciary.house.gov/uploadedfiles/competition_in_digital_markets.pdf (archived at https://perma.cc/4Z6R-RXY7)

Leswing, K (2022) Apple becomes first U.S. company to reach $3 trillion market cap, *CNBC*, 3 January, www.cnbc.com/2022/01/03/apple-becomes-first-us-company-to-reach-3-trillion-market-cap.html (archived at https://perma.cc/ST6L-KV5C)

Meta Investor Relations (no date) Marc L. Andreessen, https://investor.fb.com/leadership-and-governance/person-details/default.aspx?ItemId=67f254ec-d2aa-46e4-85e3-e3ddda492518 (archived at https://perma.cc/7GYQ-SNB2)

Nassauer, S (2022) Walmart-backed fintech startup is acquiring two firms and a new name, *Wall Street Journal*, 26 January, www.wsj.com/articles/walmart-backed-fintech-startup-is-acquiring-two-firms-and-a-new-name-11643199601 (archived at https://perma.cc/D3C7-XW8L)

Niewenhuis, L (2018) Tencent launches a social credit system similar to Alibaba's, The China Project, 31 January, https://thechinaproject.com/2018/01/31/tencent-launches-social-credit-system-similar-alibabas/ (archived at https://perma.cc/HJ8X-HJZ4)

Pejic, I (2019) *Blockchain Babel: The crypto-craze and the challenge to business*, Kogan Page, London

Pejic, I (2021) Dawn of a new frontier: Welcome to the distributed economy, The New Frontier, 10 August, https://igorpejic.substack.com/p/dawn-of-a-new-frontier?s=w (archived at https://perma.cc/SB5Q-UN99)

Perlroth, N (2021) *This is How They Tell Me the World Ends: The cyber weapons arms race*, Bloomsbury Publishing, London

Postbank (2021) Studie: Mehr als jede*r zweite Deutsche nutzt kontaktlose Bezahlmethoden, 6 July, www.postbank.de/unternehmen/medien/meldungen/2021/juli/studie-mehr-als-jeder-zweite-deutsche-nutzt-kontaktlose-bezahlmethoden.html (archived at https://perma.cc/J7FF-WU5G)

Rooney, K (2021) Andreessen Horowitz launches $2.2 billion crypto fund and is 'radically optimistic' despite price fluctuations, *CNBC*, 24 June, www.cnbc.com/2021/06/24/andreessen-horowitz-launches-2point2-billion-crypto-fund.html (archived at https://perma.cc/X5WD-VK7P)

Shopify (2020) Shopify partners with Facebook to help businesses launch branded Facebook Shops, 19 May, https://news.shopify.com/shopify-partners-with-facebook-to-help-businesses-launch-branded-facebook-shops (archived at https://perma.cc/327B-A2FZ)

Skinner, C (2018) *Digital Human: The fourth revolution of humanity includes everyone*, Wiley, Oxford

Soo, Z (2016) TechFin: Jack Ma coins term to set Alipay's goal to give emerging markets access to capital, *South China Morning Post*, 2 December, www.scmp.com/tech/article/2051249/techfin-jack-ma-coins-term-set-alipays-goal-give-emerging-markets-access (archived at https://perma.cc/LNB5-QTYN)

Statista (2022) Most popular social networks worldwide as of January 2022, ranked by number of monthly active users, www.statista.com/statistics/272014/global-social-networks-ranked-by-number-of-users/ (archived at https://perma.cc/45DX-WN8X)

The Economist (2021a) Europe is now a corporate also-ran. Can it recover its footing? 5 June, www.economist.com/briefing/2021/06/05/once-a-corporate-heavyweight-europe-is-now-an-also-ran-can-it-recover-its-footing (archived at https://perma.cc/DY8X-9BMW)

The Economist (2021b) Cloudy with a dearth of chips: How the pandemic has changed the weather in the technology industry, 30 October, www.economist.com/business/2021/10/30/how-the-pandemic-has-changed-the-weather-in-the-technology-industry (archived at https://perma.cc/3ZRV-DNGR)

Thompson, D (2012) Instagram is now worth $77 per employee, *The Atlantic*, 9 April, www.theatlantic.com/business/archive/2012/04/instagram-is-now-worth-77-million-per-employee/255640/ (archived at https://perma.cc/6QYL-E22W)

Trivedi, V (2021a) PayPal forecasts boom in QR-code payments, plans BNPL expansion, Payments Dive, 6 May, www.paymentsdive.com/news/paypal-boom-qr-code-payments-expanding-bnpl-to-australia/599680/ (archived at https://perma.cc/L2R9-R3DC)
Trivedi, V (2021b) Google Pay launches P2P cross-border payments, Payments Dive, 11 May, www.paymentsdive.com/news/google-pay-western-union-wise-p2p-cross-border/599937/ (archived at https://perma.cc/6EX7-SAKP)
Visa (2020) United Kingdom | Domestic multi-lateral interchange fees, 16 January, www.visa.co.uk/dam/VCOM/regional/ve/unitedkingdom/PDF/fees-and-interchange/uk-interchange-january-2020.pdf (archived at https://perma.cc/QTZ2-ZTAT)
Wallach, O (2021) The top 100 companies of the world: The U.S. vs everyone else, Visual Capitalist, 19 July, www.visualcapitalist.com/the-top-100-companies-of-the-world-the-u-s-vs-everyone-else/ (archived at https://perma.cc/CCM5-FPBK)
Wired (1999) The Inner Jeff Bezos, 1 March, www.wired.com/1999/03/bezos-3/ (archived at https://perma.cc/C8R3-BTCG)
World Bank Group (2017) Financial inclusion on the rise, but gaps remain, Global Findex Database shows, 19 April, www.worldbank.org/en/news/press-release/2018/04/19/financial-inclusion-on-the-rise-but-gaps-remain-global-findex-database-shows (archived at https://perma.cc/GA4J-RD4P)
Xie, S (2019) More than a third of China is now invested in one giant mutual fund, *Wall Street Journal*, 27 March, www.wsj.com/articles/more-than-a-third-of-china-is-now-invested-in-one-giant-mutual-fund-11553682785 (archived at https://perma.cc/MJ4L-LBA)

2

Railroads for a new age: birth of the blockchain

Pioneers tinker with a truth machine

Data giants were not the only ones galvanized by the idea to rewire money with technology. Much before they got in the race, a computer programmer in his mid-30s watched with curiosity at how his chosen field was transforming the world before his eyes. He was a polymath, with degrees in computer science and a Juris Doctor from Law School. A cryptographer genius with a distinct interest in economics, he was interested in far more than just lines of code or codices. One of his major obsessions was money. Unlike most hot shots and entrepreneurs of his time he was not absorbed by the question of how to make it, but where it came from, how it worked and how its shortcomings could be remedied. Money, he was convinced, was fundamental to humans. It enabled cooperation, altruism, mitigated aggression and set us apart from animals.

The young cryptographer was particularly intrigued by the characteristics of gold. Its supply was limited, its extraction burdensome. The scarcity in the market gave it its unique value. Gold was durable, portable, divisible and anonymous – superior to any other payment tool in history (Szabo, 2002). If only it could be mimicked in the digital age.

In an email describing the design of such a possible digital gold he shared his view with a few elect cryptographers. Their email addresses had found their way onto a list of brilliant computer scientists dreaming of a money fit for the computer age. The author suggested a completely decentralized cryptocurrency that needed no government to issue it, no bank to hold it and no payment processor to move it. Algorithms effectively eliminated all middlemen. The proposal was built on the so-called proof-of-work (PoW) mechanism, a design in which network participants race to solve complex cryptographic puzzles by investing massive computing power. This mechanism produces blocks with transactions, each of which is cryptographically linked to the preceding one.

I know what most of you are thinking now: it feels like bitcoin. It works like bitcoin. So, it must be bitcoin. But it isn't. The story takes place in the year 1998 and the invention described is Bit Gold, a brainchild of the exceptional Nick Szabo. Admittedly, the Bit Gold system uses many of the same technical principles as today's cryptocurrencies. These principles include PoW, one-way functions (meaning no backwards computability) and timestamping (Szabo, 2008). In fact, Nick Szabo is also the father of the smart contract idea. As a law school graduate *and* cryptographer, he was the natural candidate to invent those computer programs that are based on if-then logic (Szabo, 1996). Smart contracts are the dynamization of blockchain technology, almost as profound to the crypto world as the PoW mechanism. If you haven't heard about them yet, you will later in this book.

The first search for digital gold

Like most of us, Szabo was a product of his time. Technologically, as well as ideologically. PoW, for example, was not something Szabo invented. Rather he tweaked and patched together the work of other pioneers. In this case it was the Hashcash algorithm developed in 1997 by the Englishman Adam Back, another computer scientist in his 30s. How much of the PoW mechanism Back actually invented himself and how much was built on the work of others is still under debate; the hashing function had already been proposed by Cynthia Dwork and Moni Naor in 1992. What is clear, though, is that Hashcash was not designed to transfer money, but to be an anti-spam email concept. Or, in the lingo of IT security, 'a denial-of-service countermeasure tool' (Stradbrooke, 2021). In order to prevent spammers from sending untargeted mass emails, Hashcash forced them to pay a fee in the form of a small computational effort. While unnoticeable for the normal user, sending many emails placed a strain on a computer's resources and found its way into the sender's electricity bill.

The idea of a digital currency was also something that had been swirling around for a while before Szabo proposed Bit Gold. One of them was e-gold. Its inventor Douglas Jackson was neither a cryptographer nor an economist, but an oncologist from Florida who just couldn't stomach that Richard Nixon had ended the US dollar's peg to gold. Inflation worries kept the self-taught economist up at night. Thus, he used his autodidactic talent and the sleepless nights to learn how to code. And voila, he launched his own global financial network: e-gold. Put very simply, you buy (or rather let the market maker buy) real gold, which is then deposited. Afterwards you get the equivalent in digital gold. This was not a fringe experiment. In the 2000s e-gold rose to be the second most popular means of online payment, surpassed only by PayPal. It had more than 3.5 million accounts. In his admiration for gold, Jackson was prototypical of the early crypto-visionaries. What made him special, though, was that he still saw physical gold as part of the digital age.

Unfortunately, not all of the accounts were held by honest citizens. In the end, e-gold succumbed to the same problem that almost killed bitcoin a couple of years later: it became a tool for money laundering. In 2013 a couple of federal lawsuits eventually broke the project's neck (Mahler, 2018).

Attempts to solve the double-spend problem

The link to gold was not even there in the first notable invention of digital cash, namely eCash. In 1983 the Californian cryptography pioneer David Chaum wrote software for personal computers that was designed to make internet payments secure.

eCash had more in common with PayPal than with today's cryptocurrencies. Its major difference to bitcoin, Bit Gold and e-gold was that eCash wrapped itself around the banking system. eCash came before breakthroughs such as the PoW mechanism and it wasn't able to solve the so-called double-spend problem without intermediaries. In other words, eCash could not ensure by solely automatic computer algorithms that digital monetary value can be spent only once. Just think of a PDF that you send via email. Your recipient receives it, but that doesn't mean it vanishes from your computer or email program. For money to work, solving this double-spend dilemma is elementary. In Chaum's case, it could only be remedied by working with banks. And he did: Citi, Deutsche Bank and many others cooperated with Chaum and his company DigiCash. At one point he even sat at the table with Microsoft and turned down an offer that would have paid him $180 million and made eCash part of every PC (note the early interest of Big Tech into digital payment methods). Already in the 1980s Microsoft understood its strategically unique position, as well as the potential that loomed in the money business. But the reason Chaum eventually failed was that he was far ahead of his time. As with so many innovators before him he saw his brainchild smooth the second wave of adopters rather than having sustained commercial success.

Nick Szabo was one of those later adopters. He initially worked with Chaum on eCash. It was an obvious fit as he was preoccupied with finding a way to move money online, which did not exactly make him part of a mass movement. Yet Szabo ideologically disliked the eCash setup. The entire concept still required a central authority and middleman. And Szabo (2001, 2004, 2005) was very outspoken on how he felt about trusted third parties. Many of them such as Visa have been beneficial in the past by brokering trust between strangers and thereby enabled commerce. Yet his conclusion was that the most trusted third party was one that did not have to exist in the first place because of the way the protocol was designed. Of all the drawbacks of middlemen, he was most concerned that they were security holes.

Meet the cypherpunks

What all of the crypto pioneers have in common – except crypto-economic ingenuity and deliberately old-looking websites – is that they have been luminaries of the *cypherpunk* movement. The term is a blend of 'cyberpunk' (a futuristic, dystopian science fiction genre) and 'cypher' (an encryption method). The early movement counted a couple of hundred members who were discussing novel privacy-preserving communication methods.

The conversations did not only evolve around technology. Politics, philosophy and especially economics were debated just as fiercely. What united all of them was the belief that the freedom of the individual was the highest good. To achieve it, privacy was paramount.

Cypherpunks communicated via a mailing list of the same name in the 1990s. Its founding documents, their Manifestos (May, 1992; Hughes, 1993), were also shared that way. They made it crystal clear that (digital) privacy was the basic principle of the entire movement and the foundation of a free society.

As their name suggests, science fiction novels served as an inspiration and particularly a deterrent to what technological progress could do. Fears of dystopian uber-states have been driving much of the creativity. Yet cypherpunks embraced technology rather than demonizing it. Whatever downside it had, it certainly also offered a solution to it. In this case they saw it in information encryption (Popper, 2015).

The movement had a distinct libertarian streak. Libertarianism is a political philosophy that can be traced back to 17th-century thinkers such as John Lock, some say even to ancient China. Cypherpunks' convictions were shaped by the US brand of libertarianism prevalent in the 1970s and 1980s. It advocated civil liberties and extreme capitalism with state involvement being limited to setting the basic frame so the free market can do its magic. Those of you familiar with Ayn Rand's novel *Atlas Shrugged* (1957) will get the picture.

Free banking – minting your own money

Libertarianism had a fully fledged theory of economics attached: the Austrian School. Many of its tenets influenced the cypherpunks. One was the strong laissez-faire attitude that evoked a visceral reaction to everything that smacked of government intrusion. This was particularly concerning when it came to money or privacy matters. The other thing that made them cringe was inflation. To keep a lid on prices spiralling out of control, the Austrian School and thus cypherpunks advocated the end of fractional reserve banking and the return to the gold standard. According to the ECB (2012) this thinking should later also become instrumental for bitcoin and other cryptocurrencies.

Cypherpunks particularly revered the branch of the Austrian School championed by Friedrich Hayek, a 1974 recipient of the Nobel Memorial Prize in Economic Sciences. They shared with him the fixation on property, contracts and – above all – money.

A major pillar of Hayek's monetary theory is free banking, or as Hayek (1976) called it, 'The decentralization of money'. He postulated that governments and national banks had no God-given monopoly on minting coins and printing bills. Private companies and commercial banks should be allowed to issue their own currencies. The invisible hand would eventually make the free market converge around the best one. This thought was the prerequisite for all major crypto-projects, from eCash to bitcoin.

More eccentric influences on the cypherpunks

The worldview of cryptographers like Szabo was also shaped by another movement of the time, the Extropians. They too were tinkering with cryptography, but also with life after death. Not in a religious or philosophical sense, but a technological one. Cryonics was the buzzword of the day. Extropians were deep-freezing their bodies, and sometimes only their heads. If you think that is a crazy idea that should have stayed confined to the pages of sci-fi novels, wait. They actually dreamt of downloading the entire human mind onto a computer hard drive to store it, just in case an accident caused amnesia or killed them. Most of them being atheist or agnostic, they even proposed a new dating system that did not centre around Christ's birth. A *Wired* article (Regis, 1994) described numerous such... let's call them extravagancies. They also included the building of an interplanetary headquarters and gatherings in a commune-like fashion, despite their members radically opposing joint ownership.

It is easy to shake your head in disbelief and dismiss the Extropians as a bunch of techno-hippies. Still, it is important to keep them in mind as part of the ecosystem that shaped the world of crypto pioneers. Extropians perfectly illustrate the dynamic optimism and larger-than-life faith in technology that was prevalent in these circles. Many of their ideas invigorated and stoked the imagination of the crypto community and led to out-of-the-box ideas.

A distinctly different mindset than Big Tech

So what does all of this have to do with Big Tech? Szabo, Chaum and Back shared the same fascination with technology as Mark Zuckerberg or Steve Jobs. They dreamed about launching rockets into space just as much as the young Jeff Bezos did. And they were equally as ecstatic about artificial intelligence creating superhumans as Sergey Brin and Larry Page. And still, their worldview was fundamentally different.

The founders of the Big Five and most other tech firms had a profoundly different view on the distribution of power. Almost all of the discussions, inventions and projects of the cypherpunks were driven by a concern that centralized actors would garner too much power. While Google and Facebook see big data as a way to improve services, the cypherpunks see it as a threat to end privacy. The rejection of powerful actors even led them to reimagine the entire monetary system. A system in which data is private and the central government cannot simply pump up the money supply at will. In other words, they were suspicious of Big Government. Today, Big Banking and Big Tech have joined the list.

Consider what George Gilder (2018) bemoans as the flaws of the Google age: online security, unhinged money printing, outsized roles for regulators, powerful and concentrated networks, and the resulting proliferation of middlemen. This list could have easily appeared in one of the cypherpunk mailings. The things that terrified them in the 1980s and '90s have come to haunt today's world. Cynics might call cypherpunks radicals with more understanding of tech than of money. That might be true, but they have laid the foundation for a technology that would shake the world at a scale they could have never dreamed of.

A trust crisis and the advent of bitcoin

California, January 2009. The engineer Hal Finney was sitting in front of his four computer screens when an email pinged. He had been waiting for this one eagerly for the last couple of weeks. It was not from his boss or a colleague, but from a pseudonymous cypherpunk who happened to be on the same mailing list as him. The two had started an email exchange some time ago and this guy who went by the name of Satoshi Nakamoto had sent him a nine-page paper that outlined an electronic cash system based on peer-to-peer technology. The content of the paper was explosive. It promised nothing less than to build a completely new banking system that would not need banks. It would be anonymous. It would have its own currency. It would end inflation. And it would enable anybody to participate in it. Its name: bitcoin.

Finney, who in the past had already helped people to circumvent the official financial system, was on fire. He had discussed first-hand breakthroughs such as Bit Gold or HashCash, and David Chaum himself had introduced him to public key cryptography back in 1991. But all of those proposals eventually fell short. Nakamoto, on the other hand, seemed to have answered all the pressing questions that Finney and the cypherpunks had been trying to solve for more than 20 years.

Popularizing bitcoin within the crypto community

Finney became a fierce advocate of Satoshi Nakamoto's bitcoin concept and tried to popularize it within the community, which turned out to be sceptical at first. Finney concluded that the whitepaper was too theoretical and lacked a technical proof of concept. So he asked Nakamoto to come up with some code to run on his computer and ensure the whitepaper was not overselling. Now that code was in Finney's inbox and it would keep him busy for the day. Never mind that it was his son's birthday and that his sister-in-law had flown in from France to visit.

The email contained a link to www.bitcoin.org, a domain Nakamoto owned and where he had uploaded a simple .exe file with the first bitcoin code. The features were highly limited. Finney could see the public bitcoin addresses and his private key and he had functionalities like 'send coins'. Not that he could do that. He owned no coins, nor was he sure that coins even existed. Furthermore, he could see there were only two more computers connected to the network, both from the same Californian IP address. The digital currency hadn't exactly captured a large user base yet.

The system soon crashed and the two cryptographers emailed back and forth to eliminate some more bugs, but eventually the system stabilized. Nakamoto sent him another function, namely 'Generate Coins'. He had cautioned that mining the coins could take some time as Finney didn't have specialized equipment. Thus, Finney clicked on the function and eventually managed to attend his son's birthday celebration at a Chinese restaurant nearby.

When he returned to his computers, he had mined his first block (which was block 78 in total) and had received a reward of 50 bitcoins. He couldn't buy anything with it, nor could he sell it. Even if there was a potential buyer, the coins would have been worthless. But that didn't tarnish Finney's exuberance; after all he had just minted his first digital money (Popper, 2015).

Eventually Hal Finney, a cypherpunk and Extropian through and through, found his place in the history books as a crypto pioneer instrumental in the rise of bitcoin. After all, he had been the first person to ever receive a bitcoin transaction. Finney died in 2014, and as becomes a real Extropian, his body was deep frozen in a cryonic vault near Los Angeles.

Some speculate whether Finney was Nakamoto himself, but realistically Finney had no idea who was hiding behind the Japanese-sounding pseudonym. And neither do we more than a decade later. Many of the crypto pioneers we met before are serious contenders. In the bitcoin whitepaper (Nakamoto, 2008) On bitcointalk.org, Nakamoto also acknowledged Nick Szabo's influence. The latter has also a number of other hints pointing his way. Szabo had conceived the bitcoin precursor Bit Gold, invented smart contracts, and very shortly before the bitcoin whitepaper was published he announced on his blog that he would launch a live version of Bit Gold. Additionally, multiple forensic linguistic analyses of Nakamoto's texts came to the conclusion that they most likely originated from Szabo's pen (e.g. Grieve et al, 2014). It might also have been a collaborative project and Szabo as an eloquent law professor was simply the best candidate to write it down.

Whoever it was in the end does not make a difference. Bitcoin would have never seen the light of day without any of those pioneers, whether they were directly involved in the paper or not.

Fertile ground for the rise of a trust machine

The story of bitcoin is very telling. The pseudonymous nature of Satoshi Nakamoto, the collaborative approach in building and launching the system, the internationality of the community and the lack of an institution – God forbid the government. What is most striking, though, is the timing of the bitcoin whitepaper and the mining of the genesis (i.e. first) block. It was preceded by the largest financial meltdown of a generation. Even those people who never wracked their brains about centralization of money, power and data massively lost trust in the institutions managing our daily lives.

First of all, the big banks. As the stewards of the financial world, they were supposed to keep finance running and the economy humming. Instead, Lehman Brothers and others were using their ingenuity to create risk and financial products that destabilized the system. Second, government and regulators had failed in their primary role of checking the systemically relevant players and putting them in their place. Third, once the recession set in, central banks also became a target of anger. In order to stimulate economies around the world and to quickly recover jobs lost during the crisis, they fired up their money-printing presses. Inflation hit and savings melted away.

Centralized Big Tech had a rough time too. Its trust did not suffer from the financial crisis, but from hacks, self-inflicted recklessness and misuses of user data. In 2007, for example, Facebook launched an advertising program called Beacon that basically posted all its users' purchases onto their timelines without seeking permission first (Heiligenstein, 2022). In 2009, Google, Yahoo!, a number of other companies, as well as US law enforcement, were breached by Chinese hackers who stole personal user data (Nakashima, 2013).

It is as if the financial crisis had put cypherpunks' efforts on steroids. All their nightmares about centrally trusted authorities basically came true overnight. The middlemen economy had laid bare all its dangers. And in the years following the crisis the technology companies of the day had been driving the hypertrophy of finance too. All their payment efforts that we have seen in Chapter 1, from PayPal to Apple Pay, have simply wrapped themselves around the existing infrastructure and added a layer in which data was centralized.

bitcoin – a new protocol and currency

But what exactly is bitcoin? It is a system (bitcoin with an upper-case B) which enables and governs the flow of its native currency (BTC or bitcoin with a lower-case b). Thereby it is an alternative, self-contained monetary system. It eliminates the need for a national or central bank to issue the currency. Bitcoins are minted in a process called mining, which is specified by the bitcoin algorithm. There is no centralized institution that can influence that algorithm.

Mining works via a proof-of-work mechanism comparable to what we have seen in the last chapter with HashCash. Put very simply, participating computers to the network – also called nodes or miners – race to solve complex mathematical puzzles. Those puzzles are de facto only solvable by brute force, which means that each miner is plugging in one random value after the other. Whoever hits the winning number first is rewarded with freshly minted bitcoins. The number of issued coins is getting halved after every 210,000 blocks mined, which equals about every four years. So, whereas Finney received 50 BTC for the first blocks he mined, today's miners get 6.25 BTC. This is an extremely abridged description of PoW, so make sure to read up on it either in Nakamoto (2008) or Pejic (2019).

The bitcoin protocol enables everybody to send, receive and store value digitally in the form of bitcoins or fractions thereof. This is done in wallets. The addresses are either written on paper, stored on an external hard drive or a custodial wallet, or – if you want some really heavy mental exercise – memorized. The last two options are not recommended. Storing coins with a custodial provider such as an exchange means you are de facto not owning them. Ownership of bitcoins and other cryptocurrencies is established by having access to the coins. Access is granted via a private key, a 64-character hexadecimal number.

> This is what a typical bitcoin private key looks like:
>
> 2541B7DBCAAF4E81C6DB109A22280D375B6345DFD8F5BAD9CC7932D D82C72534
>
> Can you manage to decode the secret message behind it?

These highly complex mathematical functions and the energy that computers invest in solving them are what make bitcoin able to work on its own. Without it, it would still need banks or trusted intermediaries such as payment processors. But thanks to PoW users can trust the network instead of centralized institutions.

This is also bitcoin's key difference to Bit Gold, its most sophisticated predecessor. Bitcoin really went live, while Bit Gold did not. The reason was that Szabo did not manage to solve the double-spend problem without trusted third parties. In other words, the very heart of bitcoin was missing: the blockchain.

Definitively more than a faster horse

Bitcoin had clearly rewritten the rules by which money flows. But bitcoin was just the opening salvo. The really paradigmatic change had not happened on the application layer, i.e. the currency. After all, private money was a known concept in many parts of the world. Up until the Civil War, free banking in the sense of Hayek had proliferated in America. Banks were printing their own currencies, unbound by any federal authority. Often hopelessly undercapitalized, these banks, called Wildcat banks, issued so much money that they eventually couldn't meet their obligations. When people then wanted to pay with their banknotes and coins, they found out they were worthless. In more recent times you could argue that Airmiles and other loyalty programmes serve as a kind of privately issued currency. The airlines can themselves issue them and determine the exchange rate for services or fiat currencies. They act as central banks to their loyalty currencies.

Hence, the crypto-revolution happened in the backend, the protocol layer. The novel blockchain technology was the masterstroke that enabled cryptocurrencies. It is called that because transactions are collected into blocks, validated and then linked to the preceding block. The chain is tamper-proof, because as soon as somebody tries to alter as much as a single digit within a block, the entire chain breaks. Unlike with a normal chain, the links get stronger with every new block that is added.

The great paradigm shift

The blockchain is a paradigmatic shift from the existing systems that centrally store and process transactions. It works with distributed, shared ledgers. This means that a copy of the ledger (i.e. a list of transactions) is stored on each node of the network, making it resilient in the case of an attack. No matter how many nodes go down, as long as one of them is standing, the history of the blockchain will be accessible. All of those nodes work on one and the same chain. Thus, nobody can cheat, deny access to somebody, or rewrite history. Each attacker would have to subvert more than half of the network's power.

This is a game-changer, particularly in more complex setups. And everybody who has worked in finance can tell that there are more complex cases than simple ones. Where heavy, expensive and slow middlemen structures used to drag down the system, the blockchain cuts unnecessary layers. It is why some of the most apt descriptions for the blockchain include 'Trust Machine' (*The Economist*, 2015) and 'Truth Machine' (Vigna and Casey, 2018). And it is a lean machine too. The beauty of bitcoin also lies in its simplicity. The compactness of the whitepaper is echoed in its minimalistic code. Bitcoin is composed of only 31,000 lines of code. By comparison, Google's Chrome browser is made up of 4,490,488 lines of C++ code (Gilder, 2018). Simple machines can't do many functions, but they are highly efficient and not prone to mistakes. Hence, bitcoin was perfect for demonstrating to the world how blockchain works.

Arthur (2011) described extensively patterns of how technologies come into being and how they evolve. A key principle in his view is 'recursiveness', meaning that new inventions never appear in a vacuum but always refer to other preceding breakthroughs. Hence, the interval of innovation is continuously shortening. Bitcoin is the perfect example. Key concepts such as PoW, Byzantine Fault Tolerance, time stamping, asymmetric cryptography and many more had to be invented before Nakamoto was able to brilliantly weave them together into a tamper-proof trust machine.

Arthur goes on to sketch how the initial versions of a novel technology are always crude and that via a process of 'structural deepening', additional components are added. Those either help the new technology overcome its shortcomings or expand its functionality. This tells us that bitcoin is not the end of the road, but only a first glimpse into the potential of its underlying technology. As we will see in this book, Arthur's theory on technological development holds up for bitcoin. The cryptocurrency is the first and most solid proof of concept, but eventually more sophisticated and powerful versions of it will power the economy.

A general-purpose invention to power the economy

The blockchain can best be thought of as a 'General Purpose Invention' (Breshnan and Trajtenberg, 1995; Breshnan and Gordon, 1997). Just like the internal combustion engine or electric light it opens up the road for many sub-inventions. The internal combustion engine powers jets, helicopters, automobiles, locomotives, ships and industrial plants. Small engines such as chainsaws or leaf blowers also rely on it. Electric light was used in cars, houses and factories. It enabled street lamps as well as flashlights and countless other applications. Such general-purpose technology is the very backbone of breakneck economic growth (Gordon, 2016).

Blockchain can also be deployed in any vital industry, not just to make things more efficient but often to completely disrupt the competition. Finance is the first and most important industry to be hit. Yet the transformative power of distributed ledger technology applies to any setup where trust needs to be created among untrusting parties. Supply chain, energy, healthcare, trade, public services, data security and countless other sectors lend themselves to blockchain applications. Moreover, new developments regularly extend possible application fields. The recent NFT craze, about which you will read more later, can digitalize art and turn online gaming into a fully functioning economy.

Within each of those sectors there are countless application possibilities. Take public services. The blockchain could help health and tax departments keep citizens' data safe, it could streamline public procurement or it could be deployed to confirm diplomas and documents.

Such a disruptive cross-industry impact forebodes the arrival of a new 'techno-economic paradigm' (Freeman, 1982, 1987; Freeman and Perez, 1988). These paradigms structure economic history. Each of those extended phases is orbiting around one dominant resource: water in the industrial age, electricity and oil in the 20th century, or data in the information age. Each paradigm is set in motion by a radical technological breakthrough that makes the key resource widely affordable. Those breakthroughs are almost always general-purpose inventions. Examples of such innovation are the steam engine, the internal combustion engine and the computer. The blockchain can join this list. It brings down the cost structure for digital trust and creates digital scarcity. It lets unknown parties reach consensus on a shared digital history without building and paying an army of middlemen.

The potential has fanned the desire of many consulting firms to put a number on blockchain's impact on GDP. One of them is PwC (2020). They assume blockchain technology will directly add $1.76 trillion to global GDP per year by 2030. Of that, $433 billion falls to financial services. Probably all such forecasts are far from the actual number we will see in the future. After all, humans are terrible at anticipating exponential growth. Such predictions are still very telling because of the assumptions that underpin them. Most of the analyses, including the one by PwC, expect a hockey stick effect that will start in the mid-2020s. After a phase of slow and linear blockchain adoption, a critical mass will be reached, setting off the steep, exponential curve.

The moment banking started to listen

Much before consultants looked at how blockchain would change the economy, they looked at how it would change banking. One of the first studies that pinned down the technology's benefit for financial services came in 2015 and forecast it could save banks $15–20 billion annually, starting in 2022 (Santander InnoVentures, Wyman and Anthemis, 2015). At that time, it was hardly possible to grasp all of the use cases, let alone consider the potential in non-traditional banking business. Hence, the study only looked at cross-border transactions, securities trading and regulatory compliance. At that time a survey of Wall Street bankers found that 94 per cent of them thought the new technology had the potential to disrupt banking forever (Leising, 2015). Those were the stewards of the global financial system and they had recognized very early on the groundbreaking potential of distributed ledgers. They were not speaking about change or gradual improvement, but about disruption. And they meant it. The following year 72 per cent of banks reported that they had embarked on their blockchain journey (Deloitte and Efma, 2016).

But how did a technology invented by a handful of techno-libertarians and targeted to make banks obsolete find its way from obscure mailing lists to the boardrooms of the world's banking behemoths? Let's start from the beginning. In today's terminology we would say that bitcoin was released in an agile mode. The original code was sprinkled with errors that needed to be ironed out. New functionalities had to be added. But the community of cypherpunks and other coders kept working jointly on the software to make it ready for primetime.

bitcoin becoming (in)famous

In 2011 bitcoin started to become known and used outside of cryptographer circles. Two institutions became crucial in the expansion. The first was Mt. Gox, a cryptocurrency exchange founded by Jed McCaleb. At Mt. Gox users could buy and sell bitcoins like they did with stocks. This was a crucial step on the road to the mainstream, because without exchanges you always needed to know exactly which person you wanted to send your bitcoins to. You couldn't just go to a website and buy them.

McCaleb sold the exchange early on to Mark Karpeles. The inflection point came shortly afterwards when Ross Ulbricht joined the exchange. Ulbricht was the founder of the second institution that drove bitcoin's popularity outside of the coder community: the Silk Road market. It was a marketplace in the dark web, where the shopping categories carried labels such as 'guns' and 'drugs'. Needless to say, Ulbricht was enthralled by the possibility to circumvent the regulated payment system of banks and credit card companies. Bitcoin transactions might have been public, but users could hide behind pseudonyms. Users and investors of such sites were also quick to recognize how the new cryptocurrency could aid them.

Up to this day the image of bitcoin is determined by this early phase. At that time media and politicians jumped on the bandwagon too. Only two years after the genesis block had been mined, bitcoin had made its way to the US Senate, albeit in a negative light. In 2011 Senator Chuck Schumer, who 10 years later would go on to become the Senate Majority Leader, croaked that bitcoin was nothing else but a money laundering machine, falsely adding that it is an untraceable currency for criminal transactions. (Schumer, quoted in Jeffries, 2012). Besides exposing how little politicians knew about cryptocurrencies back then – bitcoins are the opposite of untraceable – the statement clearly shows that bitcoin was solely perceived through the lens of evading the official financial system.

At Davos in 2014, JPM Chase's CEO Jamie Dimon called bitcoin 'terrible'. The top executive of the biggest bank in the US worried about its use for illegal activities, not to mention the danger it posed to investors looking for a safe value storage (Flitter, 2021).

So, when and why did the attitude to bitcoin change? With all the lawmakers' hostility and negative press, how is possible that cryptocurrency wasn't banned? One turning point came in October 2013 at a public library in San Francisco. FBI agents captured Ulbricht in a Hollywood-style operation and took down the Silk Road marketplace. Among politicians the realization dawned that it did not take any special legislation, but that you could curb crypto's dark downsides by applying the already available legal arsenal. Bitcoin was just a means of payment, not an illicit activity in itself. If it could be regulated, say at the exchanges where fiat is swapped for cryptos, then there was no reason for a ban. Moreover, bitcoin had two features that would come in handy for law enforcement: immutability and transparency. The entire history of the bitcoin blockchain is visible to everybody and no single transaction can be altered ex-post. Today there are even companies such as Chainalysis offering automatized crypto analytics to law enforcement.

Hence, two years and one important Senate Committee hearing later, Senator Schumer changed his mind. In a tweet he hailed bitcoin as having significant potential (Schumer, 2013). The bitcoin heavyweights had managed to convince lawmakers in the 2013 hearings that it was too early to kill the technology.

Most bankers, such as Jamie Dimon, on the other hand, didn't buy in and remained critical of cryptos. Institutes like Wells Fargo, who reportedly looked into cooperation partners to build a bitcoin exchange, remained the exception and eventually didn't go through with their plans (Young, 2017). As we will see later on in the book, it would take banks years to start taking cautious steps into anything that had even the faintest smell of cryptocurrency. But they did bet big on the engine behind the new currencies.

The great decoupling

What eventually fanned bankers' imagination was the realization that the technology in the backend (the blockchain) could be decoupled from the application layer (bitcoin). The second big crypto project – Ethereum – went live in 2015 and spectacularly demonstrated that the link between blockchain and bitcoin could be broken, that the trust machine could be used in countless industries, and that blockchains could be parametrized in such a way that they were not antithetical to compliance and regulation. We will speak a lot about Ethereum in the chapters to come as it unleashed a panoply of new possibilities. For now, it suffices to say that it hinted at the Cambrian explosion of blockchain applications to come.

Neobanks turned out to be pioneers of blockchain usage. German Fidor in 2014 became the first to integrate Ripple's payment protocol (Rizzo, 2014). Ripple is a distributed ledger company that is best known for its XRP token, which for years has been among the top cryptocurrencies based on market cap. Unlike other crypto projects, Ripple Labs is geared at cooperating with financial institutions. It is often criticized by the crypto-cosmos for this aim, as well as for offering a non-blockchain-based interbank solution for cross-border transactions.

Banking behemoths were also quick to put the new technology onto their roadmaps. JP Morgan Chase, one of the fiercest critics of the crypto-realm, is among the most fervent blockchain advocates. In 2016 it launched the Quorum network, a centralized application on the otherwise decentralized Ethereum blockchain. Many other initiatives followed, including a Blockchain Center for Excellence and its own blockchain-based coin that is pegged to the US dollar. How come banks were so quick to embrace distributed ledger technology and reach such an early consensus on the topic? After all, financial institutes are often criticized for being slow moving and erring on the side of caution.

The answer might be found on the Pinterest page of Western Union, on which the company displays a money wire telegraph from 1873 (Western Union, 1873). On it we can see that somebody called C.C. Antoine has sent $300 to a Jason Ingraham in New York. For me the most fascinating thing about this historic document is the charge for the money transfer. It adds up to $9.73 or 3.24 per cent of the value sent. Through the steady technological advances of one and a half centuries we could expect these costs today to be much lower, right? Luckily, people can still send money across the country in pretty much the same fashion and we even have the same company providing the service. So, we can make a straight comparison. Let's say you want to replicate the same transaction as C.C. Antoine. You deposit the money at a counter in cash and your receiver takes it out in cash as well, just in another US city. According to Western Union's website the fee today stands at $28 or 9.3 per cent (Western Union, 2022).

Imagine paying for your TV set three times what you paid for it 10 or 20 years ago. Before emails arrived, you had to pay the post office to deliver letters and it took days or weeks. Today it is literally free. Technological progress drives down prices, but why have we seen the opposite happen with money services? How can it be that 150 years later it costs a small fortune to update the accounts at two banks when you can instantly message people around the world for free? The answer is that banking has never been digitalized. Sure, we all use banking apps to check our account balance and our iPhone at a contactless terminal to pay for groceries. Yet the backend is still designed on paper-based logic.

The big productivity booster

Banks know this and this is why they have understood like nobody else that technological leaps in the architectural layer can be extreme boosters to productivity. They can also be enablers for new offerings and new business models. In recent years banks have excessively deployed tools such as application programming interfaces (APIs) or microservices. And it is not just payment that needs a serious overhaul. I have identified seven major sectors of financial services that are likely to be disrupted by the use of blockchain technology in the coming years:

1. Payments and remittances
2. Clearance and settlement systems
3. Fundraising
4. Securities and asset management
5. (Syndicated) loans
6. Trade finance
7. Compliance – know your customer (KYC), anti-money laundering (AML), counter-terrorism financing (CTF), etc

Banks have early on been in the eye of the blockchain hurricane. Whether they wanted to or not, they had to take a stance on cryptocurrencies and blockchains. It is one thing to offer crypto services such as the purchase of cryptocurrencies. But questions abounded that required immediate decisions. Should they let crypto-businesses open bank accounts? Should they let customers transfer money to and from crypto-exchanges? On the other hand, media and pundits smelt disruption in the air. A steep rise in popularity of this alternative banking system was too good a story to pass on. That increased the pressure on incumbents as well.

Not so Big Tech. Their hand was not forced, as officially they were just the partners of established banking institutions. They were perceived as the bridge to the customer, set safely in the application layer. Whatever happened in the backend was none of their business and would not impact their business model. So far for the narrative. As we will see later, Big Tech was in fact paying very close attention. The Big Five understood that blockchain would rewrite the rules for competing in the financial system. And they also understood the power of protocol innovation. Companies such as Google or Facebook are often seen as pure application players, but in order to scale the way they did, much innovation was necessary in terms of infrastructure and protocols.

There were some IT giants that got into blockchain early. Baidu, China's largest search engine and the world's fifth-most-visited website at that time, started accepting bitcoin payments (Clinch, 2013). Only two months later the Chinese central bank cracked down on cryptocurrencies and Baidu had to stop accepting bitcoin payments. IBM has been a very early adopter of blockchain technology; since 2015 it has been a major force behind the Hyperledger project that would let private corporations benefit from centralized blockchains. Yet in the years when banks denounced cryptos, accepted the blockchain idea and actively started to get into the blockchain race, none of the Big Five publicly announced any plans for blockchain technology.

KEY TAKEAWAYS

- A unique mix of cryptographer pioneers, a techno-utopian worldview and a libertarian rediscovery of the free banking idea shaped a group called cypherpunks. The group was responsible for a number of technological breakthroughs that solved the double-spend problem when moving money online. The invention of distributed ledger technology eventually crested in the world's first real cryptocurrency: bitcoin.
- Only once cryptocurrencies were decoupled from the mechanism in the back – the blockchain – did the potential of the new trust machine come to the surface.
- Blockchain turned out to be a general-purpose invention that would power multiple crucial sectors of the economy. By creating cheap digital trust, it holds the potential to usher in a new techno-economic paradigm in which our lives also move online, including all things of monetary value.
- Banks quickly realized that blockchain technology is not only a threat to their business but can be a productivity booster in seven major financial areas. They acted accordingly.

References

Arthur, B (2011) *The Nature of Technology: What it is and how it evolves*, Free Press, New York

Back, A (1997) Hash cash postage implementation, 18 March, http://www.hashcash.org/papers/announce.txt (archived at https://perma.cc/R5Y4-8ZSS)

Breshnan, T and Gordon, R (1997) The economics of new goods, *Studies in Income and Wealth*, **58**

Breshnan, T and Trajtenberg, M (1995) General purpose technologies: 'engines of growth'? *Journal of Econometrics*, **65** (1) (January), pp 83–108

Chaum, D (1983) Blind signatures for untraceable payments, *Advances in Cryptology Proceedings*, **82** (3), pp 199–203

Clinch, M (2013) Baidu division now accepting bitcoins, *CNBC*, 16 October, www.cnbc.com/2013/10/16/baidu-division-now-accepting-bitcoins.html (archived at https://perma.cc/FT8G-BQVT)

Deloitte and Efma (2016) Out of the blocks: Blockchain: from hype to prototype, May, www2.deloitte.com/content/dam/Deloitte/nl/Documents/financial-services/deloitte-nl-fsi-blockchain-from-hype-to-prototype-out-of-the-blocks.pdf (archived at https://perma.cc/94Q5-VDBE)

Dwork, C and Naor, M (1992) Pricing via processing or combatting junk mail, www.wisdom.weizmann.ac.il/~naor/PAPERS/pvp.pdf (archived at https://perma.cc/J8PM-4P7V)

ECB (2012) Virtual Currency Schemes, October, www.ecb.europa.eu/pub/pdf/other/virtualcurrencyschemes201210en.pdf (archived at https://perma.cc/Z6JW-UU4S)

Flitter, E (2021) Banks tried to kill crypto and failed. Now they're embracing it (slowly), *New York Times*, 1 November, www.nytimes.com/2021/11/01/business/banks-crypto-bitcoin.html (archived at https://perma.cc/LTP9-MDVR)

Freeman, C (1982) *The Economics of Industrial Innovation*, Frances Pinter, London

Freeman, C (1987) *Technology Policy and Economic Performance: Lessons from Japan,* Pinter, London

Freeman, C and Perez, C (1988) Structural crisis of adjustment: business cycles and investment behaviour, in G Dosi et al (1989) *Technical Change and Economic Theory*, Frances Pinter, London, pp 38–66.

Gilder, G (2018) *Lifer after Google: The fall of big data and the rise of the blockchain economy*, Regnery Gateway, Washington, DC

Gordon, R (2016) *The Rise and Fall of American Growth: The U.S. standard of living since the Civil War*, Princeton University Press, Princeton/Oxford

Grieve, J et al (2014) Researchers uncover likely creator of bitcoin, Phys.org, 16 April, https://phys.org/news/2014-04-uncover-creator-bitcoin.html (archived at https://perma.cc/42ZM-9ZYD)

Hayek, F (1976) *Denationalisation of Money*, The Institute for Economic Affairs, London

Heiligenstein, M (2022) Facebook data breaches: full timeline through 2022, *Firewall Times*, 18 January, https://firewalltimes.com/facebook-data-breach-timeline/ (archived at https://perma.cc/6XCW-F2RT)

Hughes, E (1993) A Cypherpunk's Manifesto, 9 March, www.activism.net/cypherpunk/manifesto.html (archived at https://perma.cc/5AL9-7QBV)

Leising, M (2015) The blockchain revolution gets endorsement in Wall Street survey, Bloomberg, 22 July, http://www.bloomberg.com/news/articles/2015-07-22/the-blockchain-revolution-gets-endorsement-in-wall-street-survey (archived at https://perma.cc/8PVJ-TS3K)

Mahler, T (2018) '96 | Oncologist + Gold = Revolution? *blogwhat?* 17 October, https://medium.com/blockwhat/96-oncologist-gold-revolution-c08a8dc26880 (archived at https://perma.cc/672V-FZXG)

May, T (1992) The Crypto Anarchist Manifesto, 22 November, https://activism.net/cypherpunk/crypto-anarchy.html (archived at https://perma.cc/4NG9-FL9B)

Nakamoto, S (2008) Bitcoin: A Peer-to-Peer Electronic Cash System, https://bitcoin.org/bitcoin.pdf (archived at https://perma.cc/7WVN-QJXA)

Nakashima, E (2013) Chinese hackers who breached Google gained access to sensitive data, U.S. officials say, *Washington Post*, 20 May, www.washingtonpost.com/world/national-security/chinese-hackers-who-breached-google-gained-access-to-sensitive-data-us-officials-say/2013/05/20/51330428-be34-11e2-89c9-3be8095fe767_story.html (archived at https://perma.cc/MKL2-962C)

Pejic, I (2019) *Blockchain Babel: The crypto-craze and the challenge to business*, Kogan Page, London

Popper, N (2015) *Digital Gold: bitcoin and the inside story of the misfits and millionaires trying to reinvent money,* Harper, New York

PwC (2020) Time for trust – the trillion-dollar reason to rethink blockchain, October

Rand, A (1957) *Atlas Shrugged,* New American Library, New York

Regis, E (1994) Meet the Extropians, *Wired*, 1 October, www.wired.com/1994/10/extropians/ (archived at https://perma.cc/VF3S-2WWR)

Rizzo, P (2014) Fidor becomes first bank to use Ripple payment protocol, CoinDesk, 5 May, www.coindesk.com/markets/2014/05/05/fidor-becomes-first-bank-to-use-ripple-payment-protocol/ (archived at https://perma.cc/VR5Z-ZR38)

Santander InnoVentures, Wyman and Anthemis (2015) The Fintech 2.0 Paper: Rebooting Financial Services, www.oliverwyman.com/media-center/2015/fintech-2-0-paper.html (archived at https://perma.cc/4VPP-592H)

Schumer, C, quoted in A Jeffries (2012) Eight months after Sen. Chuck Schumer blasted bitcoin, Silk Road is still booming, *Observer*, 26 January, https://observer.com/2012/01/eight-months-after-sen-chuck-schumer-blasted-bitcoin-silk-road-is-still-booming/ (archived at https://perma.cc/7C37-V9CY)

Schumer, C (2013) #Bitcoin has significant potential. Senate Banking Committee will hear from industry & government officials at 3:30pm, 19 November, Twitter, https://twitter.com/senschumer/status/402846475409170432 (archived at https://perma.cc/8N4W-6SHH)

Stradbrooke, S (2021) Crypto Crime Cartel: Behind Adam Back and Blockstream's attempts to constrain Bitcoin, Coingeek, 18 May, https://coingeek.com/crypto-crime-cartel-behind-adam-back-and-blockstreams-attempts-to-constrain-bitcoin/ (archived at https://perma.cc/U9TQ-MFPF)

Szabo, N (1996) Smart Contracts: Building Blocks for Digital Markets, www.fon.hum.uva.nl/rob/Courses/InformationInSpeech/CDROM/Literature/LOTwinterschool2006/szabo.best.vwh.net/smart_contracts_2.html (archived at https://perma.cc/AG4N-AMXC)

Szabo, N (2001, 2004, 2005) Trusted third parties are security holes, www.fon.hum.uva.nl/rob/Courses/InformationInSpeech/CDROM/Literature/LOTwinterschool2006/szabo.best.vwh.net/ttps.html (archived at https://perma.cc/ZV9J-RJEC)

Szabo, N (2002) *Shelling Out: The origins of money*, https://nakamotoinstitute.org/shelling-out/ (archived at https://perma.cc/CY3H-STVC)

Szabo, N (2008) Bit gold, 27 December, https://unenumerated.blogspot.com/2005/12/bit-gold.html (archived at https://perma.cc/P6SA-7NPH)

The Economist (2015) Briefing Blockchains: The great chain of being sure about things, 31 October, pp 21–24

Vigna, P and Casey, M (2018) *The Truth Machine: The blockchain and the future of everything*, St. Martin's Press, New York

Western Union (1873) Money transfer form, August 25, 1873, #WesternUnion, https://co.pinterest.com/pin/183029172338781725/ (archived at https://perma.cc/HM9T-TMHZ)

Western Union (2022) Send money online, www.westernunion.com/us/en/web/send-money/start?ReceiveCountry=US&ISOCurrency=USD&SendAmount=300&FundsOut=AG&FundsIn=DebitCard (archived at https://perma.cc/8V9C-3CY2)

Young, J (2017) Why Wells Fargo tried to start a bitcoin exchange in 2013, CCN, 16 March, www.ccn.com/wells-fargo-tried-start-bitcoin-exchange-2013/ (archived at https://perma.cc/CP8U-W3X)

3

Lure of the wild: redefining the idea of money

Redefining the idea of money

While banks started to dream of beaming pounds and dollars across the world in split seconds, crypto maximalists felt not only that the initial anti-banking idea had been stolen and perverted, they also felt that banks simply didn't get the full picture. Yes, Nakamoto wanted to circumvent the financial system, and yes, he wanted to replicate scarcity in the digital world. But this was only part of the picture. While it was possible to use the blockchain with fiat currency, that was not the point. Cryptocurrencies, their advocates felt, allowed people to reimagine money from the ground up and thus get rid of the evils that had befallen fiat. At the top of that list: inflation.

We have already learned about Nick Szabo's fascination with gold, and bitcoin in particular was set to imitate the characteristics of the rare metal. The most important parallel was its limited supply. Satoshi Nakamoto capped the maximum number of bitcoins in circulation to 21 million, with the number of coins added to the system continuously halving until the new supplies dry out some time around the year 2140.

The idea was to seize from central banks a hitherto central monetary control tool. With cryptocurrencies no institution could decide to mint new money deliberately. This was supposed to be the safeguard against inflation. But the cap on the supply made fully fledged crypto coins the opposite of a functioning currency; it made them deflationary. People were buying it as a speculative asset, keeping it to themselves rather than having an incentive to use it in everyday trade.

The three key functions of money

In classic economic theory money has three key functions: it must be a store of value, a medium of exchange and a unit of account. In theory crypto-currencies can fulfil all of those criteria. In reality they don't. Fiat is doing a better job on all of those dimensions. First, take money as a store of value. What money does is to help its users transfer purchasing power from today to some point in the future. You can do that with cryptocurrencies, but what prevents them from being an *efficient* store of value is their extreme volatility. Sure, the pound or the euro lose value over time as their supply grows, but this is nothing compared to the wild fluctuations of every real crypto coin with an independent exchange rate. Buying bitcoins to hedge against inflation is the same as buying a lottery ticket.

Cryptocurrencies are not a very powerful medium of exchange either. Some retailers are beginning to accept them, but for many of those it is not much more than a PR stunt. Could cryptos become a medium of exchange if states forced their citizens to use them? This goes against the very libertarian mindset from which cryptos were born. Yet one country has made that decision and provided us with a real-life experiment. In 2021 El Salvador became the first country to declare bitcoin legal tender alongside the US dollar. The latter has had the status since 2001. Following this decision, every business must accept payment in bitcoins. Criticism rose from all sides. The IMF urged El Salvador to reverse the decision in order not to jeopardize macroeconomic stability (McDonald and Vizcaino, 2021). Meanwhile, a study found that 95.9 per cent of the population were against this move (Central American University José Simeon Cañas, 2021). Much of this disapproval stems from the shortcomings bitcoin has as a medium of exchange. The Chivo Wallet through which citizens must access their bitcoins was down frequently. Businesses and financial institutions have to invest massively into the acceptance and processing infrastructure. Furthermore, to be a valid means of exchange a currency must be widely accessible. In many corners of the world (stable) internet access and digital literacy are simply not there yet.

The third characteristic money has to fulfil is to be a unit of account. Here bitcoin and others are falling short as well. Crypto coins lack a reference value in our heads. How else can you explain that when we talk about how much somebody invested into bitcoins, we don't say how many coins they bought but how much their investment is worth in dollars. Retailers that quote their prices in cryptocurrencies update them frequently, suggesting they are in reality anchored in fiat currencies.

Money as a history of recorded debt

Defendants of traditional cryptocurrencies have realized the shortcomings and they are now increasingly talking of crypto as a 'universal unit of account' (e.g. Casey, 2021). Less abstractly, you can imagine it as a digital barter system. Crypto's initial idea was to take money back to a ledger-based model, meaning a recorded history of debt. Their argument is, rightly, that we have far too often mistaken coins, bills and other assets for the actual value, while they are just a representation and measurement thereof. Those monetary instruments were all invented because it was impossible to keep track of debt, meaning who gave what to whom. But this is exactly how the blockchain works. It is a permanent, complex ledger. When you purchase a bitcoin it doesn't move anywhere. The record (i.e. the blockchain) simply reflects that there has been a transaction and that the bitcoin you purchase can now be accessed with a different set of private keys. The argument behind it is that this new conception of money makes the store of value precept obsolete. In this view cryptocurrencies can be efficient money regardless of deflation and volatility.

Problems with this understanding are manifold. For one, it would rob central banks of very powerful tools, for example to stimulate exports and consumption or to counter economic cycles. Crises often need a 'whatever it takes' stance by governments to prevent a complete economic breakdown. Just think of when the euro was close to collapsing in 2012 or when in 2020/2021 the Covid-19 pandemic crippled literally every economy in the world.

Second, there can be no universal unit of account when it comes to money, because money is always linked to what it measures. Think of a kilogram, a mile or an hour – those are all standards that are fixed by the laws of physics. A minute or a second objectively always have the same length. But a dollar, an ounce of gold, a corporate share or a bitcoin don't. They always change with what they measure. Their value is completely dependent on what people are willing to pay for them. This is a paradox that cannot be solved by blockchain technology.

A promising new invention: stablecoins

But the crypto-sphere is brimming with other ideas. One of the most promising inventions of recent years has been stablecoins. As the name suggests, those don't fluctuate with supply and demand and are thus useless as a speculative asset. Stablecoins are pegged to a stable reserve asset and can either be centralized or decentralized. In most cases the stable asset is a fiat currency. One JPM Coin, for example, is always worth one USD and it is backed by the bank's reserves. USD Tether (USDT) has the same anchor, but is a decentralized application. DAI is a stablecoin also linked to the USD, yet it doesn't hold dollar collateral, but rather a basket of crypto-collateral.

The reserve assets could also be natural assets such as gold or oil. There are even non-collateralized stablecoins that keep the peg to an asset purely algorithmically by adjusting the supply of its tokens to the value of the reference asset. However, the spectacular collapse of the algorithmic stablecoin Terra and its sister coin Luna in May 2022 made it unmistakably clear that the future of stablecoins can lie only in secure asset reserves. Terra, among the three largest private stablecoins on the market, lost its peg to the dollar and thus set off a massive contraction of the entire crypto-sphere. Unconnected blue-chip cryptocurrencies suffered losses in the range of double-digit percentages. $400 billion in market value was wiped out within a week (Chow, 2022).

In my view, asset-backed, regulated stablecoins will be one of the most essential building blocks of a truly digital economy. They wed the advantages of blockchain-based monetary transfers to the stability of fiat. And they are the vehicle that Big Tech has tried and will try to use in order to muscle its way into the finance world. That is why we will come back to them in more detail in Chapter 8.

Gold rush and Telegram

Deep reflections on monetary theory and a libertarian utopia have been a constant in the crypto kingdom. They were driving the cypherpunks and much of the early bitcoin movement. Yet thinking about money was not what prompted the crypto-fever. It was the prospect of making it.

The early years of the bitcoin movement, however, were characterized by large failures, rather than a gripping gold rush. That does not mean that techies brimming with enthusiasm stayed alone until the industry gave birth to inspiring 'from dishwasher to millionaire' stories. The promise to reinvent money drew a completely new group to the crypto-party. While banks were giving the technology behind bitcoin a closer look, they also started to suffer from employee attrition. Bankers of all ranks smelt disruption and wanted to be on the frontlines of building a new financial system rather than improving the existing one. One prominent example was Blythe Masters, a former JP Morgan Chase executive who left the banking world in 2015 to join Digital Asset Holdings.

When I talked to Emma Todd, another former banker to switch sides around that time, she explained the allure of this new space. She had gotten bored with banking and had been looking into fintech. Though she had known about crypto since a friend had introduced her to it in 2013, she hadn't really paid much attention. It was only three years later when Todd visited a blockchain conference in Toronto that she was mesmerized by the inspirational speeches of bitcoin grandees like Andreas Antonopoulos. She was galvanized by the potential of cryptocurrencies to upend the monetary system she was working in.

But back at the bank her colleagues had no clue about it. And neither could they see why she was so animated, even after she explained it to them. 'I know it from myself. If you're not ready to hear the message, there is nothing that can be done.' She quickly realized that banking no longer held any appeal and if she wanted to work on blockchain she would have to leave the banking industry. And she did (Todd, 2022).

Asked whether it was the promise of quick money that lured burger flippers and bankers to the space alike, Todd just shakes her head: 'Back then there were very few millionaires compared to today. Some guys were making money, but mostly it was people tinkering with the technology to see where it could lead them. It was the excitement of working on something groundbreaking.'

Another characteristic of the crypto-world that has stood out ever since the birth of bitcoin is its breakneck speed – in technology, business models, but also in career development. When Todd left banking, she started with crypto-marketing, after two days went into strategy, and quickly ended up organizing countless conferences and roundtables. She later even transitioned into the mining business (Todd, 2022). Her story is quite typical of many non-coders who got in early. They played an instrumental role in broadening the appeal of blockchain technology beyond the tech community.

Self-made millionaires enter the stage

Very soon, however, 'rags to riches' stories started to pour in. You would read about average office workers who in 2010 had invested $3,000 in bitcoin, which had later turned into $25 million (Bishop, 2017) or substitute teachers who started putting $25 a week into bitcoin and ended up as millionaires with hundreds of thousands of social media followers (Schlott, 2022).

Hardly anybody personifies the promise of the crypto-success as well as Changpeng Zhao, who goes by the nickname 'CZ'. His parents emigrated from China to Vancouver shortly after Zhao was born. They lived a typical middle-class life, and as a teenager Zhao worked at McDonald's and at a gas station to support the family budget.

After studying computer science, he kicked off a stellar career working for the Tokyo Stock Exchange and Bloomberg. At the latter he was promoted three times within two years, but was so restless that he quit anyway to move to Shanghai. There he worked on high-frequency trading systems. In 2013 he learned of bitcoin by accident, namely from a poker colleague who happened to be a venture capitalist. Soon afterwards Zhao cut his teeth on various prominent blockchain projects and even sold his house in Shanghai to invest the money in bitcoin (Ambler, 2018).

Eventually, in 2017 he decided to found his own crypto-exchange: Binance. Less than seven months later *Forbes* valued his net worth at over $1 billion. More than 6 million people were using Binance, which had the technical capability of handling 1.4 million transactions per second. In addition to the powerful technical platform, Binance had issued its own token at exactly the height of the hype. Revenue and employee numbers skyrocketed so quickly the company couldn't get a lease for an adequate office. Landlords looked at Binance's tax records from the preceding year, and judging by them the company wasn't even able to cover the lease for one month (Ambler, 2018).

It was stories like these that fanned the media frenzy and turned venture capitalists, entrepreneurs, and Average Joes looking for a quick buck into cryptophiles. The money going into cryptocurrencies snowballed in 2017. Investment titans such as Marc Andreessen and Peter Thiel showered projects with millions. IT professionals started buying mining chips and earning rewards in their spare time. Cab drivers, students and salesmen tried to emulate their friend or cousin who had bought some bitcoins two years ago and was now cruising around in a Lamborghini. They came from all walks of life and all continents, but they were all gripped by the same basic human instinct: the fear of missing out. People around them were getting rich, seemingly out of thin air. They needed to get onto the bandwagon before it raced past them.

The explosion in popularity even stunned some of the earliest travellers to the crypto-cosmos. George Selgin, who today is the director emeritus of the Center for Monetary and Financial Alternatives at the

Cato Institute, was one of the select few whose name was on the early cypherpunk mailing lists in the 1990s. This is even more remarkable considering Selgin was an economist in a space run by techies. Nick Szabo (2018, 2019) calls Selgin's work on free banking 'very inspirational' and repeatedly stresses him as a big influence on the crypto-movement. Yet not even Selgin could have anticipated where those thought experiments would end up two decades later:

> Back then it was just some intriguing but hypothetical discussions on pseudonymous money. I did not imagine at the time that any prospective private money that was neither a commodity nor a redeemable claim to something else of value could get off the ground. I certainly did not anticipate how popular such a medium could become. (Selgin, 2022)

A libertarian channel fans the hype

The images evoked by the crypto-boom struck a chord with most people because they were so familiar. Metaphors of bitcoins as digital gold and stories of overnight wealth paralleled the imagery that had driven gold-seekers to the coasts of California in the middle of the 19th century. The stories of findings of bitcoin's shiny equivalent on America's West Coast had spread extremely quickly through a very recent invention of the time: the telegraph. In many ways that communication revolution had enabled the gold rush.

Fast-forward to the 2010s and you might expect that digital gold-seekers would organize themselves via the communication channels of the day. Social media such as Facebook and Twitter or messenger services like WhatsApp and iMessage would be perfectly suited to pitch new crypto-businesses, raise capital and recruit talent. None of it happened. At least not on the scale that would have driven the new gold rush. Instead, most new coins that got minted lured investors via telegrams. Admittedly those telegrams had nothing to do with the 19th-century technology, but were a new messaging service of the same name, and explicitly not provided by tech titans. Telegram was founded in 2013 by two Russian brothers with an affection for

Edward Snowden. The messaging app soared to questionable prominence when the likes of ISIS terrorists used it to prevent government agencies from snooping on their communication and even using it as a marketing channel (Auchard, 2015).

But why did Big Tech squander the opportunity to become the central communication hub for a movement that was about to revolutionize finance, their biggest target industry? Many argue that Telegram was simply technologically better suited. Users could have multiple accounts, build APIs to feed real-time crypto exchange rates into the platform, and choose between exclusive groups and public channels.

Yet two things were really driving crypto-enthusiasts to Telegram. First, Big Tech explicitly steered clear of cryptocurrencies. Facebook and Google even prohibited advertisements for new coin offerings. As we will see later, they understood the disruptive force of the blockchain, but decentralized power is simply something their DNA does not support. Unsurprisingly, discussions about and promotions of new coins also avoided the private spaces of these crypto-hostile applications.

The second reason for Telegram's appeal was its ideology. Rooted deeply in the libertarian worldview, it was exactly the opposite of Big Tech and its massive aggregation of power. Telegram is a communication channel explicitly anti-government and explicitly pro-privacy. It does not harvest troves of customer data. It does not build digital profiles of its users to run through AI algorithms. And it does not sell user data to advertisers. Telegram even moved its headquarters multiple times to avoid governmental pressure to reveal its users' communications. Though not a decentralized organization, Telegram instantly appealed to the crypto-community.

When creating an account, users don't have to reveal their phone numbers as they do with WhatsApp. Starting a fundraising project is much simpler than on Kickstarter. And all communication is fully encrypted. The focus on privacy transcended mere ideological sympathy. Many projects operated in dark grey areas, but even for those seeking to be compliant with the law, it was easier said than done. The legality of cryptocurrencies at that time in most jurisdictions was an unsettled matter. And as new coin offerings were mostly global projects, they certainly reached into territories with hostile legislation towards everything that had the faintest smell of a crypto-asset.

In short, the images of crypto-millionaires popularized by the media made the hunt for prosperity spread on Telegram like wildfire. Adventurers headed for untamed crypto land. Being part of private – and thus limited – Telegram groups made them feel ahead of the curve and privy to a great investment opportunity. While participants in the groups were limited, the number of groups was not. As more and more money poured in, a crypto gold rush broke out. It pushed up coin prices and the media swooned again.

Encountering bulls and bears

In 2017 crypto-investors were not treating themselves with new cars or first-class flights for Christmas. In December their assets had started to lose their Midas touch and fears of the bitcoin bubble bursting were taking hold. Things got worse over the next couple of months. In January 2018, the Japanese exchange Coincheck announced a hack of $500 million. Studies started to confirm anecdotal evidence: most new projects were outright fraud (see Chapter 5). Starting in East Asia, regulators reacted and initiated crackdowns on crypto-trading. Wall Street bosses pitched in, making public their disregard for bitcoin. Mass psychology triggered a gargantuan sell-off.

In the course of 2018, the crypto-market disintegrated. Its bellwether, bitcoin, was down by 80 per cent. This was not the first bear market bitcoin had encountered. In 2011 it had lost 92 per cent of its value; in 2015 it was down by 84 per cent. But back then there were few exchanges, no Main Street investors and the market cap was miniscule. This time the crypto winter slashed $700 billion in market value and burned bitcoin's – and even the blockchain's – image in front of the eyes of an attentive public (Rooney, 2018).

Survivors of the great crypto-winter

The bursting of the bubble was akin to a natural selection process of the free market in which the most resilient and promising companies survive. Emma Todd's MMH Technology Group was one such company. It was an important strategic decision that made her survive the mass extinction of crypto start-ups. The fatal mistake of most entrepreneurs was a lack of asset diversification. What killed them was not that the market interest for cryptocurrencies disappeared. The real problem was that they had all of their money in bitcoins, Ether and other coins. When the value of these crypto-assets plummeted by 80 per cent, all of a sudden they weren't able to pay their employees and suppliers. The capital they owned became worthless and many went bankrupt.

Following the advice of Anthony Di Iorio, the co-founder of Ethereum, Todd had made sure to have two to three years of expenses in fiat currency and hence her company was able to survive even a long crypto winter. The other important thing was not to become disenchanted and to continue working as if the market hadn't collapsed (Todd, 2022).

The industry shakeout was impressive as the crypto-prices stayed low until the start of a new bull market in 2020. At the end of 2021 bitcoin stood at above $60,000 apiece, more than tripling its value from before the crypto-winter of 2018. Yet the cycles between bull and bear markets are extremely short in the blockchain world. The aforementioned collapse of the Terra stablecoin in April 2022 set off another carnage of crypto-value.

If you remember Zhao, the founder of Binance and burger flipper turned billionaire, you will recall that he earned his first billion in less than seven months. But his story didn't stop there. At the beginning of 2022, *Forbes* estimated the 44-year-old's fortune at $96 billion, which made Zhao the world's 19th-wealthiest person and the richest crypto magnate. In the wake of the Terra collapse in May 2022 his net worth plummeted to $17.4 billion *within one month*.

Zhao's rollercoaster ride is highly characteristic of the crypto-tycoons. They own most of their wealth in crypto-assets or their products are directly linked to the fortunes of the market, say in trading fees for crypto-assets. Mostly they have both dependencies. Hence, crypto wealth is as volatile as its exchange rates. And it is not just the ups and downs of the market that make crypto-wealth more dynamic or fleeting.

Alphabet splurges on blockchain

Despite all of the hype around cryptocurrencies and blockchain, tech titans remained suspiciously tight-lipped about it. This was unusual, given that they brim with enthusiasm every time new tech such as AI or virtual reality enters the stage. Their silence reminded me of the time before Amazon launched its cloud arm Amazon Web Services (AWS) in 2006. Cloud was the hype of the day, yet Amazon introduced AWS with little fanfare. Today, the subsidiary could be described as the world's computer, running the largest cloud by far and earning the company some $18 billion in revenue each quarter, while still growing at around 40 per cent (Novet, 2022).

Fast-forward a decade and a familiar picture emerges. Instead of their communications departments, tech juggernauts let their money speak. While most of the investment was done in-house and thus remains invisible, it was one tech giant in particular that opened its wallet to external companies: Alphabet.

Google's parent company Alphabet became the world's second-largest investor in blockchain start-ups between 2012 and 2017. It pumped more money into the space than highly active banking investors like Goldman Sachs (Kharpal, 2017). A closer look at the companies receiving the funding tells a lot about Alphabet's strategy at that time and how it has expanded in the last five years.

Some blockchain investments were apparent. Storj is such a case. The company works on a decentralized cloud storage system, meaning that it makes data centres more efficient. Alphabet participating in its $3 million seed financing round in 2017 is like Mastercard investing in payment applications – obvious.

But things get more interesting. Google Ventures (now called GV) had invested early on in Ripple, a company that was very far away from data centres, search or any other field that could be considered a Google core competence. Ripple is specialized in improving settlement, in particular for cross-border transaction. So why would Alphabet take such a bet? Simply a good investment opportunity? Hard to believe. In 2013 when Google Ventures financed Ripple its odds of turning a profit were far from what they were years later, when others such as Standard Chartered or SBI Holdings got on board. Perhaps the idea was to create an Alphabet cryptocurrency? Kevin Rose, who back then spearheaded the investment, admits he never believed Ripple would make it as a currency but rather it would be a means for settlement (quoted in Loizos, 2020). Not only is that settlement none of Alphabet's traditional business, it is not even close to the user or application interface. Settlement is deep bank territory. The investment marked a watershed moment in Big Tech's race for finance. For the first time a silicon giant grabbed for a finance area completely out of its reach.

Could the partnership with Ripple simply be an anomaly? It could, if it had been an isolated case. Also, it is crucial to understand how Alphabet invests its money. The holding company does have a later-stage investment arm called Google Capital (or CapitalG) which is focused first and foremost on pure financial gains. GV, on the other hand, gets in early and is more strategic than CapitalG. An investment by GV means that the technology is not just being observed in detail by Alphabet, but that the company is willing to spend lavishly to bring it into its universe.

Revealing acquisitions and partnerships

Alphabet's foray into finance didn't stop with Ripple. It also financed LedgerX (Chavez-Dreyfuss, 2017), which in 2021 was acquired by FTX US Derivatives. LedgerX was a crypto derivative clearing organization. Once more, not exactly a field for a tech company to traditionally toil around in.

In July 2018 Alphabet announced it would partner with the blockchain expert Digital Asset (Roberts, 2018), a well-funded start-up led by the aforementioned Blythe Masters, a former JP Morgan banker.

Digital Asset is focused on breaking down data silos in financial services by employing distributed ledger technology. Their highest-profile project is the Australian Securities Exchange's (ASX) switch to distributed ledgers, scheduled for 2023. Like Amazon or Microsoft, Alphabet sees blockchain's future in the cloud. Through Digital Asset, it gains access to a proprietary programming language called DAML, with which the data colossus can build smart contract apps itself and license those to other companies.

The same year, Alphabet partnered with BlockApps, another cooperation that enables companies to rapidly deploy blockchain solutions via the Google cloud (BlockApps, 2018).

Those early investments have a common pattern. For starters, each of the target companies builds its business on centralized blockchains. Hardly any of them even have the faintest smell of traditional cryptocurrencies. Moreover, they were all start-ups that held crucial technology assets. And lastly, all of them were challengers of the traditional banking system, while at the same time seeking to cooperate with banks. Ripple and Digital Asset both built their business model on collaborating with established finance players. It clearly shows Alphabet's ambition to become the blockchain engine for the financial world.

Alphabet's investment strategy takes a turn

Alphabet kept its wallet open over the years. However, its blockchain investment strategy took a turn. While it stayed committed to building the distributed, cloud-based backbone of the finance industry, in 2021 it also started pouring money into classic crypto firms. Google Ventures took part in a $120 million funding round of blockchain.com, the most widely used wallet for crypto-assets (LedgerInsight, 2021).

Later that year Alphabet, through its subsidiary CapitalG, invested in another crypto-native company called Digital Currency Group (DCG). DCG is a conglomerate of several crypto-heavyweight companies and also holds significant crypto-assets. In the second-largest crypto-investment round ever, Alphabet contributed $100 million (Vigna, 2021). Investing in DCG shows Alphabet's belief not just in one particular company that might help it build a powerful blockchain product, but in the future of the crypto-sphere. As we will see later on, this is the result of a general wave stoked by the rise of decentralized finance and increasing regulatory clarity. More important to notice is that Alphabet recognizes the rising market demand for decentralized digital assets and might in future latch it to its centralized systems. Its banking strategy does not end with the backend.

KEY TAKEAWAYS

- Cryptocurrencies fell short of effectively fulfilling the three key functions of money: store of value, medium of exchange and unit of account. They thus evolved from means of payment to investment assets. This did not kill the hype around cryptocurrencies; on the contrary, it fanned it.
- Stablecoins, i.e. digital currencies with their value pegged to stable assets such as fiat money, crystallized as a promising alternative for moving money. They merge the advantages of traditional currencies with blockchain technology and thus offer a huge potential that Big Banking and Big Tech have understood quickly.
- To grasp Big Tech's blockchain strategy, look at where its money goes. As the second-largest investor in distributed ledger technology, Alphabet seeks to become the blockchain engine for the entire financial realm, not just payments. Yet its later investments in crypto-assets show that this does not mean it will yield the application layer. The battle for finance will be waged on multiple levels.

References

Ambler, P (2018) From zero to crypto billionaire in under a year: Meet the founder of Binance, *Forbes*, 7 February, www.forbes.com/sites/pamelaambler/2018/02/07/changpeng-zhao-binance-exchange-crypto-cryptocurrency/?sh=2eae86a11eee (archived at https://perma.cc/YQ6J-4HL3)

Auchard, E (2015) Islamic State makes Telegram messaging app a major marketing tool, Reuters, 18 November, www.reuters.com/article/france-shooting-telegram-idCNL1N13C2YG20151118 (archived at https://perma.cc/M5C3-9BXB)

Bishop, J (2017) Meet the man traveling the world on $25 million of bitcoin profits, *Forbes*, 7 July, www.forbes.com/sites/bishopjordan/2017/07/07/bitcoin-millionaire/?sh=b4aedec62615 (archived at https://perma.cc/WKA9-XFMT)

BlockApps (2018) BlockApps partners with Google Cloud platform to provide rapid-deployment blockchain solutions, Press Release, 23 June, https://blockapps.net/blockapps-partners-google-cloud-platform-enterprise-blockchain-solutions/ (archived at https://perma.cc/M38W-T3J3)

Casey, M J (2021) How crypto becomes money: A new theory for a universal digital barter system, CoinDesk, 12 November, www.coindesk.com/policy/2021/11/12/how-crypto-becomes-money/ (archived at https://perma.cc/G56J-6X78)

Central American University José Simeon Cañas (2021) La población salvadoreña opina sobre el bitcoin y la situación socioeconómica del país, *Boletin de prensa Año XXXV*, No. 5, https://uca.edu.sv/iudop/wp-content/uploads/Boletin-BTC-Coyuntura-2021-2.pdf (archived at https://perma.cc/Z4CC-2FJ8)

Chavez-Dreyfuss, G (2017) Bitcoin options exchange raises $11.4 million in funding, Reuters, 22 May, www.reuters.com/article/us-ledgerx-exchange-funding-idUSKBN18I0B9 (archived at https://perma.cc/M677-PN99)

Chow, A (2022) The real reasons behind the crypto crash, and what we can learn from Terra's fall, *Time*, 17 May, https://time.com/6177567/terra-ust-crash-crypto/ (archived at https://perma.cc/462V-76WX)

Forbes (2022) Profile: Changpeng Zhao, www.forbes.com/billionaires (archived at https://perma.cc/HNM2-G6KV); World's billionaires list 2022, www.forbes.com/profile/changpeng-zhao/?list=billionaires&sh=7dd9baef6277 (archived at https://perma.cc/KZN5-SGGH)

Kharpal, A (2017) Google and Goldman Sachs are two of the most active investors in blockchain firms: Report, *CNBC*, 19 October, www.cnbc.com/2017/10/18/google-goldman-sachs-investors-blockchain.html (archived at https://perma.cc/WE2A-PVFV)

Ledger Insights (2021) Google Ventures backs Blockchain.com $120 million funding, 18 February, www.ledgerinsights.com/google-ventures-backs-blockchain-com-120-million-funding/ (archived at https://perma.cc/S5B2-LC3B)

Loizos, C (2020) Kevin Rose on health apps, crypto and how founders get through this time with their sanity intact, TechCrunch, 16 May, https://techcrunch.com/2020/05/15/kevin-rose-on-whats-next/?guccounter=1 (archived at https://perma.cc/5ELA-VRCW)

McDonald, D and Vizcaino, M (2021) IMF sees risks after El Salvador makes bitcoin legal tender, Bloomberg, 10 June, www.bloomberg.com/news/articles/2021-06-10/imf-sees-risks-in-el-salvador-law-making-bitcoin-legal-tender (archived at https://perma.cc/SZ7U-8UGM)

Novet, J (2022) AWS growth accelerates in quarter marred by outages, *CNBC*, 3 February, www.cnbc.com/2022/02/03/amazon-web-services-earnings-q4-2021.html (archived at https://perma.cc/ZTY5-E8WU)

Roberts, J (2018) Google expands blockchain push with digital asset tie-up, Fortune, 23 July, https://blog.digitalasset.com/news/google-expands-blockchain-push-with-digital-asset-tie-up (archived at https://perma.cc/LZ26-38DR)

Rooney, K (2018) Bitcoin is down more than 80% from last year's high, nearing its worst-ever bear market, *CNBC*, 26 November, www.cnbc.com/2018/11/26/bitcoin-nears-its-worst-ever-bear-market-down-more-than-80percent-from-the-high.html (archived at https://perma.cc/RWA5-7QW3)

Selgin, G (2022) Personal interview, 28 April

Schlott, R (2022) Four ordinary people share how they got rich from crypto, *New York Post*, 5 February, https://nypost.com/2022/02/05/how-cryptocurrency-made-these-four-ordinary-people-rich/ (archived at https://perma.cc/XB5B-4657)

Szabo, N (2018) Dr. Selgin was on the mailing list with Wei Dai and myself where in 1998 cryptocurrency (bit gold, and a bit later b-money) was invented. His description of free banking was very inspirational and informative, Twitter, 24 July, https://twitter.com/NickSzabo4/status/1021650312350691328?s=20 (archived at https://perma.cc/4K6C-24F2)

Szabo, N (2019) Nick Szabo on cypherpunks, money and bitcoin, *What Bitcoin Did Podcast #163*, 1 November, www.whatbitcoindid.com/podcast/nick-szabo-on-cypherpunks-money-and-bitcoin (archived at https://perma.cc/3LY5-3FXJ)

Todd, E (2022) Personal interview, 20 April

Vigna, P (2021) Digital currency group wants to be crypto's standard oil, *Wall Street Journal*, 21 November, www.wsj.com/articles/digital-currency-group-wants-to-be-cryptos-standard-oil-11635764400 (archived at https://perma.cc/3V63-8X9Q)

4

Two roads ahead: centralization

Ideology clash: to decentralize or not to decentralize?

'I definitely personally hope centralized exchanges burn in hell as much as possible.' That was the unmasked answer Vitalik Buterin (2018), the founder of Ethereum, gave when he was asked about centrally run cryptocurrency exchanges. His allergic reaction displays how emotionally charged the debate on centralization really is. And given the ideological roots of the cypherpunks and the reasoning in Nakamoto's whitepaper this is not surprising.

But what exactly does decentralization mean? Unfortunately, it is probably the most misused term when it comes to blockchain, so let's go beyond the gossip and into the heart of the matter, the nub of the mystery. Centralization has nothing to do with who can use the network. Nor has it anything to do with where the data is stored. Whether data is located on one server or disseminated across a network of 10,000 nodes is a matter of *distribution*, not decentralization. This is why we talk of all blockchains as distributed ledgers; they are always operated by multiple nodes of the network.

Centralization is about who gets to *confirm* transactions. To understand centralization it is necessary to understand blockchain consensus. This is basically the mechanism by which the blockchain network agrees on which version of the blockchain to continue working on. The task of blockchain nodes is not to verify a block – every node could do that by itself – but to agree on which version of the blockchain is the right one. Only the version upon which most nodes agree becomes the collective truth.

> Compare the logic to this analogous scenario: you borrow $50 from me, and I record that transaction in my notebook. If I want the money back after one year, you wouldn't accept my notebook as proof. If, however, we both had a notebook in which we confirmed that I gave you $50 – say by scribbling a signature at the bottom of the pages – then we would have a shared, confirmed understanding of the truth. It would be a way of preventing different versions of the truth from coming into existence.

The consensus mechanism is the heart of blockchain. It protects the chain from splitting, a scenario called forking in blockchain lingo. This happens when you have two diverging versions of the truth. Being the first blockchain, bitcoin has set people's expectations of how a blockchain works. While bitcoin's consensus mechanism might be the most popular one, it is just one among many. In its Proof-of-Work (POW) mechanism massive computing power is burned to weed out malicious participants. Others such as Proof-of-Stake (PoS) require a different kind of commitment, for example by investing into the network's tokens. But all of these mechanisms are linked to some kind of cost because they can all be summarized as decentralized consensus mechanisms. This means that everybody is free to join the network as an active validator.

The scenario in which you borrow $50 from me is a centralized setup. The two of us agree on the transaction and both record it in our notebooks. No other party can join. If, however, we want to expand the network we can let other people also supervise the transaction. They would record in their notebooks that I gave you $50. As long as we approve each of those recorders of the transaction it is still centralized. Let us imagine I don't hand you the bill behind closed doors, but slip it into your hand at a public square and everybody is free to record it. This would be true decentralization.

Closed, open, private and public blockchains

Note that the distinction of closed vs open networks does not refer to who can validate transactions. Rather it refers to whether people or companies can use the services of a network without approval, say to transfer crypto-assets. Therefore, a bank that offers blockchain-based cross-border payments *only to its customers* would be considered closed.

Sometimes blockchains are also described as private and public. Again, this has nothing to do with validation, but it specifies whether the reading rights for the ledger are restricted. In an open network like bitcoin everybody, even non-users, can scan the ledger for its history.

In short, if there is a privileged party that decides who gets validating power in the network, it is called a centralized blockchain. Sometimes it is also referred to as a permissioned blockchain. Unlike decentralized or permissionless blockchains, this setup requires trust in those who run the network. I need to know that the entity in charge will not let scoundrels decide which transactions are legitimate and which are not.

Is centralization a matter of degree, not kind?

Centralized blockchains are more than enhanced databases. They still mean that institutions are giving up power, because the nodes they nominate must not necessarily be under their control. Compare it to a president nominating a Supreme Justice. The president will choose somebody close to him who is likely to decide the way he would. But as soon as the Justice is confirmed the president has no formal control anymore. On top, blockchains are immutable. In some centralized designs they are even public. It is nothing compared to the current omnipotence of companies and banks when it comes to their data.

The question of whether a central authority controls who operates the network is critical. It ensures the present and past legitimacy of transactions. Yet it is also important what happens in the future and how the ledger develops. Here the question is who controls the code. Is it open source or proprietary?

Even from these very superficial considerations it becomes clear that decentralization comes in many different hues. It is not a simple yes/no question. Also, unlike bitcoin, most protocols are actually born as highly centralized applications. As Chapter 7 shows in more detail, many projects start as actual LLCs, others have a number of privileged signers, and yet others such as Ripple only slowly add more external validator nodes. Decentralization is a journey in which very few travellers actually make it to the end.

This absence of a clear distinction between centralization and decentralization has led many commentators (e.g. Roubini, 2018) to doubt the honesty behind the touted libertarian ideology. Greed, not idealism, they claim, is the major driver of the hype.

Crypto-enthusiasts retort that those pushing for centralized blockchains don't understand the very idea of the technology. Nakamoto did not invent this magic trust engine to improve the efficiency of databases. And most refuse to even call them blockchains, but resort to the term Distributed Ledger Technology (DLT).

Technology, however, does not always follow the path its creators envisioned. Once you put it out there, the market will automatically shape it into its perfect form. Those who understand the groundbreaking potential of blockchain like to compare it to the internet. But they don't (want to) see all the parallels. As Georgia Tech professor Ian Bogost (2020) splendidly illustrates, the internet began as a decentralized idea too. Visionaries perceived it as a liberating force that could bring down the gatekeepers of communication. Circumventing journalists and publishers, everybody could publish unfiltered and in real time. 'Information wants to be free' was the battle cry uttered by internet pioneer Steward Brand (1987). Yet as soon as cyberspace became commercially interesting, centralization kicked in. The likes of Facebook and Google became the new gatekeepers, far more powerful and far more concentrated than anything seen in the pre-digital age.

Problems with decentralization

Decentralization defenders put forward one special selling proposition: only decentralized blockchains can create trust out of thin air; only they can accommodate a model without a privileged party. But this total algorithmic trust comes not only at the cost of computing power or other investments the miners have to make, but also at the cost of processing speed. Nakamoto set the block size at one megabyte and put in place a mechanism that allows the network to mint only one block approximately every 10 minutes.

This is the very heartbeat of bitcoin. But it is a slow heartbeat whose low pulse fatally limits the number of transactions that can get verified. Bitcoin can process seven to eight transactions per second. Visa, Mastercard and other payment giants can handle multiple thousand times more. There is no easy fix for that. Make the block size larger and the risk of splitting the chain increases. Reduce the 10-minute gap and the supply of coins will be exhausted very soon because Nakamoto capped it at 21 million to make sure there is no inflation. Other decentralized coins such as bitcoin Cash or Litecoin have improved performance, but the output is still nowhere near current payment systems or centralized blockchains.

Speed is one problem of decentralized consensus. Energy is the other. According to the Cambridge Centre for Alternative Finance (CCAF) the bitcoin network annually burns through 119.47 terawatt hours of electricity (as measured in 2022). Is that a lot? Yes. You can liken it to the entire energy consumption of countries such as the Netherlands, Austria or Argentina. Every year the countries used for comparison grow bigger, despite bitcoin still languishing at the fringe of the financial system. A move into the mainstream could not be handled by either the chain or the planet.

It is widely known that bitcoin gobbles insane amounts of energy, but its environmental impact goes much farther than that. The hardware it uses provides a monstrous CO_2 footprint. Miners, that is nodes participating in the PoW verification, need highly specialized equipment. Computer chips that are extremely efficient in performing repetitive tasks such as plugging in values and are sometimes specifically geared for mining have to be swapped in ever shorter cycles. On average the specialized hardware lasts 1.29 years and then it turns into electronic waste. The bottom line is that one bitcoin transaction is equivalent to trashing two iPhones. Toxic chemicals and heavy metals end up in the soil; air and water get polluted (de Vries and Stoll, 2021).

Shortcomings beyond speed and energy consumption

Bandwidth and storage demands are high too. Downloading the bitcoin ledger, which you have to do if you want to mine, will cost you 407 GB of storage space as of May 2022 (YCharts, 2022). As more transactions are added to the record every day, the storage space needed is permanently increasing. Other blockchains occupy even more hard drive space.

bitcoin was blockchain's first proof of concept. It introduced a paradigmatic change; it was not its task to create the most efficient solution. So, it would be unfair to judge all decentralized applications based on bitcoin's capacities. When the first car was introduced, it had the marvellous power of 0.55 kW and rolled on three wheels (Mercedes-Benz, no date). One-and-a-half centuries later car demand is ever growing and manufacturers are still finding ways to tweak them. Similarly to cars, PoW blockchains are becoming more resource-efficient. Today large amounts of data are often stored off-chain, with only pointers and references of the data stored within the blockchain itself.

But as fascinating as the improvements to our automobiles have been, the core functionality is still to take people from A to B, where the distance between the two is usually short. No matter how fast the car becomes, people will always travel by aeroplanes to farther-away places, even to closer ones if they are pressed for time.

The performance gap between decentralized and centralized blockchains is comparable to that between cars and jets. Even if bitcoin can improve its transactional throughput by 1,000 per cent it would still only stand at about 70 transactions per second. Now compare that to centralized applications, in particular *Project Hamilton*, by The Federal Reserve Bank of Boston (Boston Fed) and the Massachusetts

Institute of Technology's Digital Currency Initiative (MIT DCI). The research project on central bank digital currencies managed to cram as many as 1.7 million transactions into one second (Federal Reserve Bank of Boston, 2022).

The efficiency debate is certainly the most important one, but there are a number of other caveats that, if forgotten, can break projects. For example, a decentralized blockchain might easily fail to take off. If you cannot mobilize a sufficiently large number of users to act as validators, the blockchain will be unsecured. Platform ignition failure is the result. Bitcoin and Ethereum would never inspire so much confidence were it not for the thousands of globally dispersed nodes.

Furthermore, there are characteristics of decentralized blockchains that are not necessarily weaknesses, but make it useless for certain setups. When choosing the setup, it is incumbent to determine whether the use case can tolerate outdated or wrong data. In other words, does the data lend itself to being immutable? Another crucial question concerns transactional transparency. Does the data for the application need to be available to everyone? Is there any harm in having public data, meaning that everybody is able to track the transfer of assets between accounts?

Big Tech and Big Banking saddle up

It was an unusual problem that Sundar Pichai and his top deputies had to wrestle with in their weekly Monday meetings. Google, for years one of the world's most popular employers, was seeing more and more managers and top talent hand in their resignations. The problem became so pressing that at the end of 2021 it had become a matter for the CEO.

It was not that Google had lost its allure as a good place to work or had gone through a scandal that could have repelled its workers. Google was still a highly trusted brand, offered a decent work environment and was continuously tinkering with all sorts of thrilling futuristic technology. By all measures it should have been the very top of the hill for everybody whose work was even remotely connected to

IT. The big problem was rather that a generation of new companies were mushrooming, which like a magnet pulled in the brightest talents: crypto start-ups (Wakabayashi and Isaac, 2021).

But the switchers were no hardcore cyperphunks like David Chaum or Nick Szabo. That brain drain was driven by techies' fear of missing out on astronomic money. It was an entirely new Californian gold rush. This demonstrates that many of Big Tech's top performers actually believe so firmly that the future will be decentralized that they are willing to give up high-paying and prestigious jobs. Google and others may carry centralization in their genes, but not in all of their employees. The ideological rift becomes more visible the more popular crypto becomes.

Founder and CEO of Twitter Jack Dorsey retired from the social media giant in order to focus on his other well-known venture: the fintech Square. Making unmistakably clear that he sees the future with blockchain and Web3 he renamed the company *Block*. The father of Meta's Libra, David Marcus, quit his job in order to co-found the bitcoin start-up Lightspark.

On the benefactors' side are companies such as Mysten Labs. Founded by four former Facebook employees, Mysten Labs seeks to build the infrastructure for Web3 – or put differently, a competitor to Ethereum. The 20-person team has since received millions from the likes of Andreessen Horowitz. Today four out of five employees come from companies such as Google, Facebook or Netflix (Wakabayashi and Isaac, 2021).

Banking incumbents have been witnessing this trend for years. For their employees it was even more natural to take their industry know-how and build up challengers with more efficient technology. Remember Blythe Masters, the former JP Morgan banker who quit Wall Street to run Digital Asset? Examples such as these abound and now that Big Tech is starting to pay attention to the blockchain, so do its employees.

The difficult relationship of blockchain and AI

But why is it that Big Tech and Big Banking are so incompatible with decentralization? There are a few different reasons. Banks have always enjoyed a privileged position due to the special regulatory scrutiny they were exposed to. The banking licence and state guarantees have turned banks into institutions of trust that had to collect the monetary value (and data) of their customers in-house. They were liable for them and their very licences to operate depended on the proper handling of customers' assets and on the fulfilment of systemically relevant tasks. Identifying and obstructing cashflows to terrorists or enforcing sanctions require full control of the system, just as the safeguarding of money does.

For tech giants, on the other hand, centralization is essential for the business model. Take data away, and the Jenga tower falls apart. Gilder (2018) breaks down Google's worldview and why it is antithetical to decentralization. It has its own theory of knowledge according to which the way we learn is through analysing big data. This means that the actor who does the analysis must collect the data centrally so that it has enough of it to make valid deductions. Part of the worldview is also a theory of mind. The brain is seen as fundamentally algorithmic. Hence, computers can also produce knowledge autonomously if only given enough data. The crucial tool here is artificial intelligence, which is far superior in processing capacity to human brains, the AI priesthood claims. Hence, Google has pivoted to the AI-first mantra. This is complemented by Google's technological vision, which is centred around cloud computing. In order to capture data and bring it to its power plants, i.e. data centres, it is best if they are stored on them right away as people and corporations use cloud services. Finally, the worldview is completed with a theory of money and value. Knowledge and the internet are supposed to be free. Customers don't pay for search, navigation, email or calendars. At least they don't pay in dollars and pounds. This ensures that the well of data that keeps the Google machine operating never runs dry.

Google might be the paragon of Big Tech, but most of the Big Five see the world along those lines. Apple and Microsoft are somewhat of an exception. Microsoft has a very distinct B2B model and Apple makes most of its revenue from hardware. But what unites them all is their theory of knowledge. They all learn through big data, and big data can only happen when you hoard data centrally. Embrace a decentralized blockchain, and you don't own that data. Your core competence is core no more.

Even beyond issues of centralization and distribution, blockchain and AI have opposing tenets. 'The former is immutable, the latter probabilistic and adaptable. The blockchain is transparent and tamper-proof, the decision-making process of AI is often a puzzle' (Pejic, 2019).

The very culmination of the centralization paradigm can be seen in Alphabet's frantic effort to combine – not merge – the two buzzy technologies. Alphabet owns London's AI start-up DeepMind, which has secretly exchanged sensitive patient data with the British National Health Service (NHS) for some time. After the practice became public, DeepMind (2017) said it would use centralized blockchain technology. This would create a robust audit trail for collecting and exchanging the data that would then be processed by its artificial intelligence algorithms.

A patent tsunami washing over open source waters

Banks and tech giants have both saddled up and are riding in the same centralized blockchain direction. This is evident in the setup they are choosing – permissioned blockchains. It is evident in their distinct focus on infrastructure – cloud computing. And it is evident in the way they are trying to protect their investments – patents.

Decentralized blockchain protocols are by nature open-source projects. Of course, there are companies that contribute more code than others and many key actors try to steer the projects into certain directions, but everybody is free to use it, and unlike with protected intellectual property there are no licence fees incurred. Centralized blockchains are the opposite. Hence, it is also tech and banking titans that dominate the roster of blockchain-related patents.

Up until 2017 traditional finance players were filing the most blockchain patents. Bank of America spearheaded the list ahead of Mastercard. Then IBM took over the lead, filing multiple times the number of patents Bank of America did. In 2018 Alibaba started to yank out application after application and eventually its patent applications dwarfed even those of IBM, reaching over 200 in 2020 (Baker, 2020; KissPatent, 2020).

The more active Big Tech and Big Banking became, the more it exposed the ideological rift running along the line of centralization. Whereas bitcoin had set out to eliminate institutions of trust, tech saw an opportunity to become one. Similarly, banks saw a possibility to become more efficient if they only squeezed the blockchain into their centralized worldview. In it there needs to be a trusted – and liable – manager of the network that sets up the rules and decides who gets to join. The meteoric rise in crypto activity proved them right as it exposed the weaknesses of fully decentralized or permissionless blockchains. Scalability, costs, speed – three fatal failures that rendered a mass deployment unthinkable.

To everybody but the most die-hard crypto-buffs it became quickly clear that the nature of money would not be fundamentally altered. Instead, cryptocurrencies were increasingly regarded as assets. Yet while banks and tech companies doubled down on centralized setups, the crypto community rushed to exploit blockchain's hidden potential.

KEY TAKEAWAYS

- Two broad categories of blockchains exist: centralized vs decentralized. Centralization does not refer to where data is stored or processed, but to who gets to confirm transactions. While cryptocurrencies have a decentralized setup, banks and tech giants prefer centralized ones due to scalability, lower costs and higher speed. Moreover, in this setup they get to keep control over the chain.
- Centralization is a matter of degree. There are numerous governance decisions a blockchain creator has to make. Companies and banks must choose the mechanisms according to their corporate goals.
- Another crucial decision is whether to go with an open-source protocol or to build proprietary technology. Tech companies and banks often prefer the latter, which is why they have been the most active in filing blockchain patents.

References

Baker, P (2020) Alibaba on track to be the largest blockchain patent holder by end of 2020: Study, CoinDesk, 17 September, www.coindesk.com/markets/2020/09/17/alibaba-on-track-to-be-the-largest-blockchain-patent-holder-by-end-of-2020-study/ (archived at https://perma.cc/HY23-G5CX)

Bogost, I (2020) So much for the decentralized internet: A recent Twitter hack probably didn't scare you. Here's why it should, *The Atlantic*, 26 July, www.theatlantic.com/technology/archive/2020/07/twitter-hack-decentralized-internet/614593/ (archived at https://perma.cc/GJZ5-W9LE)

Brand, S (1987) *The Media Lag: Inventing the future at MIT*, Viking, New York

Buterin, V (2018) Vitalik Buterin: 'I definitely hope centralized exchanges go burn in hell', *TechCrunch Blockchain Conference in Zug*, YouTube, 6 July, www.youtube.com/watch?v=sBcdpTsvDnk (archived at https://perma.cc/VU8M-8W5N)

Cambridge Centre for Alternative Finance (2022) Cambridge bitcoin Electricity Consumption Index: bitcoin network power demand, dynamic list, https://ccaf.io/cbeci/index (archived at https://perma.cc/65XL-F2X9)

DeepMind (2017) Trust, confidence and verifiable data audit, *DeepMind* blog, 9 March, www.deepmind.com/blog/trust-confidence-and-verifiable-data-audit (archived at https://perma.cc/6GL7-3G3Q)

De Vries, A and Stoll, C (2021) Bitcoin's growing e-waste problem, *Resources, Conservation and Recycling,* **175**, December, www.sciencedirect.com/science/article/abs/pii/S0921344921005103 (archived at https://perma.cc/3SMC-UTWK)

Federal Reserve Bank of Boston (2022) Project Hamilton Phase 1: A high-performance payment processing system designed for central bank digital currencies, Whitepaper, 3 February, www.bostonfed.org/publications/one-time-pubs/project-hamilton-phase-1-executive-summary.aspx (archived at https://perma.cc/C5FZ-QUH7)

Gilder, G (2018) *Life after Google: The fall of big data and the rise of the blockchain economy*, Regnery Gateway, Washington, DC

KissPatent (2020) The current state of blockchain patents: A comprehensive study by KISSPatent, https://kisspatent.com/blockchain-patents-study (archived at https://perma.cc/H7JT-32VB)

Mercedes-Benz (no date) 1885–1886. The first automobile, Company History, https://group.mercedes-benz.com/company/tradition/company-history/1885-1886.html (archived at https://perma.cc/M25Y-J3QH)

Pejic, I (2019) Why blockchain and AI haven't clicked yet, *Kogan Page Blog*, 13 June, www.koganpage.com/article/blockchain-and-ai (archived at https://perma.cc/X56J-BKB7)

Roubini, N (2018) Blockchain isn't about democracy and decentralisation – it's about greed, *Guardian*, 15 October, www.theguardian.com/technology/2018/oct/15/blockchain-democracy-decentralisation-bitcoin-price-cryptocurrencies (archived at https://perma.cc/B665-QGRL)

Wakabayashi, D and Isaac, M (2021) The new get-rich-faster job in Silicon Valley: Crypto start-ups, *The New York Times*, 20 December, www.nytimes.com/2021/12/20/technology/silicon-valley-cryptocurrency-start-ups.html (archived at https://perma.cc/YKG3-SY8T)

YCharts (2022) Bitcoin Blockchain Size, dynamic list, https://ycharts.com/indicators/bitcoin_blockchain_size (archived at https://perma.cc/8UD3-JA32)

5

Land rush: crypto-economics

Ethereum and other Swiss Army knives

Vitalik Buterin was one of the least likely people to drop out of college without a degree. At the age of four the Russian-Canadian's favourite toys were Excel spreadsheets. At seven he taught himself Mandarin, which he speaks to this day. His touted IQ: 257. Buterin was a prodigy whose talent was nurtured. His parents sent him to a private school; his teachers put him in classes for gifted kids. At the University of Waterloo he became the assistant to the top-notch computer scientist – and cypherpunk – Ian Goldberg (Martin, 2022).

In 2011 his father introduced him to bitcoin. Sceptical at first, Buterin started to write articles for the blog *Bitcoin Weekly*, earning him $1.50 per hour. The same year he co-founded the influential *Bitcoin* magazine. He had caught the crypto-bug and eventually dropped out of university as his new hobby was taking up most of his time (Buterin, 2019).

After leaving university, Buterin travelled the world to learn all about cutting-edge projects in the crypto-space. A journey to Israel was particularly formational as he met entrepreneurs who were experimenting with coloured coins for different purposes. They were broadening the blockchain idea, no doubt, but for Buterin this did not go far enough. He sought to build a general application machine, one that was not limited to highly specific use cases. The result: the Ethereum blockchain (Buterin, 2019).

Back in North America, he applied for a Thiel fellowship. Peter Thiel, PayPal co-founder and Silicon Valley luminary, regularly offers a select few under-22 year olds a launchpad for their world-changing ideas. The catch: they need to quit college to start a two-year-long programme in which they realize their project.

The jury liked Buterin's proposal and the enormous potential he ascribed to Ethereum, but they didn't trust Buterin would have the charisma and business acumen to really pull off a project with a global impact. After all, he was only 19 years old when he wrote the Ethereum whitepaper (Buterin, 2014). Luckily for both sides they changed their minds and made Buterin one of the 12 fellowship recipients. The young genius now had a $100,000 budget to bring his brainchild to life. The result would not only make him the most famous Thiel fellow, but the largest celebrity of the blockchain world. In 2015 the genesis block of the open-source blockchain was mined.

A Turing-complete machine

Ethereum was revolutionary because it was a blockchain that enabled an entire economy instead of a single use case. It devised a new programming language called Solidity that was Turing-complete, meaning that all types of applications could be programmed on top of the blockchain. Ethereum is a Swiss Army knife that can handle all kinds of digital assets and digital identities, not just cryptocurrencies. It is like the operating system on your smartphone.

Ethereum was not the only network to peel apart the blockchain idea from bitcoin and use it for the transfer of assets other than money, but it was the most profound. Its appeal stems on the one hand from its Turing-completeness, and on the other from the high degree of standardization that is highly attractive to developers. Driven by the Ethereum Enterprise Alliance (EEA), which defines technical specifications, open standards are created to enhance interoperability and Ethereum adoption.

Handling all kinds of assets is already a giant leap forward, but the real magic behind Ethereum is how these are transferred. Whereas with bitcoin users could only initiate their transfer manually, in

Ethereum this can be completely automatized on-chain. Buterin equipped Ethereum with smart contract capability as envisioned by Nick Szabo some 20 years earlier.

Smart contracts are computer protocols that sit on top of blockchains. They are not necessarily contracts in the legal sense but more generally can be viewed as if-then scenarios that are coded onto a blockchain. Think of them as a rule engine with the ability to automatically execute actions based on triggers. This capability has earned smart contracts the nickname 'blockchain 2.0'. Business agreements can be executed completely by algorithms. So smart contracts are the very foundation of an economy that largely runs without human intervention.

> One example of such an event-driven program is flight insurance. Imagine you had a bad experience with an airline and you have a feeling your next flight might get delayed again. You can purchase an insurance that reimburses you if that really happens. You lock $10 worth into a digital vault, the insurer locks in $200. If the flight is delayed, you walk away with the entire pot, otherwise the $210 is pocketed by the insurance company. The innovation is that you don't have to rely on an insurance agent to greenlight the claim and manually initiate the transfer. The smart contract does that for you.

This is not a hypothetical use case. The Swiss insurer AXA started such an experiment in 2017 built on the Ethereum blockchain. In 2019 the company aborted the project, citing a lack of market appetite for the product (Wood, 2019). But the problem runs deeper than that.

Of oracles and gas fees

Every smart contract relies on at least two interactions with the off-chain world. For starters, it needs to be set up by programmers. Let us assume that all parties agree on the logic of the contract and that the code is created error-free. Both those things are mammoth tasks but for simplicity's sake say both are accomplished. The second link to the off-chain world is the triggers of the on-chain execution. These third-party data feeds are known as oracles.

In the flight insurance scenario, the decisive question becomes this: where does the data come from that tells the smart contract whether the claim was legitimate or not? Most friction with insurances occurs when they decide a customer's claim is not covered for some reason. They could claim the delay might be due to a *force majeure*, an incident beyond their control. Or they could use a medical reason or a security concern as an excuse. If it is the insurance company feeding information into the oracles, then the blockchain does not really offer a benefit anymore. In other use cases these interfaces might be easier to manage. If a smart contract sells your bitcoins the moment their value falls below $20,000 apiece, it is straightforward. The smart contract simply calls the recent values of an exchange like Coinbase.

The contracts are executed by the Ethereum Virtual Machine (EVM). Rather than being a physical computer, the EVM is the sum of the miners' computing power. To power the machine the Ether currency serves as gas. If you want the network to execute your application, you have to pay a transaction fee in Ether, also known as a 'gas fee'. As with a physical machine, the fee is determined by two variables: by the current gas price and by the amount of gas used. The more complex the execution, the higher the gas consumption.

Downsides of powerful machines

Of course, being so versatile does not come without drawbacks. A Swiss Army knife might perform the same tasks as a knife, a pair of scissors and a screwdriver, but by combining those functionalities the tool might break more easily. Complexity of a system always means that it is more susceptible to errors, quite simply because there are more parts that can potentially break and because they are interdependent. If one breaks, the others break with it. Bitcoin, on the other hand, was designed to do one specific thing: transfer monetary value without intermediaries. It has never been hacked. Its system had no bugs that could have jeopardized the project.

Furthermore, bitcoin's code base is qualitatively far better than that of Ethereum. The Institute for Crypto Code Review analysed 170,000 lines of bitcoin code and 35,000 lines of Ethereum code, before scoring them on a scale ranging from -5 to +5. Bitcoin ended up at 2.53 points, whereas Ethereum scored only 1.69 points. Twenty-five per cent of the Ethereum code could use some rework; 2 per cent was flagged as critical. Even Litecoin, an early bitcoin clone, had a slightly more solid code base than Ethereum (Sandner, 2018a, 2018b).

Ethereum is a platform on which decentralized applications can be built. Each of those poses an additional risk for vulnerabilities. Ergo, even if there is no issue with the underlying Ethereum code, applications on top can become compromised. Researchers from Singapore and the UK (Nikolic et al, 2018) analysed almost 1 million Ethereum smart contracts and found 34,200 of them to have vulnerabilities. That is a whopping 3.4 per cent. To be sure, this does not endanger the basic underlying chain, but it can give the entire project a bad reputation. This was the case with the 2016 DAO hack, in which a vulnerability of the smart contract code let attackers drain funds worth $50 million. DAO stands for decentralized autonomous organization, a potent smart contract application we will discuss later. The 2016 DAO, which confusingly was also called DAO, was the first notable of its kind, but the hack led to a fundamental dispute on how to handle the attack. Eventually it even resulted in the splitting of the chain into Ethereum and Ethereum Classic.

The birth of alleged Ethereum killers

Another drawback of Ethereum is that it is frequently overloaded. This makes the execution of smart contracts rather expensive compared to competing platforms. Others on the market were quick to note the enormous potential Ethereum had tapped. So, a number of well-funded competitors reached for a piece of the pie, trying to remedy Ethereum's shortcomings.

The former Morgan Stanley analyst Arthur Breitman and his wife Kathleen formed one such challenger in 2017 called Tezos. It received a larger crowdfunding than any previous crypto-project. After a series of legal problems, it is now listed on many big exchanges. Its selling point: Tezos is natively built on Proof-of-Stake (PoS) validation.

Two rather similar smart contract-enabled platforms are Cardano and EOS. Just like Tezos, they are both permissionless but thanks to PoS offer much higher scalability than Ethereum. Cardano was initiated by Charles Hoskins, one of Ethereum's co-founders. EOS was a by-product of Dan Larimer's Steemit, a blockchain-based social media application that rewards successful content creators with its native token.

NEO is a different type of competitor. Thanks to its distinct focus on on-chain identities it is regulator-friendly. This was the precondition for its unparalleled success in China, its domestic market. The project was launched in 2014 under the name AntShares – no connection to Ant Financial – before it was rebranded as NEO in 2017.

The Ethereum competitor with the most gravitas is Hyperledger Fabric. It is a protocol that covers a similarly broad functionality range as Ethereum, but it does so by deploying centralized blockchains. The Hyperledger initiative is an open-source hub founded by Linux in 2015 and since steered by the non-profit Hyperledger Foundation. It serves as the home for various DLT applications, with Fabric being its most prominent one. Hyperledger Fabric doesn't have a native currency. Its permissioned nature appeals to corporations who want, and in most cases are required by law, to retain control of their application. Fabric's velocity is respectable. While Ethereum can handle about 15 transactions per second, Fabric was designed to do around 3,000 transactions per second, though researchers have even suggested methods to bring up that number to 20,000 (Gorenflo, Lee and Keshav, 2019).

Hyperledger's main flaw is that applications built on the chain are often not interoperable with each other. This prevents it from being the global blockchain platform underpinning tomorrow's economy. Fabric is modular and configurable. It comes with multiple pluggable options, meaning that the company implementing it can choose parameters that fit its current systems. A company could define by itself things such as in which format to store dates. This boosts onboarding and has a high appeal to legacy-ridden enterprises, but eventually it results in many siloed solutions.

Many of the numerous Hyperledger members are behemoths such as American Express, Swift and JP Morgan Chase. Tier-two tech (e.g. IBM, Oracle, Huawei, Lenovo, SAP) is also strongly represented. Yet only one of the Big Techs is to be found there: Microsoft (Hyperledger, 2022). Microsoft has always been the odd one out of the Big Five when it comes to blockchain strategy. It has, for instance, been one of the founding members of the Ethereum Enterprise Alliance (EEA), demonstrating that its focus had been solely on the backend.

Despite the rise of these 'Ethereum killers', as they are often dubbed by the press, Ethereum is still the de facto gold standard when it comes to smart contracts, at least among the permissionless applications. Its currency Ether still holds firmly the second place of all cryptos when it comes to market capitalization. Besides the investors, many banks and companies trust in its security. Yet all this will be in vain if Ethereum fails to improve its efficiency. This is why Vitalik Buterin and the EEA have for years been working to switch the consensus mechanism from a PoW to a PoS model. It is a delicate matter, like swapping the engine of a train at full speed. Since September 2022, instead of plugging in values to hit the right value, Ethereum validators have to stake 32 Ether coins or more that they don't get back in case of bad behaviour. Of those nodes the winners are chosen at random. The more coins a node has, the higher the likelihood of solving the block (Ethereum.org, 2022).

Rise of the token economy

The impact of a technology correlates with the size of the problem it solves. Bitcoin disposed with the double-spend problem; Ethereum eliminated the 'Tragedy of the Commons'. In an influential essay of the same name, ecologist Garrett Hardin wrote in 1968 about 19th-century farmers grazing their cows on common land. His conclusion was that shared resources will ultimately become exhausted if they are unregulated. Individuals seek to maximize their own benefits, even if it is to the detriment of the common good. Hardin's thesis justifies the role of external governance in regulating scarce resources constituting a public good. Today the term commons refers also to intangible resources such as free speech or technical infrastructure. The blockchain is such a common good. Everybody conducting transactions relies on it, but participants could block it for others by using it excessively.

Ethereum and comparable blockchains that constitute a shared infrastructure solve this dilemma with something called tokens. Put simply, tokens are digital assets native to a blockchain. They are units that can be transferred on the network and their movement is tracked by distributed ledger technology (Token Alliance, 2018).

Tokens are created on-chain, transferred on-chain and managed on-chain. They are always blockchain-secured, transferable and programmable. Yet though they don't exist in the off-chain world, they can be used to represent external assets such as real estate or fiat currency on the blockchain.

A token always means *digital scarcity*. It cannot be multiplied, copied or modified. Thus, it is the exact opposite of other digital goods that can be altered at will. Also, as part of smart contracts the usage of tokens can be automatized. Put sloppily, tokens are programmable money. Sloppily, because it doesn't have to be money they represent. Tokens come in all shades. Some of them represent natural assets such as gold or oil, other tokens stand for securities such as bonds or stocks. And yet others tokenize intangibles such as human attention. They can be fungible, say a cryptocurrency, whereby every unit is identical to any other. Or they can be non-fungible (NFTs) and represent unique digital art or collectibles. Tokens can entitle users to voting rights too. To mention a more profane one, football clubs like Arsenal in London or the Italian Juventus are issuing fan tokens that give their supporters a vote on things such as team bus designs.

Utility tokens sustain the ecosystem

Not all tokens are equally important. The most fundamental token to an ecosystem is called a utility or ecosystem token. All others are secondary and do not work without the underlying ones. The utility token is the one that solves the tragedy of the commons. Ethereum's

Ether is the prime example. Those who seek access to a common-pool resource, in this case Ethereum's platform and its virtual machine, must have a buy-in or stake in the commons. Utility tokens are needed to pay the network nodes to process their secondary token.

Whether a token is a utility makes all the difference to regulators. Tokens not considered a utility must conform to the harsh rules of security issuance. Except for Ether there are few tokens that the Securities and Exchange Commission (SEC) has accepted as utilities. But even more importantly, utility tokens are an elementary cog in the token economy. They are the basic layer on which all other tokens and applications depend. The Basic Attention Token (BAT), for instance, is a reward users receive for watching ads on the Brave browser. But the execution of smart contracts that move the BAT token requires the blockchain's native token Ether. Miners are paid gas fees in Ether for providing their processing power that feeds the giant Ethereum Virtual Machine and processes the smart contracts.

In economic terms, this means that all-purpose machines such as Ethereum profit from every successful new token. Every time a secondary token such as the BAT is purchased and transferred, it also feeds the value of the underlying utility token. Ethereum's great appeal is its standardization that allows for interoperability among the secondary tokens. For fungible tokens the standard is called ERC-20. It ensures that one token is always equal to all others.

The Ethereum blockchain is open, non-profit infrastructure. Open basically means that anybody can join as a validator node without approval, i.e. Ethereum is decentralized or permissionless. Non-profit means that Ethereum is not a corporation that seeks to realize profits for shareholders, but very much like the Linux Foundation has the goal to let as many people as possible access a public network that will improve their lives.

That does not mean that tokens and applications built on top of it cannot monetize their products. Tokens are comparable to paid API keys. Any developer wishing to use those APIs needs to buy the tokens and use them within the decentralized protocol. It is comparable to the rise of the internet. The basic protocols such as the web protocol http or the email protocol SMTP are open like Ethereum. They were built by universities and non-profit organizations. Yet tech companies, including the Big Five, coded proprietary software that sits on those protocols. Those are the profit turbines of the internet age.

The applications that are built on top of blockchains such as Ethereum are known as DApps, which is short for decentralized applications. Think of it as a Facebook or YouTube app, only that it does not reside on a centralized Big Tech server, but on many distributed nodes that are not controlled by one entity. To achieve that, DApps rely on tokens and smart contracts.

Initial coin offerings

To understand the token economy, it is also crucial to look at how tokens are issued. This happens in an event called an initial coin offering (ICO). Like the eponymous IPO it is an investment vehicle that provides the project with the necessary funds to roll out the solution and market it. It is an extremely efficient way to raise capital as it gives founders immediate access to liquidity, cuts bureaucracy and can easily tap funds worldwide.

Issuers do not have to sell off all pre-mined tokens within the ICO. They can set aside some tokens, either for themselves to gain from uptakes in price or as incentives for later users of the platform. The BAT token, for instance, set aside one pool to lure users but also another one to reward developers who are improving its open-source software. ICOs are not limited to secondary tokens. The underlying – or primary – tokens such as Ether are sold to raise money in very much the same fashion as secondary tokens. Take the Ethereum competitor EOS, which some have jokingly nicknamed 'Ethereum on Steroids' because it is a platform on which other tokens can be built just like Ethereum. It raised more than a whopping $4 billion by selling its tokens (Volpicelli, 2022).

The ICO process starts with a whitepaper, a document in which the founders of the project outline their undertaking and why investors should get on board. In contrast to the IPO, very few countries have specifications on what such a whitepaper should look like, or who is liable for the project and the funds. In that regard ICOs are more akin to a crowdsourcing campaign than an IPO.

Investor protection is close to zero. A study by Satis Group at the height of the ICO boom in 2018 reached a devastating conclusion: 81 per cent of all ICOs were outright scams and only 8 per cent were eventually listed at a serious exchange. No wonder the ICO craze had died away by 2019, but emerging regulation makes the space more attractive again, as Chapter 9 shows.

The rise of Ethereum led to a proliferation of decentralized blockchain applications. Every industry took notice and smelt possible disruption. For financial services it meant that more than just the movement of money was under siege. While bitcoin and early other cryptocurrencies could be easily fended off, even dismissed, the token economy opened the door for most major banking domains to be tackled.

The automation of finance – from smart contracts to DAOs

On first glance the New York start-up R3 shares much with other successful blockchain challengers: grandiose claims to revolutionize finance, hundreds of millions of dollars raised from reputable investors and a highly powerful platform at the core of its offering.

Yet R3 is everything but an ordinary blockchain company. It started in 2014 as a consortium backed by more than 60 banks (R3, 2022). Bank of America, BNP Paribas, JP Morgan Chase, Goldman Sachs, Deutsche Bank, Barclay's, UBS Group, Morgan Stanley, Banco Santander – it is an impressive roster. Alongside the banking behemoths members included regulators such as the Bank of Canada or the Hong Kong Monetary Authority. R3 was a powerful response from the banking sector to the challenge it faced from blockchain technology.

The birth of a banking-first smart contract platform

In 2016 R3 launched its Corda platform for finance, which two years later was also made available for enterprises. Just like Ethereum, Corda has smart contract capability. It can run so-called CorDapp code on a powerful virtual machine.

But there is one major difference that marks Corda as a banking platform: it is centralized. The bank deploying it gets to decide on who gets to validate transactions. There are a number of further characteristics that set it apart from the classic permissionless blockchains. For example, the transactions are not batched in blocks but processed in real time. Plus, you don't need hundreds of nodes to have a reliable consensus mechanism; the chain can reach an agreement by as few as two parties. Those characteristics resulted directly from the proximity to centralized institutions. Many in the crypto-world just can't stomach this adjustment of the original technology. They see it as a perversion of the original blockchain idea, which was to get rid of banks. One former employee even complained about the management wearing suits (Behrens, 2018).

Corda's permissioned setup pushes the advancement of blockchains into a banking corset. Unlike its permissionless peers it can perform complex transactions to ensure scalability, privacy and compliance with regulation. On Corda, banks and companies can use corporate firewalls and have other features considered exotic in the blockchain world. Support 24/7 and predictable release schedules are something you will not find on Ethereum and EOS. Table 5.1 shows how Corda compares to its other two major contenders.

A number of banks have left the R3 consortium for other blockchain initiatives but that didn't stop the growth of its ecosystem. R3's blockchain Corda now underpins much of the financial system, including the trade finance consortia Marco Polo and Voltron, the blockchain-agnostic Nasdaq and central bank digital currency pilots. Yet it does not have a monopoly on finance. Banks are using Corda just as well as Hyperledger. They are even finding ways to build compliant applications on permissionless blockchains such as Ethereum. While we see a concentration around a handful of platforms the race is too early to call. But it is clear that financial players are harnessing any concept the crypto-world churns out.

Real-life examples abound. The interbank messaging network SWIFT, which enables the transfer of money between more than 11,000 banking institutes, ran a proof-of-concept on blockchain for cross-border payments. The French asset manager Meta Capital

TABLE 5.1 Summary of the top three smart contract-enabled blockchains

	Ethereum	R3 Corda	Hyperledger Fabric
Use case focus	Music and content distribution, digital currency or asset-backed tokens, gambling and online gaming, attention tokenization	Started in finance but expanded to corporate applications more generally	Supply chain, supplier inventory management, voting
Governance	Ethereum Foundation and developers	R3 consortium	Linux Foundation
Centralization	Permissionless	Permissioned	Permissioned
Cryptocurrency	ETH	n/a	n/a
Consensus type	PoW (→PoS)	Pluggable – only parties involved in the transaction validate	Pluggable – it is sufficient if a part of the network is involved
Provider experience	High	Medium	High
Execution costs	High	Low	Medium
Interoperability	High	High	Low
Trx/second	15	170/1.678	3.000–3.500

tokenized over €350 million worth of real estate assets and introduced an automatic, smart contract-based KYC (know your customer) check. The open banking expert Finastra started a syndicated lending platform called Fusion LenderComm. Leading banks such as BNP Paribas, Société Générale and NatWest have joined the pilot, which makes it easier for them to provide joint funding for large infrastructure projects. Syndicated loans can have more than 1,000 funders, hence having a joint ledger as a transparent single source of truth is an enormous step forward.

This illustrates perfectly how Big Banking and Big Tech have let the early crypto daredevils go their way with decentralized blockchains, and eventually the features they came up with were a boon to the centralized players as well. Yet while smart contracts, tokenization and stablecoins did not do away with centralized banks or corporations but made them more efficient, another invention was threatening to obliterate them. Three letters pose an existential threat to the organization as we know it: DAO.

Decentralized autonomous organizations (DAOs)

The acronym DAO stands for decentralized autonomous organizations. These are organizations run completely by algorithms and are the next level of smart contracts. They neither require staff nor incorporation, yet DAOs are more than smart contracts. Instead of being mere operations, DAOs also have their own funds to manage so they are more akin to a corporation.

Just like smart contracts, DAOs exist in every industry. They have been around since 2015, as first introduced by Dan Larimer, who had founded a number of important crypto-companies such as BitShares, Steemit and EOS. Today, application fields are exploding. MolochDAO, for instance, pools money to provide grants to those advancing the Ethereum platform. Cultural DAOs let fans come together to purchase digital art collections and display them in virtual museums. Other DAOs are set up to manage the proceeds of the exploitation of intellectual property rights. Gamers use them to transact with in-game collectibles. Yet the most important DAOs can be found in decentralized finance (DeFi). Many DeFi protocols are set up so that investors can, for example, pool their money and lend it out to those willing to lock up their crypto-assets as collateral. The DAO does the lending, securing the collateral, collecting the interest payments and dispersing the gains to the investors – all fully automatically.

And this is how a DAO comes into being: in the beginning the founders set out the rules of how the DAO will function. What will its purpose be? How will it make money? How will it disburse money? How will protocol changes be decided upon? You get the point. Hundreds if not thousands of such questions have to be decided on, but the beauty of a DAO is that once answered, the logic can be coded into a smart contract. It then works completely autonomously. No need for managers or operative staff. It is the leanest possible organization. Human errors: gone. So are fraud attempts; code is incorruptible.

In a nutshell, DAOs enabled a completely new and self-contained economy built on top of the blockchain layer. The technical possibilities sparked the wildest imaginations. Why stop with the economy if regulation, rules enforcement and the judiciary could all be managed instantaneously and automatically? If brokers and payment processors could be cut, why not petty bureaucrats? While those things remain utopian aspirations for now, the technological breakthroughs have laid the foundation for DeFI.

KEY TAKEAWAYS

- Ethereum was a revolutionary blockchain as it can handle all types of tokens and can execute smart contracts. Those are if-then scenarios coded on top of a blockchain.
- Though a number of decentralized Ethereum competitors are rising, most corporate blockchains are built on either Ethereum or the more centralized alternatives Hyperledger Fabric and Corda. The latter is particularly popular with banks.
- When building smart contracts, corporations must take into account oracles, i.e. interfaces from the on-chain to the off-chain world, as well as the inflated complexity and number of vulnerabilities.
- Smart contracts enable decentralized autonomous organizations (DAOs). Those require neither staff nor incorporation but can execute many tasks performed by companies. DAOs can autonomously lend money, provide insurance cover and invest somebody's crypto-assets. Banks and tech titans must not underestimate those challengers as they can compete with a unique cost structure for isolated services.

References

Behrens, A (2018) Blockchain startup R3 could burn through $100 million in just two years, sources claim, *Blockchain News*, 11 June, www.the-blockchain.com/2018/06/11/blockchain-startup-r3-could-burn-through-100-million-in-just-two-years-sources-claim/ (archived at https://perma.cc/T9QL-7NNZ)

Buterin, V (2014) Ethereum Whitepaper, https://ethereum.org/en/whitepaper/ (archived at https://perma.cc/S3K6-AG4W)

Buterin, V (2019) Vitalik Buterin, About Me, https://about.me/vitalik_buterin (archived at https://perma.cc/S3FS-DM7R)

Ethereum.org (2022) The Merge, 15 September, https://ethereum.org/en/upgrades/merge/ (archived at https://perma.cc/RXZ6-JCGR)

Gorenflo, C, Lee, S and Keshav, L (2019) FastFabric: Scaling hyperledger fabric to 20,000 transactions per second, arXiv, 14 March, https://arxiv.org/pdf/1901.00910.pdf (archived at https://perma.cc/TTA3-EC6L)

Hardin, G (1968) The Tragedy of the Commons, *Science: New Series*, 162 (3859) (13 December, 1968), pp 1243–48, www.jstor.org/stable/1724745 (archived at https://perma.cc/S6D4-9638)

Hyperledger (2022) Members, dynamic list, www.hyperledger.org/about/members (archived at https://perma.cc/H5CD-WXLX)

Martin, K (2022) Exploring Vitalik Buterin Net Worth 2022, The co-founders of Ethereum, *Key Management Insights*, 20 March, https://keymanagementinsights.com/vitalik-buterin-net-worth-2022/ (archived at https://perma.cc/6H74-SHDF)

Nikolic, I et al (2018) Finding the greedy, prodigal, and suicidal contracts at scale, arXiv, 14 March, https://arxiv.org/pdf/1802.06038.pdf (archived at https://perma.cc/LT7D-R2WM)

R3 (2022) About R3: History of R3, dynamic list, www.r3.com/history/ (archived at https://perma.cc/S8H6-DKKR)

Sandner, P (2018a) Ethereum: Why the code needs to be improved, Medium, 20 May, https://philippsandner.medium.com/ethereum-why-the-code-needs-to-be-improved-926833b42656 (archived at https://perma.cc/86E9-844F)

Sandner, P (2018b) Bitcoin: Higher code quality than Ethereum, Medium, 22 July, https://philippsandner.medium.com/bitcoin-higher-code-quality-than-ethereum-d8f98b6958f0 (archived at https://perma.cc/RVX7-9QJG)

Satis Group, quoted in Seth, S (2018) 80% of ICOs are scams: Report, Investopedia, 2 April, www.investopedia.com/news/80-icos-are-scams-report/ (archived at https://perma.cc/29BK-LMH6)

Token Alliance (2018) Understanding digital tokens: Market overviews and proposed guidelines for policymakers and practitioners, 9 August, https://digitalchamber.s3.amazonaws.com/Understanding-Digital-Tokens-08_09_2018-Web.pdf (archived at https://perma.cc/8TGG-AFAN)

Volpicelli, G (2022) EOS was the world's most-hyped blockchain. Its fans want it back, *Wired*, 18 May, https://bit.ly/3t1Kic3 (archived at https://perma.cc/5L8P-BW7T)

Wood, N (2019) AXA withdraws blockchain flight delay compensation experiment, Ledger Insights, 11 November, www.ledgerinsights.com/axa-blockchain-flight-delay-compensation/ (archived at https://perma.cc/4TN5-QGSC)

6

DeFi unicorn stampede

DeFi and the return of crypto

After a long phase in which the values of cryptos languished and most illegitimate and weak projects were weeded out, BTC, ETH and their followers roared back. The former reached an all-time high of over $67,000 apiece in November 2021 (CoinMarketCap, 2022c). But the return of crypto was not the result of the price rally of BTC. What had happened?

Partly responsible for it was the increased regulatory clarity, but the major drivers were the new functionalities and the promise they held for the financial industry. Features such as smart contracts, tokens and DAOs got polished, technically as well as organizationally.

More importantly, the features were potently combined to address more complex financial use cases. The applications that emerged en masse were dubbed DeFi, short for decentralized finance. This host of emerging financial technologies did not stop at using blockchains and smart contracts to transfer value and improve the efficiency of financial processes. DeFi also promised new financial operations that were not possible with fiat money or physical assets such as real estate. Thanks to a layer of blockchain-based tokens, DeFi includes financial instruments such as flash loans, synthetic assets and decentralized insurance.

Major DeFi characteristics

DeFi is always built on a blockchain. As the name suggests, it must be a decentralized application, meaning that none of the centralized or permissioned blockchains count. Some have concluded that this is the only decisive characteristic and thus every permissionless cryptocurrency constitutes DeFi. But the World Economic Forum (2021) has come up with the best definition so far. According to the WEF, DeFi must have four key components:

1. **Financial services or products:** The protocols in question must be directly responsible for the transfer of value, not only information such as price feeds.
2. **Trust-minimized operation and settlement:** This means that DeFi must run on public, permissionless blockchains. It also means that the blockchain in question must be equipped with smart contract capability so that the transfer of funds is automatized.
3. **Non-custodial design:** The account owner has complete control over the funds. There is no company or organization that has access to the fund's private keys. Whatever happens to the funds is only a matter of what the owner has agreed to in the smart contract.
4. **Programmable, open and composable architecture:** Each DeFi application has to be built on open-source code and thus can easily be linked to other applications via accessible interfaces. It is comparable to open banking or the EU's PSD2-mandated compatibility between banking applications.

Elements 2 and 4 make it clear that cryptocurrencies cannot be seen as DeFi in the narrower sense. Under this definition the first DeFi was neither bitcoin, nor Ethereum, but the infamous 2016 DAO that got hacked. It took a couple of years until the concept of DAOs recovered from the shock and was rediscovered by savvy coders and entrepreneurs. Only in the so-called DeFi summer of 2020 did it find its way back into the headlines, when DeFi protocols such as Uniswap saw a hundredfold increase in their trading values over a couple of months.

The difficulty of measuring DeFi volume

A key metric to gauge how well the space is doing is the so-called TVL. This stands for the total value locked in the tokens. At the end of 2021 the TVL stood at $189 billion, which is a yearly increase of 767 per cent. The vast majority of the value locked in DeFi ($115 billion) is in Ether, followed in distant second by BSC ($21.9 billion), as well as Terra, Solana and Avalanche – the only other blockchains that meet the $10 billion hurdle (Herrera, 2021).

Though TVL is the metric most often used, it can be very deceiving. A TVL growth of 1,000 per cent might lead you to believe that there is a tenfold increase in DeFi activity. What happens in reality, however, is that by an uptick in DeFi activity the Ethereum price soars as it benefits from the increased demand. The TVL rises by the mere fact that the underlying asset's value increases. This means that in dollar terms the boost seems to be multiple times higher than it actually is.

More protocols for the DeFi world

As dominant as Ether seems, it has lost the quasi-monopolistic position it had at the beginning of the DeFi wave. When Ethereum pushed its scalability limit, costs for DeFi applications soared and eventually we saw the rise of a multi-chain paradigm. Legitimate applications could now also be built on competing protocols such as Solana or Avalanche. Thanks to native wallets and DApps, as well as much more efficient consensus mechanisms, they have become serious contenders.

Together with NFTs and games – which we will examine in Chapter 12 – DeFi makes up the decentralized app (or DApp) space. The number of active wallets using DApps exploded in 2021, growing by a factor of seven and eventually reaching 2.7 million at the end of the year (Herrera, 2021).

And popular non-blockchain companies started charting DeFi territory too. Even (semi-)Big Tech is open to the idea. Twitter recently launched a crypto-division (Lyons, 2021). Square, also a brainchild of Twitter CEO Jack Dorsey and one of PayPal's fiercest competitors, has been renamed Block and unveiled plans to open a decentralized exchange (DEX). DEXs in general saw a rise of 550 per cent in 2021 (Elliot, 2021). DEXs play an important role in expanding the DeFi space as they are linking people seeking assets to participate in the DeFi space with those selling them. The promise of DeFi is best summed up in a tweet by Tyler Winklevoss (2020), founder of the Gemini cryptocurrency exchange and a crypto-heavyweight: 'Software is eating the world. DeFi is the software that is starting to eat Wall Street.'

DeFi layers and where to compete

The complexity of the DeFi ecosystem is multiple times higher than that of cryptocurrencies. To find the major challengers of the financial system, it is crucial to distinguish between the key layers of DeFi. It is also essential for each firm vying to be part of the financial value chain to determine where it wants to compete. The DeFi stack pyramid in Figure 6.1 illustrates the different layers and their dependencies. Each layer is built on the ones beneath it.

FIGURE 6.1 The DeFi stack pyramid

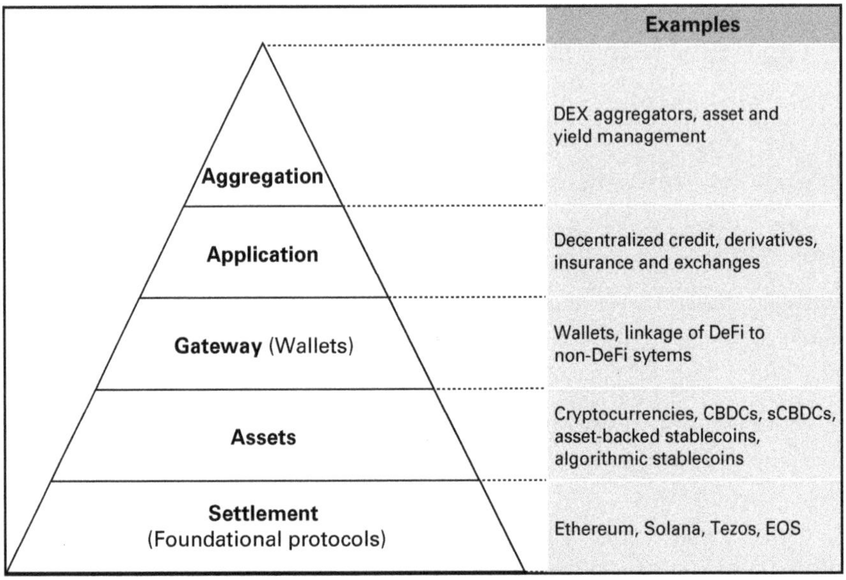

Adapted from the World Economic Forum, 2021

The footing is composed of the settlement layer. These are the foundational protocols such as Ethereum or Solana. They are the crypto-heavyweights that will be powering the DeFi economy. This is the layer where basic rules are set, security is guaranteed and things such as velocity and costs are determined.

Above it is the assets layer, representing the tokens used to move value on the chain. Here we find two major categories: first the pure crypto assets such as the tokens of the underlying settlement layer (e.g. Ether). The second category consists of all sorts of stablecoins, ranging from CBDCs and synthetic or sCBDCs to privately issued stablecoins. They represent the link from the digital to the traditional financial system as there is a peg to government-issued fiat currencies. This peg can be sustained either algorithmically or by the stablecoin issuer locking up reserves.

Then the assets go through an optional gateway, which is represented by wallets in which you can hold and manage your assets. They are the portal to access all kinds of digital asset services. Just like with your online banking app today, the functionality and the user experience will be decisive. While DeFi wallets have come a long way in terms of usability, we are still at the beginning of what is possible. Instead of only seeing my balance, it could become the cockpit from which I can operate and combine all of the applications in which my assets are locked.

Wallets are also the place DeFi and traditional finance will be bundled. The target of banking incumbents and tech aspirants must be to become a platform or a hub that connects all financial services. The perfectly suited place for that is the gateway layer. Ergo, Big Tech and banks must work towards developing potent wallets that can handle crypto assets, physical assets and all kinds of other financial services. Those few that succeed will remain the primary financial managers of their customers, get complete transaction data and can extract rents from providers that connect their apps to their platform.

The layers at the top of the DeFi stack pyramid are made up of applications and the aggregation thereof. Similar to the smartphone, these layers will be the most diverse and sustain most competitors. The vast majority of DeFi applications today fall into one of five big categories.

The five major DeFi application categories

Decentralized borrowing and lending

Credit was the first application field and is the prime example of DeFi-caused disintermediation. In traditional lending the bank takes deposits from savers and lends them to credit seekers. The interest rates for savers are close to zero and in some countries even below that. At the same time many unsecured loans are issued with double-digit interest rates. The difference represents the bank's margin. Thanks to automatic DeFi lending mechanisms, that margin goes directly to credit givers and seekers. People are lending to each other without the need for a bank, either directly in a peer-to-peer fashion or by pooling the money.

Banks check the customer's credit bureau scores, income, past payment behaviour and a host of other variables to determine whether they are credit-worthy. They also calculate the maximum credit amount and the appropriate interest rate for the customer's risk profile. Not so in DeFi. Most loans are over-collateralized and thus the risk assessment becomes obsolete. Many DeFi lenders don't even require a KYC (know your customer) process in which customers have to properly prove their identity.

A typical DeFi lending example is Aave, a liquidity protocol based on Ethereum smart contracts that works with pooled funds. Borrowers deposit collateral that is significantly higher than the loan they take out of the protocol's reserves (Aave, 2020). Those providing capital receive a token that represents their deposit plus the interest rate. The token also determines the interest they earn, all based on supply and demand. If more people borrow than provide funds and the reserve shrinks, interest rates are adjusted accordingly to balance the supply and demand again. Lenders and borrowers can swap the tokens back to their assets any time. Should the value of the collateralized coins plunge – say because the value of ETH drops precipitously – the smart contract would automatically sell off the assets once they reach a predefined threshold. This hedges against possible (chain) defaults (for details on the interest rate mechanism see Aave, 2021).

Even unsecured lending is possible in the form of flash loans. Assets are borrowed for interest and have to be paid back within the same block. If the borrower fails to do so, the transaction is automatically reversed (Wharton, 2021).

Decentralized exchanges (DEXs)

Most value in the crypto-world has changed hands through exchanges such as Coinbase or Binance. But those are all centralized institutions, run and managed by a team that is more or less liable for the company they own. In any case, people must lay their trust in them, which is exactly what crypto-enthusiasts don't want. Thanks to smart contracts and DAOs, automatic and non-custodial alternatives known as DEXs are possible.

The most widely spread form of DEXs are automated market makers which get by without order books. Instead, asset holders dedicate assets for trading and thus earn yield from traders. An algorithm sets prices automatically according to supply and demand. Every time a token is bought, it gets removed from the liquidity pool, which triggers an automatic price adjustment. Hence, these matching engines replace traditional market makers. And brokers are cut altogether (Wharton, 2021).

Uniswap is among the best-known DEXs. It is a typical automated market maker protocol built on Ethereum. The business model behind the protocol is that traders pay a fee which is then distributed to liquidity providers. Another prominent DEX is a fork of Uniswap called SushiSwap that allows larger participation of the community via a governance token.

Decentralized derivatives

In its most basic form, a derivative is a token linked to another asset or group of assets. Those advanced financial instruments could be futures, options or prediction markets. What links them is that they all work with incentivized collateral pools. And just as with lending, DeFi derivatives are always overcollateralized to reduce the risk.

Some applications such as Synthetix let users create synthetic assets. Those can be made up of cryptocurrencies, fiat currencies, stocks or commodities. They are collateralized by tokens that are locked into smart contracts that also define the agreements and incentive mechanisms.

Augur is an example of a prediction market. With this DeFi application users can bet on economic events, sport matches and things such as election results and the weather. Thanks to DeFi, you don't need traders, clearing or futures commission merchants.

Decentralized insurance

Technically speaking, insurance is also a form of a derivative as you are betting on a negative impact in the future. The difference is that the trigger for the insurance payout depends on an oracle, which means some input from the off-chain world.

Insurance is a wide field, and while you can theoretically decentralize almost every insurance scenario, DeFi insurance has come to mean specifically the protection of risks that are inherent in DeFi applications. Those might include a cover against software bugs, protocol hacks or incentive system failures. Probably the most important covered risk is hacking. According to REKT (2022) between May 2021 and May 2022 DeFi hacks amounted to more than $3 billion worth of assets, of which less than a third was recovered. This shows the exploding relevance of DeFi insurance.

A typical DeFi insurer is Nexus Mutual, where you can buy cover against hacks from DeFi exchanges as well as smart contract bugs. The idea is that the insurer has a wide enough pool of premiums through which the insured risks can be spread.

Aggregation of applications

Summing up, we have looked at the settlement layer (e.g. the Ethereum blockchain), the asset layer (e.g. Ether coins), the gateway layer (wallets) and the application layer (e.g. credit or insurance) of DeFi. Above the applications resides only the aggregation layer.

To be highlighted here are DEX aggregators, as well as asset and yield management tools. DEX aggregators automatically and permanently scan all current DEXs to find the best exchange rates. Asset and yield management tools basically automatize what human asset managers do, namely build portfolios, keep a certain portfolio balance, invest your assets and so on. The consulting function of bankers and asset managers could be significantly threatened by DeFi algorithms.

Zapper, Rotki and Zerion – there are already many examples of portfolio trackers and managers, but the importance of such aggregation services will grow exponentially with the growth of the layers below. In this regard wallets will also be crucial. They might become the place where users access the aggregation services and manage their entire DeFi activity in one place.

Money LEGO

Carlota Perez is a researcher who has spent much of her scholarly life studying techno-economic paradigms and the shifts from one paradigm to another. A far-reaching conclusion of her work is that financial innovation transforms our economy just as much as big technological breakthroughs do. Hence, it is especially important to pay attention to the *type* of financial innovation. Perez (2003) groups them into five major categories:

1. Instruments to provide capital for new products or services (e.g. bank loans or venture capital).
2. Instruments for growth or expansion (e.g. bonds).
3. Modernization of financial services themselves (e.g. ATMs or e-banking).
4. Profit-taking and spreading investment and risk (e.g. IPOs, derivatives or hedge funds).
5. Instruments to refinance obligations or mobilize assets (e.g. swaps or futures).

DeFi is so significant because its applications don't just disrupt one of the above categories, but every single one of them. Stablecoins change the way capital is provisioned. Collaterized crypto-lending and token offerings are new instruments to finance growth. Decentralized exchanges and the distributed ledger idea more broadly paradigmatically change financial services themselves. Decentralized insurance and derivatives disrupt the fourth category. And in the following paragraphs we will also see how DeFi services are combined to change the ways obligations are refinanced and assets mobilized.

DeFi means a paradigmatic overhaul of existing financial services, as well as an explosion in novel applications that were formerly impossible with fiat money. But it also means that an end to the fragmentation in financial technology could be in sight. Lex Sokolin (no date) predicts that 'We are a stone's throw away from the global financial industry running on a common software infrastructure.' This has primarily to do with the open and interoperable nature of DeFi.

The genius thing about DeFi applications is that they can all be combined and automatized. I am not referring solely to the application aggregators discussed in the last chapter, but the modules' compatibility with each other more generally. That is what has earned DeFi the nickname 'LEGO of money'. DeFi loans could be one brick, DeFi insurance another. They can easily be plugged into one another and then sold via a DEX, which is yet another brick. Or DeFi credit instruments can themselves be securitized and traded on a DEX. A stablecoin and fiat currencies could be combined to a DeFi derivative, which in turn could become collateral in a DeFi loan that becomes subject to a prediction market, is insured decentrally and traded on a DEX. The possibilities are endless, as are the number of DeFi bricks that can be combined.

Network effects

Composability and compatibility have leveraged network effects to drive the DeFi explosion. It is similar to what we have seen with the open banking movement or the PSD2-mandated API opening for banks in the EU: once you can access and use existing modules (i.e. third-party applications), innovation and new functionalities explode. Economies of scale effects are no longer a barrier for innovative young firms. This openness also exploits the principle of virality: each new feature inspires and enables a host of others. At the same time programmers do not have to build the tools from scratch. In its open-source spirit, DeFi offers standardized APIs, smart contract libraries and a stack of security tools.

Compatibility is ensured by using the same settlement layer and assets. Most applications run on Ethereum's ERC-20 token, which is the most popular standard for issuing and trading tokens on the blockchain. You can compare it to a standardized API. And there are even attempts to build a compatibility layer to glue together transactions between applications based on different settlement protocols, say Solana and Ethereum (Chawla, 2021).

Systemic risks resulting from compatibility and composability

This combination can represent a systemic risk, especially with the many possible levels of derivatives. Increased connectivity comes with decreased visibility. Most applications are over-collateralized, but if the ratios are adjusted, if more applications and users enter the space and if DeFi includes more complex, real-life assets such as real estate, no one will have a complete risk overview. Once too many LEGO bricks are stacked on top of each other, the construction might come crashing down like a Jenga tower.

The second risk is 'financial contagion' (Gudgeon et al, 2020). Much more dangerous than applications being interconnected is the layered pyramid structure as shown in the DeFi stack illustration. If there is an issue on one of the lower layers – say the settlement one – it would also crash all layers built atop it.

Dangerous bugs in the underlying protocols

While the Ethereum blockchain has proven remarkably resilient, there are always scenarios in which even those foundational protocols might face shortcomings. Ethereum's switch from PoW to PoS could have had unforeseen consequences.

And other popular Ethereum competitors are less tested yet. In September 2021, for instance, the Solana network was down for 17 hours, in which its SOL tokens could neither be sold nor bought. The reaction of Anatoly Yakovenko, a co-founder of Solana Labs, revealed that the danger of financial contagion is real. He said to Bloomberg that most of the people running blockchains are volunteers and hence those networks will always suffer from bugs (Yakovenko, quoted in Bloomberg, 2021). The stark reactions that followed the statement showed that Silicon Valley's 'move fast and break things' mantra doesn't work with financial services.

The chain gang

We started the last chapter by looking at financial innovation and techno-economic paradigms and we have later seen DeFi's powerful capabilities that could usher in a new era of financial services. And whatever is true for DeFi is exponentially true for the blockchain in general. Centralized as well as decentralized distributed ledgers will make digital trust easily and cheaply accessible throughout the economy. Every time in history a new paradigm took hold, the builders of the new economic system rose to become the stewards of the new age. So it was with Big Tech in the internet age, and so it will be with blockchain titans in the trust age.

While Alphabet, Meta and other tech and banking giants are cultivating the technology to stay on top, the rise of blockchain-native contenders has irreversibly started. The question is just who will get a grip on the market first.

Yet identifying those new challengers is tricky as we have new market rules. Even the indicators by which we measure the heft of companies are different in the blockchain age. If you go according to pure yearly revenues, the top 10 list (Johnston, 2021) is dominated mostly by mining pools and companies that are in some way connected to the classic cryptocurrency universe, say exchanges or mining chip manufacturers. And the least of the companies are publicly traded, so you can't use the stock-based market cap either. You could look at company valuations in investment rounds, but I doubt that would have helped at the turn of the millennium to identify Google or Facebook as global goliaths in waiting.

Instead, it makes sense to analyse the market with the DeFi stack pyramid (Figure 6.1). For this purpose that model can basically be applied to all blockchain businesses, even those with a centralized setup. Each layer will bear a handful of giants, and not all layers are equally important. The deeper down you go, the tougher the competition, yet the higher the gains thanks to platform economic mechanisms.

The application and aggregation layers

This is the area where we will see most blockchain applications spring up, but these are also the layers that will sustain most companies. It is comparable to the multitude of web portals or mobile applications; each of them can specialize in a certain niche, or cater to a large audience, yet the number of those applications that could become new Big Techs is highly limited. Prime examples of application-focused tech titans are Amazon and Facebook, as well as Tencent in China. First, because they have conquered mega-industries such as retailing and communication, and second, because they have been diversifying to more strategic areas. Just think of Amazon's venture into cloud computing or Tencent's WeChat becoming a super-app that can handle so much more than messaging.

With blockchain this is very similar. At the moment the largest companies are somehow connected either to mining or crypto-trading. Mining will be continuously losing importance as blockchains migrate to other consensus mechanisms such as PoS or are built in a centralized fashion. Trading will remain relevant, but by itself it might never become a mainstream application comparable to shopping or chatting.

Coinbase, the largest crypto exchange in the United States, has understood that limitation very well. It has tackled more strategic applications, and joined the consortium running USD Coin, which is one of the most important private stablecoins on the markets and is compatible with all major DeFi protocols. Coinbase is also looking into payment infrastructure that will allow merchants to accept cryptocurrency and at the same time it has issued a card jointly with Visa. Hence, instead of focusing on narrow use cases (managing crypto assets), Coinbase is seeking to underpin a wide array of economic activity.

The internet was officially invented in 1983; it took some 30 years and the painful bursting of a bubble until the lords of the new age crystallized. Given that the first bitcoin block was mined in 2009, it is still too early to call the race for the next killer application. It is remarkable, however, how fast the market capitalizations are skyrocketing. Uniswap, the largest DEX, within six months (October 2021–April 2022) has grown more than 39 times in size and reached a market cap of $22 billion (Coinmarketcap, 2022a, which is more than many mid-sized banks (CompaniesMarketCap, 2022a).

Gateway and tool layer

Integration, aggregation and interoperability are major hurdles in a blockchain. Strictly speaking, this is not necessarily an on-chain layer, but still crucial to making the blockchain protocols work. Gateways are often the glue that connects applications onto blockchains and they enable the use of certain assets.

One exemplary company in this layer is ConsenSys. It helps corporations use the Ethereum blockchain by appropriating it. Let's say you need to ensure the privacy of your users or you need to build compliance mechanisms. These are functionalities not supported by the plain Ethereum blockchain, so there are companies that help build applications or gateways to connect Ethereum with the company's system.

In 2020 ConsenSys acquired Quorum, a permissioned implementation on the Ethereum blockchain that JP Morgan Chase had built (ConsenSys, 2020). You can imagine Quorum like a travel adapter you use to make your electricity plug fit. It is a layer that helps you connect things that were not initially designed to fit. ConsenSys has become the gold standard when it comes to Ethereum development. And it has taken this position as a springboard to venture into other layers too, for example by backing a number of ICOs.

The need for implementation is even larger with centralized blockchains. And this is where the divide between the new challengers and Big Tech gets highly visible. While integration services in centralized and decentralized blockchains require similar competencies, say programmers versed with blockchains, tech giants are focusing on permissioned applications. IBM has grown into a leader in corporate blockchain integration, but all based on Hyperledger Fabric.

Enterprises are not the only ones needing gateways. Wallets are non-blockchain-based software that help end-customers manage assets such as cryptocurrencies and NFTs. As I have mentioned before, wallets could be the smartphones of the blockchain finance age. They are likely to become the central cockpit to manage applications and assets. Again, ConsenSys has captured the high ground so far. Their wallet, Metamask, is the biggest non-custodial Ethereum wallet, with more than 10 million users (ConsenSys, 2021). And Coinbase has announced its rival wallet as well. These are still early days, so expect banking and tech giants to come up with their own powerful wallets soon. Indeed, we will see in Chapters 8–12 how both groups are systematically preparing to launch what I call super-money engines. Those are powerful hubs that can handle all types of assets and have advanced transaction execution capabilities.

Settlement and asset layer

This is the layer that might produce the most serious rivals to Big Tech and Big Banking. Think of them as the Microsofts, Alphabets and Apples of the blockchain age. Each of these three has a broad product portfolio, but with Windows, Android and iOS they also own the very foundation on which all other activity runs.

It is exactly like that with foundational blockchain protocols. If I use an application to trade a crypto asset or use another one to purchase a piece of digital art, the underlying network participates.

To perform the operation users must pay some kind of fee. On top, every application built on the original blockchain needs to buy and swap that primary token. This drives up investor demand and thus the price and market capitalization.

Many settlement protocols vie to dominate this space. Some more prominent names include Tezos, Solana, EOS, Avalanche, Polkadot, Cosmos, Binance Smart Chain, Algorand and NEAR. These are all blockchains that are smart-contract compatible.

But the undisputed number one is Ethereum. At the beginning of 2022 its market cap stood at $250 billion (CoinMarketCap, 2022b), which even today is not so far away from the tech titans that hover between $500bn and $2.5bn. Alibaba ($241bn) and IBM ($118bn) have even smaller market caps (CompaniesMarketCap.com, 2022b), as do many major banks. JP Morgan Chase has the only comparable market cap with $370bn (CoinMarketCap, 2022a). The trust in Ethereum seems imperturbable too thanks to its long track record. On top, interoperability and provider experience are extremely high thanks to the first-mover advantage.

Outside of the world of DeFi, the settlement layer could be dominated by the likes of Hyperledger Fabric and R3 Corda. Both chains are decentralized and much more efficient as they don't require a cumbersome consensus. It is difficult to compare their footprint to Ethereum, as no native tokens are minted and sold in centralized setups, but Hyperledger Fabric is *the* blockchain standard for enterprise applications. Tech companies such as Tencent, IBM and Oracle are all members of the Hyperledger Foundation. R3's Corda, on the other hand, is the largest blockchain ecosystem for building banking applications. R3 is almost exclusively financed by big banks and some regulators.

Closely linked and equally important to the settlement protocols are the assets that are used. The native assets of these underlying protocols will be far from the only ones. Here the battle will not just be waged between young fintech challengers and commercial banks, but also tech titans and central banks. It is a battle so central to the future of finance, that I will be discussing it until the end of the book. Chapter 8 describes the most hubristic Big Tech push to conquer finance yet, namely Facebook's Libra Coin. It was envisioned as a stablecoin pegged to a basket of currency and designed to rewrite the global currency system. At the same time central banks are fighting back by issuing digital fiat in the form of CBDCs, and the question is on the table whether to allow private stablecoins at all, and if so with which regulation.

Corporate models in an open-source, autonomous age

Now you might wonder, why we are talking about new giants, when many of these 'companies' are decentralized and not really companies at all? Some of them, such as ConsenSys or R3, are classic, profit-oriented corporations, but what about Ethereum or MakerDAO?

With Windows or iOS the mode was straightforward. You had a company that invented code, protected it and tried to have it run on as many devices as possible. The marketing approach was tricky, because you needed to appeal to two sides of the market: developers that make your platform more attractive, and users that pay for the services. But at least the business model was clear.

Ethereum and MakerDAO present two different approaches. The Ethereum Enterprise Alliance is a non-profit foundation that steers the blockchain towards the common good. You can compare it to the Mozilla or Linux foundation with one important difference: the founders usually hold large quantities of the initially minted coins, which makes them profit from the value appreciation of the tokens. This happens automatically once the acceptance for their blockchain standard rises.

Hyperledger is somewhat similar, as it is an open-source hub initiated by the Linux foundation to foster the proliferation of standards for corporate blockchain implementation. However, there are no native tokens, which means that it is closer to classic non-profit foundations than to Ethereum.

With DAOs the picture is blurrier. MakerDAO, for example, is a DeFi lending protocol that collateralizes crypto-assets into a stablecoin called DAI. Like all other DAOs it is a joint project based on algorithms. No executives, no legal status, no concentrated ownership and thus no threat to Big Tech and Big Banking, correct? Read on. In Chapter 7 we will expose complete decentralization as a chimera, which even if achieved could be particularly vulnerable to Big Tech.

Big Tech powerhouses in the clouds

The hungry herds of unicorns galloping through the Wild West of decentralized finance seem like an indomitable force. They are spurred on by seemingly endless capital supplies. Funding of blockchain start-ups exploded in 2021, shooting up by 713 per cent to a total of $25.2 billion. Of the 47 blockchain unicorns, 40 were born in 2021. For the first time more than 1,000 big deals were done per year and the number of blockchain deals for DeFi companies almost doubled. Blockchain mega-funding rounds, i.e. deals worth more than $100 million, climbed by almost 2,500 per cent (CBInsights, 2022). The total market cap of digital assets reached $3 trillion at the end of 2021, up from $14 billion five years earlier, according to the US Treasury Secretary (Yellen, 2022).

It seems neither banks nor regulators can easily tame them. Yet tech giants can. They own the very land unicorns are running on: giant data centres. If protocols and applications are the veins and arteries of the digital age, the endless racks of servers and switches are its muscles.

For most unicorns it is impossible to leave Big Tech's ranch. Good luck asking a Silicon Valley venture capitalist for investment to build your own infrastructure. There is an unshaken consensus that you use one of the big clouds and focus on the application layer. This has been the tried-and-tested recipe for start-ups to grow into valuable companies. Instagram and Netflix showed how quickly start-ups can soar to multi-billion-dollar companies with a handful of employees and a backend managed by AWS (Gilder, 2018). In the blockchain age venture capitalists accept newcomers to transcend the application layer and dare to venture onto the protocol level, but don't think they will get money to build their own data centres. This is why Big Tech will always have a grip on promising start-ups.

True, blitzscaling companies can benefit tremendously from the on-demand resources and scaling possibilities of the gargantuan infrastructure run by Amazon, Alphabet or Microsoft. But if business does not pick up as expected or the ratio of paying and non-paying customers is poor, it can break start-ups' necks all the faster. Compare it to a restaurant owner renting a prime location in the city centre. Profitability is much higher than somewhere in the suburbs, but if a pandemic hits or you lose key personnel, the enterprise's resilience is much weaker. The high fixed costs will kill the business quickly. A pandemic might not keep crypto- and DeFi-companies up at night, but the price swings will. A crypto-winter could wipe out promising enterprises overnight. The value of a token might fall precipitously; the need for expensive cloud resources does not.

The lords of the cloud, on the other side, are nonplussed by crypto-cycles. In a bull market entrepreneurs flood their ecosystems. When the mood turns bearish, they cannot simply take the app or the network down. But does Big Tech really care about blockchain in the cloud?

AWS and Azure bring blockchain to their data centres

In 2017 I wrote in the *American Banker* that not fintechs but data behemoths such as Google or Amazon will be the major drivers for blockchain to go mainstream. One of my arguments was that their cloud muscle would grow into the backbone of many of the world's blockchains, regardless of whether centralized or decentralized. In November the CEO of Amazon's cloud computing arm AWS Andy Jassy (quoted in Lardinois, 2017) explicitly denied that blockchain will be on the company's agenda in the near future. Fast-forward just some months and the picture looked very different. AWS had introduced two major blockchain products, and on its website it bragged that it had the 'largest global infrastructure for building end-to-end blockchain solutions' (Flores, 2017).

The first product is called Amazon Quantum Ledger Database (QLDB). As the name suggests, it is a ledger that records and saves each new entry into an immutable journal, very much like a typical centralized blockchain. QLDB is a cryptographically secured transaction log in the cloud. As opposed to traditional databases, it works on an append-only principle leveraging blockchain's immutability. This makes it perfect for auditing, compliance and other regulation.

It has to be noted, though, that Amazon does not consider QLDB a blockchain, acknowledging that it is run centrally. Yet its second product is one: Amazon Managed Blockchain. Crypto-maximalists would also object to calling this a blockchain, because there is, after all, a centrally managing entity in the middle. But Amazon Managed Blockchain allows users to leverage open-source platforms in order to either build a private network or join a public one. It runs most major frameworks including Ethereum, Hyperledger Fabric and R3's Corda. Simply explained, this is how Amazon Managed Blockchain works: an AWS partner develops a blockchain app on, say, Hyperledger Fabric and then deploys it on AWS infrastructure. From there it can be scaled like any other cloud application.

Furthermore, AWS struck an important deal with R3, the banking-backed start-up building Corda (R3, 2017). Thanks to Corda, enterprises can deploy CorDApps onto the AWS cloud. Note here that AWS specifically chose to start its blockchain journey with a partner that is vying to master the banking world, not an all-purpose actor. This all neatly fits into Amazon's broader strategy of targeting financial services. After all, it is offering more financial products than any other of the Big Five.

But Amazon was actually late to the party. The first tech giant that understood the cloud's potential for blockchain was the one that had shown the least interest in financial services up to that point: Microsoft. It early on realized that it could use its Azure platform to offer so-called Blockchain-as-a-Service (BaaS). Similar to Software-as-a-Service, the company rents out functionality. For its customers there is no initial investment for physical IT infrastructure such as servers, nor for installing or maintaining software. Blockchain becomes easily accessible even for companies that can't build the expertise themselves. That is why Google and AWS have taken over the BaaS model for their cloud offerings as well.

Needless to say that Azure is one of the three biggest blockchain clouds and can handle most major protocols, including many financial use cases. For example, Microsoft has supported the Bakkt platform, an ecosystem for digital assets. In June 2019 it created a blockchain tool for Bank Hapoalim, running on its Azure cloud. Hapoalim thus became the first Israeli bank to give bank guarantees by using blockchain technology (Solomon, 2017). Others such as Nasdaq, who are mainly concerned with blockchain interoperability, chose Azure to pursue a multi-blockchain strategy with a ledger-agnostic implementation.

Alphabet transcends the Blockchain-as-a-Service model

Google Cloud has grown into the third big BaaS provider. Just as with its investment strategy in the beginning, Alphabet was highly focused on closed and permissioned blockchains, but began to warm up to open-source platforms such as Ethereum. In the blockchain cloud wars it is essential to strike as many deals as possible with app developers to make one's cloud more attractive than those of competitors. Part of this strategy is also to nurture developer talent. Hence, Google Cloud offers tools such as the *DevOps and Blockchain Developer Bundle* or certification exams that help newcomers build expertise in the Google environment. The more of these services they use, the more they get bound to Google's cloud. The search giant puts its full understanding of double-sided markets on display.

Google Cloud is going one crucial step further than simply providing the managed hard- and software environment on which other blockchains can run. Take for example its involvement with the video streaming service Theta Labs. Google became one of the few validator nodes, meaning that it has an active role in confirming transactions and steering the network. The company is keen on rolling out this strategy of becoming an active participant of blockchain networks. Google reached further agreements with smart contract platforms

EOS and Hedera Hashgraph. Both are more centralized challengers for the dominant Ethereum protocol and both now have validator nodes hosted in the Google cloud.

That Google Cloud, AWS and Microsoft Azure are running such a breadth of BaaS services shows not only their intention to power tomorrow's trustless economy, but also the vital demand for blockchain applications. In that sense BaaS turns a decisive proxy battle in the larger cloud wars. Alphabet still has some catching up to do with AWS and Azure in terms of market share. The search colossus might dominate the investments in blockchain start-ups, but when it comes to the cloud Amazon reigns supreme.

Why not Azure? The news came in May 2021. It was well hidden on the Microsoft documentation site (Altimore, 2021) but that couldn't change the fact that it was dynamite to the blockchain cloud wars: out of nowhere Microsoft had announced the end of its Azure blockchain service. It said it would not accept any more deployments on the blockchain and companies that were using it – JP Morgan Chase, Starbucks, Xbox, among others – were asked to migrate to Quorum. Quorum, you might remember, is the Ethereum-based, open-source protocol once conceived by JP Morgan Chase and later bought by ConsenSys. Many thought that was it for Microsoft, that its blockchain ambitions were buried. But little did they know that Microsoft would roar back on another blockchain front, as we will see in Chapter 12. The rise of the metaverse, a new frontier built on blockchain technology, will hand Microsoft a huge advantage as the company is a leader in hardware and gaming interfaces.

Could banking blockchains also end up in tech titans' clouds?

So how well does this dominance in the cloud translate into influence in the blockchain space? Extremely well. In fact, the stampeding unicorns have secretly already been tamed by the Big Tech cowboys. AWS alone runs about a quarter of all Ethereum nodes (Stevens, 2019).

Moreover, running nodes with hosted providers gets easier and easier. In 2021 Amazon also launched its Managed Services for Ethereum, which saves developers time and effort and so strengthens

Amazon's say in the crypto realm. The concentration trend will be irreversible, as the next chapter shows.

Having a large number of nodes run by a centralized company undermines the very idea of decentralized networks. In the most extreme scenario, distributed apps could be shut down by a central authority in that they just turn off the cloud servers on which the apps are hosted. Even worse, the controlling authority could validate transactions in its own favour or, contingent on the governance setup, could steer the further development of the chain.

Unlike blockchain unicorns, traditional banks are fortunate (or unfortunate – it depends on whom you are asking) to have their own data centres. This has made them largely independent from the cloud powerhouses. Whether it stays like this will be determined by how well cloud providers and banks appropriate the blockchain. Glancing to China we see that even large banks are starting to agree to migrate their operations to Big Tech's data centres if just the benefits are large enough.

In 2010 the Chinese government banned foreign cloud providers. Out of necessity Alibaba launched OceanBase, an in-house cloud that was capable of powering the incredible transaction volumes of Alipay and its digital bank MyBank. The cloud became so appealing that it soon processed the operations of hundreds of clients including banks such as the state-owned ICBC or China Construction Bank. The functionalities grew bigger, blockchain capabilities were included, and eventually OceanBase became the largest BaaS provider in China. It will even handle the blockchain-based digital yuan issued by the central bank, but more of this later (DigFin, 2021).

Banks can draw a number of lessons from this cloud dominance:

1. Banks' own data centres can be a huge asset if only they are well funded and properly managed.
2. The reason own clouds often have a competitive advantage is because of the lower cost structure and the sharp focus on adherence to laws and banking rules.
3. For smaller banks joint datacentres could form a banking cloud out of Big Tech's reach.

Merging old and new territory

If there is any such thing as a digitally native technology, it is the blockchain. Its very essence is to generate digital scarcity. With every new feature that refined the technology it opened up new possibilities and the industry became overbearingly self-confident. So confident that it now grabs for the off-chain and even offline world.

Rather primitive examples of the bridging to the physical world include bitcoin ATMs and crypto cards. Those already have a long tradition. The term bitcoin ATM is misleading as they are more than cash disbursement machines. Instead, a bitcoin ATM is an internet-connected kiosk where people can purchase or sell bitcoins without going through a classic exchange. They generate a QR code on their phone's wallet and scan it so the system knows which address to send the tokens to. Then users can feed the machine with paper bills or tap a credit card. Bitcoin ATMs can also work the other way around; users can sell their cryptocurrency and receive cash from the machine.

This is not very disruptive. Neither are crypto-credit cards. Basically, they are conventional payment cards going through the big card schemes, but users get some rewards in crypto-tokens for using them. Some of them are pre-paid cards where you first have to buy the native crypto token, but that does not hide the fact that crypto-reward cards are simply adding a layer onto payments instead of slashing them. Credit card companies are part of the picture, just as well as issuing banks.

DeFi and DAOs reaching for the physical world

Over time the means to connect the physical world to the chain have become more sophisticated, with DAOs a prime vehicle for this ambitious endeavour. Traditionally, DAOs were DeFi protocols that helped people pool their money and invest it in a crypto-native field, say stake it to earn rewards or lend it to people paying interest. Then art lovers used it to purchase expensive NFTs. They left the traditional financial ecosystem but still remained focused on what was happening on the blockchain.

That began to change when memes on the web surfaced poking fun at DAOs' seeming omnipotence. Sotheby's, the prestigious auction house, had put up for sale the last privately owned copy of the US Constitution. And the joke on social media was, what if some crypto guys chipped in to actually buy the document. Memes featuring the actor Nicolas Cage spread like wildfire. In a Zoom call some of these crypto guys met, had a quick laugh and then decided to actually give it a try. Jonah Ehrlich, who was on the call and later became one of the initiators, recalls the breakneck speed of events that followed. They set up a website and a Discord, got in touch with museums and within seven days their bidder at Sotheby's had almost $50 million at their disposal (quoted in Patel, 2021).

To be precise, the DAO had crowdfunded about $47 million worth of Ether from more than 17,000 individual contributors. In the end, that turned out to be just slightly too little. US billionaire and Citadel founder Ken Griffin snatched the copy from under the DAO's nose. He dished out a record $43.2 million. ConstitutionDAO had set its bidding limit at $43 million, because it still needed to put aside funds to manage the asset in the real world. This was the big difference from former DAOs that solely handled on-chain assets. Their major task was to hold crypto-collateral and move it around according to what the smart contracts dictated. But with the US Constitution you had to provision for its physical security, set up off-chain insurance contracts and talk to museums interested in displaying it.

These analogous tasks were also what earned projects such as ConstitutionDAO much criticism. In the end, the entire project still required a high-trust environment to get started. Investors had to place trust in the founding team of ConstitutionDAO that initially decided via multi-signature wallets, meaning that the founders rather than the holders of the $PEOPLE token decided the direction of the project. And Ehrlich himself admitted that they planned to turn the DAO into a non-profit organization (Patel, 2021). Eventually, the failed bid for the US Constitution demonstrates the growing ambition, but also reveals the limits of autonomous organizations.

And still the physical world will soon be linked to the blockchain. The driving force, however, will not be art aficionados or collectors of rare items, but the banking world. One telling initiative is MakerDAO. Though it has grown into one of the biggest players on the market, there are only so many crypto-assets you can turn into collateral. So MakerDAO has to bridge the gap to the physical world in order to become a financial player of serious heft.

And eventually MakerDAO did accept Ethereum tokens that represent pools of real estate or shares therein. It signed multiple deals involving traditional assets. One of the biggest was with Société Générale, a major French bank that requested a loan worth $20 million. Those are the first tentative steps in which banks and DeFi players experiment with legal frames, processes and ecosystems. As Christensen (quoted in Marsh, 2019) concludes: 'There is so much to be done before the crypto ecosystem becomes this big self-sustaining economy.' But the trend is irreversible.

KEY TAKEAWAYS

- Decentralized finance (DeFi) is called the 'LEGO of money' due to its compatibility and composability. While it opens up a panoply of opportunities, it also magnifies systemic risk in a barely regulated area.
- With the DeFi stack pyramid companies can pinpoint on which layer they want to compete. Dominance in the asset, settlement and gateway layers is most rewarding but these layers will bear only a handful of market leaders. Most competition will happen on the level of applications.
- Big Tech will eventually target all layers, but Amazon, Alphabet and Alibaba have already conquered the infrastructure layer. AWS alone runs about a quarter of all Ethereum nodes. Banks will be faced with the decisive question of whether to build their blockchains in Big Tech's clouds or their own data centres.
- There are early signs that DeFi is growing beyond being a mere finance niche. The first major banks are starting to lock real-life assets onto blockchains and dropping them into DeFi protocols.

References

Aave (2020) Aave Protocol Whitepaper V1.0, Github, January, https://github.com/aave/aave-protocol/blob/master/docs/Aave_Protocol_Whitepaper_v1_0.pdf (archived at https://perma.cc/BPK3-DG9B)

Aave (2021) Borrow Interest Rate, *Aave Docs*, https://docs.aave.com/risk/liquidity-risk/borrow-interest-rate (archived at https://perma.cc/7X3S-PZL7)

Altimore, P (2021) Migrate Azure Blockchain Service, Github, 1 September, https://github.com/Azure-Samples/blockchain/blob/master/abs/migration-guide.md (archived at https://perma.cc/LUB9-XUDB)

CBInsights (2022) State of Blockchain, Global 2021, https://bit.ly/3lD3ecU (archived at https://perma.cc/XP4G-8663)

Chawla, V (2021) Ethereum virtual machine now compatible with Solana via Neon Labs, Crypto Briefing, 20 July, https://cryptobriefing.com/evm-now-compatible-with-solana-neon-labs/ (archived at https://perma.cc/Y8C3-CH8S)

CoinMarketCap (2022a) Uniswap, dynamic list, https://coinmarketcap.com/currencies/uniswap/ (archived at https://perma.cc/7VZN-DBTT)

CoinMarketCap (2022b) Ethereum, dynamic list, https://coinmarketcap.com/currencies/ethereum/ (archived at https://perma.cc/QP3P-AAUQ)

CoinMarketCap (2022c) Bitcoin, dynamic list, https://coinmarketcap.com/currencies/bitcoin/ (archived at https://perma.cc/UA8Q-LTSW)

CompaniesMarketCap (2022a) Largest banks and bank holding companies by market cap, https://companiesmarketcap.com/banks/largest-banks-by-market-cap/ (archived at https://perma.cc/4ZM6-J4NK)

CompaniesMarketCap (2022b) Largest tech companies by market cap, https://companiesmarketcap.com/tech/largest-tech-companies-by-market-cap/ (archived at https://perma.cc/U3G7-HCC3)

ConsenSys (2020) ConsenSys acquires Quorum® platform from J.P. Morgan, Press Release, 25 August, https://consensys.net/blog/press-release/consensys-acquires-quorum-platform-from-jp-morgan/ (archived at https://perma.cc/BL6Y-WXAQ)

ConsenSys (2021) MetaMask surpasses 10 million MAUs, making it the world's leading non-custodial crypto wallet, Press Release, 31 August, https://consensys.net/blog/press-release/metamask-surpasses-10-million-maus-making-it-the-worlds-leading-non-custodial-crypto-wallet/ (archived at https://perma.cc/8WS6-78Y4)

DigFin (2021) Ant may be more relevant to China's banks than ever, DigFin, 28 June, www.digfingroup.com/ant-oceanbase/ (archived at https://perma.cc/X22Y-F889)

Elliot, S (2021) DeFi trading volume on large DEXs has jumped 550% in 2021 so far: Chainalysis, Decrypt, 9 November, https://decrypt.co/85570/defi-dex-trading-volume-chainalysis-report-2021 (archived at https://perma.cc/N8B7-9ET8)

Flores, A (2017) AWS is investing in blockchain through our partner community, *AWS Partner Network (APN) Blog*, 20 December, https://aws.amazon.com/blogs/apn/introducing-aws-blockchain-partners/ (archived at https://perma.cc/9VDB-LAER)

Gilder, G (2018) *Life after Google: The fall of big data and the rise of the blockchain economy*, Regnery Gateway, Washington, DC

Gudgeon, L et al (2020) The decentralized financial crisis. In 2020 Crypto Valley Conference on Blockchain Technology (CVCBT), pp 1–15, IEEE

Herrera, P (2021) 2021 Dapp Industry Report, DappRadar, 17 December, https://dappradar.com/blog/2021-dapp-industry-report (archived at https://perma.cc/MR82-4AQG)

Johnston, M (2021) 10 biggest blockchain companies: COIN, MNXBF and BTCM lead the 10 biggest blockchain companies list, dynamic list, Investopedia, 21 December, www.investopedia.com/10-biggest-blockchain-companies-5213784 (archived at https://perma.cc/C8Y2-GYNK)

Lardinois, F (2017) Don't expect AWS to launch a blockchain service anytime soon, TechCrunch, 29 November, https://techcrunch.com/2017/11/29/dont-expect-aws-to-launch-a-blockchain-service-anytime-soon/ (archived at https://perma.cc/C939-YU4D)

Lyons, K (2021) Twitter is launching a dedicated crypto team, part of its push toward decentralization, *The Verge*, 10 November, www.theverge.com/2021/11/10/22774501/twitter-crypto-dedicated-team-dorsey-square-decentralization (archived at https://perma.cc/NX6P-Y94Z)

Marsh, A (2019) Crypto rebels trip over each other en route to financial utopia, Bloomberg, 5 October, www.bloomberg.com/news/features/2019-10-05/crypto-rebels-trip-over-each-other-en-route-to-financial-utopia?sref=-3REHEaVI (archived at https://perma.cc/3E48-UXQD)

Patel, N (2021) From a meme to $47 million: ConstitutionDAO, Crypto, and the future of crowdfunding, *The Verge*, 7 December, www.theverge.com/22820563/constitution-meme-47-million-crypto-crowdfunding-blockchain-ethereum-constitution (archived at https://perma.cc/3TGK-J7M5)

Pejic, I (2017) BankThink: Tech giants will not be silent about blockchain for long, American Banker, 18 May, www.americanbanker.com/opinion/tech-giants-will-not-be-silent-about-blockchain-for-long (archived at https://perma.cc/YTB3-B7M2)

Perez, C (2003) *Technological Revolutions and Financial Capital: The dynamics of bubbles and golden ages*, Edward Elgar Publishing Limited, Cheltenham

R3 (2017) R3's Corda becomes one of the first DLT platforms available on AWS Marketplace, Press Release, 5 December, www.r3.com/press-media/r3s-corda-becomes-one-of-the-first-dlt-platforms-available-on-aws-marketplace/ (archived at https://perma.cc/PV4G-XLCX)

REKT (2022) REKT database, dynamic list, https://defiyield.app/rekt-database (archived at https://perma.cc/2K2X-7R36)

Sokolin, L (no date) Blockchain for Decentralized Finance (DeFi)? ConsenSys, https://consensys.net/blockchain-use-cases/decentralized-finance/ (archived at https://perma.cc/26M5-DTM9)

Stevens, R (2019) A quarter of Ethereum nodes run on Amazon Web Services, yahoo!finance, 26 September, https://finance.yahoo.com/news/quarter-ethereum-nodes-run-amazon-164044333.html?guccounter=1 (archived at https://perma.cc/T7KU-YY9Q)

Solomon, S (2017) Bank Hapoalim, Microsoft join forces on Blockchain technology, *The Times of Israel*, 6 September, www.timesofisrael.com/bank-hapoalim-microsoft-join-forces-on-blockchain-technology/ (archived at https://perma.cc/BUC6-W63T)

Wharton (2021) DeFi beyond the hype: The emerging world of decentralized finance, May, https://wifpr.wharton.upenn.edu/wp-content/uploads/2021/05/DeFi-Beyond-the-Hype.pdf (archived at https://perma.cc/5B4W-64SX)

Winklevoss, T (2020) Software is eating the world. DeFi is the software that is starting to eat Wall Street, Twitter, 7 December, https://twitter.com/tyler/status/1335969161248387072?lang=en (archived at https://perma.cc/6WY3-LXLJ)

World Economic Forum (2021) Decentralized Finance (DeFi) Policy-Maker Toolkit, White Paper, June, www3.weforum.org/docs/WEF_DeFi_Policy_Maker_Toolkit_2021.pdf (archived at https://perma.cc/Z4QZ-4GE2)

Yakovenko, A, quoted in Bloomberg (2021) What the Solana blackout reveals about the fragility of crypto, Bloomberg, 18 September, www.bloomberg.com/news/articles/2021-09-18/solana-trading-how-outage-reveals-vulnerability-of-crypto-blockchains (archived at https://perma.cc/M5XN-JB5Z)

Yellen, J (2022) Janet L. Yellen remarks on digital assets, press release printed in *Traders Magazine*, 12 April, www.tradersmagazine.com/featured_articles/janet-l-yellen-remarks-on-digital-assets/ (archived at https://perma.cc/N38G-WZ3Z)

7

The decentralization delusion

Who runs the crypto-DeFi show?

On 1 October 2021 many crypto-believers awoke to a souring tweet by Robert Leshner (2021), the CEO of the long-time DeFi darling Compound Labs. It read:

> If you received a large, incorrect amount of COMP from the Compound protocol error:
> Please return it to the Compound Timelock (0x6d903f6003cca6255D85CcA4D3B5E5146dC33925). Keep 10% as a white-hat.
> Otherwise, it's being reported as income to the IRS, and most of you are doxxed.

The story actually starts two days earlier when many users of the Compound protocol had won the jackpot without ever playing the lottery. A bug in the protocol – a total of two lines of code was broken – accidentally transferred COMP tokens worth some $80 million to random Compound users. The tokens were not owned by other users. They came from a token pool set aside to reward miners later on (Thurman, 2021).

Leshner's tweet set off a storm of indignation. On his own Twitter page the crypto-community went wild. While many chose to express their ridicule in memes and gifs, most were simply upset. One user (Hallam-Baker, 2021) accused them of extortion.

There are many things to unpack here. First is the communication. Imagine your bank's core system runs into a bug and transfers thousands of dollars into your account. The bank's CEO publicly threatens to report you to the authorities if you do not remedy a mistake you were not even responsible for. The bank could pack up and close its doors forever. There is no marketing department that could spin this issue. In the case of Compound, it is much worse. Compound Labs has hailed decentralization, autonomy and immutability as the holy grail of finance. Its vision is to have a DAO run the protocol completely without outside intervention. And now Leshner takes such an outsized role? After the crypto-industry fought reporting requirements by claiming it doesn't have the information, all of a sudden it can turn its users in?

To many this tweet made crypto's entire anti-banking argument look like a pretence to replace the old lords of finance with geeky, but equally powerful tech founders. Yet not to all. Some observers celebrated the success of decentralization. It was exactly Leshner's desperate tweet that proved his impotence, as well as the immutability of the ledger. Had he been a banker he could have unilaterally reversed the transaction. Instead, he had to turn to threatening, and later to begging.

And still, one tweet killed much of the idealism that Nakamoto and so many others had built. The episode exposed the willingness of founders to flout crypto-ideals and quickly resort to centralization tendencies under pressure.

The static machine that never was

It is one of the most stubborn myths that decentralized blockchains such as bitcoin have been coded and launched at one point in the past and ever since are machines that run perpetually without any servicing or development. In Chapter 4 we likened bitcoin to the first car, inefficient in many ways but proving the very concept that a combustion engine-powered construction could bring you from A to B. Other coins such as Ethereum or Ripple could be seen as new car models, but that doesn't mean the first model stays as it is. A tail light could break and you would have to replace it. Or imagine you are not happy about the grip at a higher speed and you decide to use broader tyres. If you drive the car for the first time when it rains, you might figure to add windshield wipers. Or lawmakers could complain about the rising number of casualties in traffic accidents and demand you add seatbelts.

The car needs engineers to propose new features and figure out how to add them. It needs executives who decide which of them to add, which materials to use and at what cost. It also needs mechanics to eventually upgrade the features. And it also needs mechanics to fix parts that are broken and to perform regular check-ups. Often those groups are in disagreement and have opposing interests.

Open-source decentralized blockchains and cryptocurrencies work in much the same way. Sometimes security patches are needed, other times the regulatory landscape evolves. And here and there developers come up with ideas to improve the protocol, say to make transactions faster. We can broadly distinguish between three stakeholder groups in decentralized protocols.

First, the miners. They have a very clear financial incentive to decide about future changes in the protocol. They invest in assets for a blockchain – say mining equipment – and need to make a return via freshly minted coins. If, for example, the rate at which blocks are mined is halved, then this also halves their income.

The second group are venture-backed businesses in the ecosystem such as exchanges or wallet providers. Sometimes their interests align with those of the end-users, but not always.

And the third group are the developers that are tasked to contribute updates to the code. Yet while bitcoin is open source, not all of the coders are volunteers. Some of them are paid, especially lead developers. Sometimes non-profit companies such as the MIT Digital Currency Initiative or the bitcoin Foundation pick up the tab, but sometimes this is also done by for-profit companies like Blockstream.

The best example of the dynamism in a blockchain's development is what came to be known as bitcoin's Civil War. Ever since bitcoin started gaining popularity, scalability was a problem that core developers were trying to solve. In 2017 some of them suggested doubling bitcoin's block size from 1MB to 2MB. Others even suggested 8MB. Another group advocated sticking with the 1MB limit but suggested reaching scalability instead by deploying a protocol on top of bitcoin called the Lightening Network. This would have moved much of the consensus activity off-chain. The size of transactions would have shrunk and thus more of them could have been crammed into a block. Ergo, there would be no need to increase the block size. However, this in turn would have hurt miners, which is why they were opposed to it. It might seem like a detailed discussion, but it is a perfect illustration of the different interest groups at work.

Eventually the civil war ended in the most extreme form, namely a hard fork. This means that bitcoin split into two incompatible chains, the original bitcoin (BTC) and bitcoin Cash (BCH), which has an 8MB block size. BCH is still around, but the BTC version is the one dominating the market cap lists.

On the necessity of chain governance

But after all, there is a democratic way of voting on how to proceed with the network, right? The block-size debate and rolling back the DAO hack were decided by the miners. And DeFi in particular stands for *decentralized* finance where decisions are taken by the network, doesn't it? As users of the decentralized exchange UniSwap learned in July 2021, there is a difference between theory and practice.

Uniswap had been growing so successfully that it had attracted the attention of regulators. They worried about the synthetic assets that were exchanged over the platform. Synthetic assets are tokens linked to traditional money instruments like stocks. Hence, the SEC warned that this kind of asset possibly constitutes a security itself and thus must be overseen by the SEC. Uniswap has been designed to be run by a DAO, meaning that the network would have to vote on how to react to the SEC's warning. In theory, the members of the Uniswap DAO use its native token UNI to vote on changes. But that's theory. What happened in reality was that Uniswap Labs, the company that launched the DAO, restricted access to certain tokens single-handedly by limiting access through its interface (Casey, 2021). So, while in theory everybody could participate (i.e. it was decentralized) and the blockchain protocol gave all token holders voting rights, another layer (i.e. the interface) could be built on top that restricted those basic rights. Thus, the project wasn't truly decentralized.

The smart contract governance models

Even the best DeFi can't get around the central problem of 'algorithmic incompleteness'. Just like with a traditional contract, a smart contract can never cover all contingencies and there needs to be a way to make alterations after it is signed (Aramonte, Huang and Schrimpf, 2021).

There are three types of smart contract governance. First, the idealized decentralized model, in which token holders vote directly for smart contract changes. Second, the partially decentralized model. This is a proxy setup in which a number of signers decide in lieu of the token holders. And third, the centralized model in which token holders have no say at all. Instead, it is the coders directly who decide how to rewrite the smart contract (World Economic Forum, 2021).

Of course, this is a very idealized and simplified categorization. Crucial governance questions include who can vote on which proposals exactly, what kind of thresholds are implemented, how do you change the governance process itself, are there admin keys, how are these stored, and so on. But as the examples of Uniswap and Compound illustrate, most crypto-applications are far from the idea of decentralization proclaimed on the project's websites. It is certainly far away from what we have in mind when talking about a revolutionary DeFi-space. Or do you imagine a DAO to be steered by developers with master keys that allow them to change the protocol at will?

> MakerDAO is another major DeFi protocol that is a DAO in name only. It is the largest decentralized lending platform, with its own stablecoin called the DAI. Post-launch it established the Maker Foundation because the founder Rune Christensen realized that without clear leadership it would never reach the targeted adoption. Yet from the outset the Maker Foundation was designed as a temporary tool to reach scale before it dissolves, meaning that eventually absolute control would be handed to the network. Christensen has even laid out a concrete plan to transition to a real DAO (Dale, 2020). However, despite all of the good intentions such a transitioning phase inevitably always requires trust in the founders, which stands in opposition to the initial idea of putting trust in algorithms only.

The follow-through remains to be seen. But let us give DeFi founders the benefit of the doubt and say they really target complete decentralization and complete autonomy. What happens if this is achieved? Certainly not what crypto-utopians tell us, so hold your hats.

Pay-to-play consensus

A stone's throw away from Reykjavik airport and along Iceland's countless geysers and waterfalls four industrial buildings stretch into the plains. They resemble a large farm, and a farm they are. Yet not to grow chicken or cattle, but to mint virtual coins. Inside, countless aisles of server racks are flashing lights. The noise they produce is nothing short of that of smokestack industries. Hundreds of thousands of GPU processors whirr along the countless fans that cool them. On the ceiling six mega-turbines spin with the power of 360 washing machines (Mallonee, 2019). Welcome to Enigma, one of the world's largest bitcoin mining farms.

Genesis Mining, the company running Enigma, boasts on its website that it is the largest provider of bitcoin-hashing power in the world, servicing far more than 2 million customers (Genesis Mining, 2020). Enigma is also characteristic of big mining farms. They burst with highly specialized equipment and are built where energy is cheapest. Despite Iceland's low energy costs, Enigma's electricity bills exceed $1 million per month (Mallonee, 2019).

Anybody who has seen pictures or videos of Alphabet's data centre in Dalles, Oregon, or some other location, will immediately know where my argument is headed. If it weren't for the pipes on the ceiling in Google's colours, you couldn't tell whether you are in a centralized Big Tech data centre or in a bitcoin mining farm. The servers might be performing different operations, but the infrastructure is pretty similar. If PoW really were to become the future, as crypto-hardliners still believe it will, it is very easy to imagine Big Tech's data centres being remodelled or expanded to dominate mining very quickly. They have all the trump cards in their hands. Yes, they still need a majority of the nodes to rule the network, but what would prevent tech titans from simply keeping on adding mining nodes? After all, no single user nor mining company could rival Alphabet's or Amazon's cost structure. And even if it did, Big Tech has the big pockets to win a battle that would hand them control over their most coveted industry.

Most probably, however, PoW will play a marginal role in the future of finance. It simply doesn't scale sufficiently to power the new economy, which is also why Big Tech has ignored mining so far. Many crypto-believers understood this shortcoming early on and have thus worked on alternative ways of getting the network to agree without a centralized authority. Many alternative consensus mechanisms emerged. In proof of capacity, for example, miners 'pay' with hard drive space. The more hard drive space they allocate to the network, the higher your chances of mining the next block and thus getting the rewards. Proof-of-burn works somewhat similarly, except that miners have to destroy ('burn') their coins by irretrievably sending them to a wallet address. The more they burn, meaning the more they invest, the higher their chances of mining the block.

None of these alternative validation mechanisms has picked up, except one: Proof-of-Stake (PoS). Instead of investing in heavy mining equipment, nodes invest in native coins. For each block they can choose how many of the coins to stake. Again, the higher the investment, the more likely they are to get rewarded. If miners behave against the interest of the network, for example work on two versions in parallel, they lose all the staked coins.

Many have criticized PoS for tilting the scale towards big nodes, but in reality every decentralized consensus mechanism does this. Each way of agreeing is a pay-to-play scheme and the higher your investment, the more likely you are to earn from it. This in turn exacerbates the already existing imbalance. Whether miners must buy super-fast computer chips, foot enormous energy bills, provide hard drive space or buy token equity, those with the deepest pockets pool decision power.

This is the inevitable nature of decentralized blockchains. There must be a barrier that protects the network from people without any stake in the legitimacy of the project. This is the reason why bitcoin needs farms like Enigma that invest heavily in highly specialized equipment. GPUs and ASICS chips are solely used for mining and they need to be exchanged for more recent and thus more potent chips frequently. This is the buy-in that protects the blockchain from malicious users.

Why Proof-of-Stake plays into the hands of Big Tech

As mentioned above, PoS is winning the race as the successor of PoW. The last nail in PoW's coffin is Ethereum's switch to PoS. The de facto backbone of DeFi and the crypto economy, Ethereum will tilt much of the industry in favour of PoS.

And herein lies an even bigger opportunity for Big Tech. If there is anything that technology leaders have more of than servers and data centres, it is capital to invest. In fact, Apple has been reported to have an (inverted) cash problem. It is sitting on $202.6 billion in cash and struggles to get rid of it fast enough. Alphabet, Microsoft, Amazon and Meta keep $169.2 billion, $132.3 billion, $86.2 billion and $54.8 billion in cash respectively (Krantz, 2022). With so much money at hand, tech titans could buy up the majority of the native cryptocurrency, say Ether, and thus be effectively running the blockchain. Never mind the number of nodes and their equipment.

Sure, in the event of such a coin-purchasing campaign prices would shoot up and make acquiring Ether much more expensive. But even if the IT giants don't manage to gain the majority at once, obtaining a big chunk of the power means they would gain massive rewards from running the financial system. And in time they could increase their share of voting power in the network.

The race is already on. Mastercard has started buying Ether coins as it sees Ethereum as a key infrastructure for both the financial and non-financial world. Moreover, it has funded ConsenSys, a strategic enabler in the Ethereum ecosystem. And there is evidence of big players such as JP Morgan Chase and Walmart buying Ether. This is true for tech titans too. In a study of 10,000 Ether-holding wallets, Adam Cochran (2020) found that some of them belonged to Microsoft, IBM and Amazon.

According to the Bank for International Settlement (Aramonte et al, 2021), at the end of 2021 big financial players each held between $150 million and $380 million in crypto-equity. And research by BCG Platinion shows that 55 per cent of banks and insurances are assessing DeFi applications, while 23 per cent have already tested them (Harrison, 2021). The study works with a broad definition of DeFi, but it demonstrates that crypto is gaining acceptance across financial companies.

Whichever way it turns out, centralization seems inevitable. And it plays into the hands of Big Tech. Whether centralized blockchain setups dominate in the first place, or PoW roars back, or the PoS mechanisms revolutionize finance, technology companies have never been better suited to become masters of finance.

Treacherous concentration

The Wild West stood for individual liberty and the absence of a strong government, yet it took centrally run trains to conquer the vast space. And crypto enthusiasts are now awaking to a similar truth. You can disregard permissioned blockchains by banks and corporations, but even the most permissionless projects end up in the hands of a select few.

Concentration is inevitable as a network becomes bigger and more professional. We have seen it happen on tech giants' cloud platforms and we have seen the concentrating nature of the pay-to-play consensus. Consolidation happens on other levels too.

Concentration in wallets

The initial goal of cryptocurrencies of distributing power and wealth to many instead of concentrating it in the hands of few is failing. Whales, i.e. investors that own more than 1 per cent of the circulating supply, are grabbing an ever-larger part of the pie. This is true for most major cryptocurrencies. The top 10 BTC addresses hold 6.12 per cent of all available coins (BitInfoCharts, 2022). An estimate by the US Bureau of National Research shows that the 1,000 major investors own about 3 million BTC or one-seventh of all coins in circulation (Makarov and Shoar, 2021). With Ether the consolidation is even more advanced. Seventeen per cent of Ether is concentrated in just 10 wallet addresses (Cochran, 2020). The trend is worsening. A look at more recent figures shows 24.13 per cent being held by the top 10 addresses at the beginning of 2022 (Etherscan, 2022). Ergo, technical decentralization does not equal commercial decentralization.

Many of those big coin holders are custodial services that hold coins for investors, but technically speaking, whoever owns the private keys, owns the coins. Either way, decentralization looks different.

Concentration in mining pools

The need for expensive, highly specialized gear skews mining towards big players. There are steadily over 10,000 nodes actively mining bitcoin. In the summer of 2021, there was even an all-time high of over 13,000 of them (Avan-Nomayo, 2021). This means a node could run for years before solving a block first. Hence, nodes are joining their forces in mining pools. They aggregate their hashing power and whichever node of the pool wins the reward shares it with the network. This makes cashflows more predictable and investments easier.

Yet mining pools have a downside. In 2020 Bloomberg reported that the five largest mining pools had more than half of the world's hashrate under their control (Kharif, 2020). In 2021 the number was already down to four (Blockchain.com, 2022).

If, as I have claimed earlier, the PoW gets replaced by PoS, does all of this matter? It does. PoS is not exempt from concentration. In 'Delegated Proof-of-Stake' participants can pool their staked coins in order to boost their odds for rewards. The mechanism and the result are similar to that of mining pools.

Concentration in geographies

In the last section we visited the Enigma mining farm in Iceland, built strategically where the environment is cold and electricity cheap. It is the major cost driver that makes mining economically viable or not. In past years China provided 50–75 per cent of the global hashing power (Statista, 2022). Many crypto-critics have thus fretted that China might take control of the network. What happened was the opposite. China didn't perceive bitcoin to be of geopolitical interest, but rather a threat to internal stability. After China banned mining for the third time in 2021 – and cracked down hard on it – the global mining landscape was jumbled. The Cambridge Centre for Alternative Finance (2022) found the US to be the major beneficiary. Its share of the global hashrate jumped from 26.2 per cent in June 2021 to 42.7 per cent in August.

Anybody pondering setting up or working on a PoW blockchain does well to take into account this geographic concentration as it highlights the fragility of the PoW model. While many hail PoW as having paramount security standards, it is particularly vulnerable to two factors: unexpected regulatory crackdowns in major markets and upticks in energy costs. Both slash the number of active miners which in turn degrades the security level.

For PoS mechanisms geographical concentration is less of a problem. While they are still highly dependent on whether certain countries allow their currencies and tokens, they are not significantly impacted by energy prices. Ethereum's switch to PoS saves the network 99.95 per cent of all energy consumed (Ethereum.org, 2022). Centralized blockchains on the other hand are neither subject to energy price dependence nor to regulatory interest. Governments set up laws for concrete applications such as cryptocurrencies, but not for the mechanisms in the back.

Concentration around the network

Bitcoin's first pitch was the death of the middlemen. The promise was twofold: get rid of centralized institutions and get rid of intermediaries altogether. Yet as time passed more and more layers were built on top of cryptocurrencies. Decentralized on-chain mechanisms have given rise to centralized players that run the crypto ecosystem with little competition. Specialized hardware providers design ASIC chips for mining only. Exchanges and wallets are usually traditional companies that take custody of investors' coins. Payment processors like BitPay enable e-commerce shops to accept cryptocurrencies as a payment method. Yet other companies install bitcoin ATMs in shopping malls to let customers buy crypto without having to use their computers. Companies such as Chainalysis or BitAML, on the other hand, analyse transactions and do research for law enforcement.

Most of the ecosystem does business in the conventional way and centralizes crucial data the blockchain sought to decentralize. It doesn't help that data is distributed in an on-chain transaction, when it is aggregated at a payment processor that makes crypto-purchases possible. Hackers still have a central vector of attack. Neither does it help that bitcoin is pseudonymous when Chainalysis can link that pseudonym to your identity. So, when integrating blockchain into your enterprise, it is vital not only to look at the on-chain mechanism, but also at the off-chain environment. Native blockchain advantages such as trustless consensus or pseudonymity can be annulled by what you do with the data once they leave the blockchain.

The pendulum is swinging back to a centralized and concentrated world. While DeFi and PoS are certainly set to process parts of the financial world, that will not stop centralization from happening.

Whether in terms of infrastructure, investment, decision power or simply the off-chain ecosystem, the original utopian dream is over. Yet while in a pre-blockchain era the finance gatekeepers were harshly regulated, regionally dispersed banks, tomorrow it could be a handful of global tech giants with a 'move fast and break things' mantra. Their market worth is higher than most countries' GDPs and sometimes their brands and their content are more trusted than governmental institutions.

KEY TAKEAWAYS

- Even decentralized blockchains are not static machines. Various interest groups try to influence the direction of the protocols.
- Just like blockchains, smart contracts need a governance model, which can fall into one of three groups: decentralized (token holders vote directly), partially decentralized (proxy setup with limited number of signers) and completely centralized (no say for token holders). Governance models might evolve from one group to the other.
- Technological decentralization does not lead to commercial decentralization. Concentrations of users and power occur in wallets, mining pools, geographic regions and off-chain enterprises that live off the blockchain economy.
- Each consensus mechanism is eventually prone to concentration as it follows a pay-to-play scheme. This benefits tech giants that already have huge data centres (PoW consensus) and unparalleled cash reserves (PoS consensus). Banks could obtain influence over a decentralized network the same way. At the moment, however, both groups are focusing on building centralized solutions and becoming compatible with decentralized ones.

References

Aramonte, S, Huang, W and Schrimpf, A (2021) DeFi risks and the decentralisation illusion, *BIS Quarterly Review*, 6 December, www.bis.org/publ/qtrpdf/r_qt2112b.pdf (archived at https://perma.cc/Z6HQ-FJAH)

Avan-Nomayo, O (2021) Bitcoin network node count sets new all-time high, *Coin Telegraph*, 15 July, https://cointelegraph.com/news/bitcoin-network-node-count-sets-new-all-time-high (archived at https://perma.cc/J7Z9-QXW3)

BitInfoCharts (2022) Top 100 richest bitcoin addresses, BitInfoCharts, dynamic list, https://bitinfocharts.com/top-100-richest-bitcoin-addresses.html%20 5.1.2022 (archived at https://perma.cc/E3E3-8Y8S)

Blockchain.com (2022) Hashrate distribution, dynamic list, www.blockchain.com/charts/pools (archived at https://perma.cc/Z78Z-YCLV)

Casey, M (2021) Money reimagined: Can DeFi stay decentralized? CoinDesk, 30 July, https://old.coindesk.com/money-reimagined-can-defi-stay-decentralized (archived at https://perma.cc/7MB4-6BH7)

Cambridge Centre for Alternative Finance (2022) Bitcoin Mining Map, dynamic list, https://ccaf.io/cbeci/mining_map (archived at https://perma.cc/JM3B-LYJZ)

Cochran, A (2020) The 10k audit, Medium, 29 April, https://medium.com/@adamscochran/the-10k-audit-42c100dd32bb (archived at https://perma.cc/VCR9-V9YZ)

Dale, B (2020) MakerDAO Foundation Plots Its Own Demise, CoinDesk, 4 April, www.coindesk.com/tech/2020/04/03/makerdao-foundation-plots-its-own-demise/ (archived at https://perma.cc/43Q7-C94Z)

Ethereum.org (2022) The Merge, 15 September, https://ethereum.org/en/upgrades/merge/ (archived at https://perma.cc/HPJ8-NJ4H)

Etherscan (2022) Top Accounts by ETH Balance, dynamic list, https://etherscan.io/accounts/1 (archived at https://perma.cc/PDH9-L4H9)

Genesis Mining (2022) The world's leading Hashpower provider, dynamic site, www.genesis-mining.com/about-us (archived at https://perma.cc/3AMC-P3RD)

Hallam-Baker, P (2021) Are you aware that threatening to dox people to the IRS unless they give you money is called extortion? You might think you have a moral claim but that doesn't make a difference. If you think you have a legal claim, your sole recourse is the courts, Twitter, 1 October, https://twitter.com/hallam/status/1444024317365325827 (archived at https://perma.cc/2HSV-QUAM)

Harrison, P (2021) Why traditional banks are embracing DeFi to catch up to challenger banks, *The Fintech Times*, 16 April, https://thefintechtimes.com/why-traditional-banks-are-embracing-defi-to-catch-challenger-banks/ (archived at https://perma.cc/VT2E-8ANA)

Kharif, O (2020) Bitcoin's network operations are controlled by five companies, Bloomberg, 31 January, www.bloomberg.com/news/articles/2020-01-31/bitcoin-s-network-operations-are-controlled-by-five-companies (archived at https://perma.cc/EG42-892T)

Krantz, M (2022) 13 firms hoard $1 trillion in cash (we're looking at you big tech), *Investor's Business Daily*, 3 February, www.investors.com/etfs-and-funds/sectors/sp500-companies-stockpile-1-trillion-cash-investors-want-it/ (archived at https://perma.cc/WY2W-ZFXB)

Leshner, R (2021) If you received a large, incorrect amount of COMP from the Compound protocol error: Please return it to the Compound Timelock (0x6d903f6003cca6255D85CcA4D3B5E5146dC33925). Keep 10% as a white-hat. Otherwise, it's being reported as income to the IRS, and most of you are doxed, Twitter, 1 October, https://bit.ly/3LJewal (archived at https://perma.cc/D5GL-KNUB)

Makarov, I and Shoar, I (2021) Blockchain analysis of the bitcoin market, *NBER Working Paper Series 29396*, October, www.nber.org/system/files/working_papers/w29396/w29396.pdf (archived at https://perma.cc/N82M-GY7U)

Mallonee, L (2019) Inside the Icelandic facility where bitcoin is mined: Cryptocurrency mining now uses more of the Nordic island nation's electricity than its homes, *Wired*, 3 November, www.wired.com/story/iceland-bitcoin-mining-gallery/ (archived at https://perma.cc/24C2-2CN7)

Statista (2022) Distribution of bitcoin mining hashrate from September 2019 to January 2022, by country, dynamic list, www.statista.com/statistics/1200477/bitcoin-mining-by-country/ (archived at https://perma.cc/U872-MZGK)

Thurman, A (2021) Compound Founder Says $80M Bug Presents 'Moral Dilemma' for DeFi Users, CoinDesk, 1 October, www.coindesk.com/tech/2021/10/01/compound-founder-says-80m-bug-presents-moral-dilemma-for-defi-users/ (archived at https://perma.cc/KUZ3-WKK2)

World Economic Forum (2021) Decentralized Finance (DeFi) Policy-Maker Toolkit, Whitepaper, 30 June, www3.weforum.org/docs/WEF_DeFi_Policy_Maker_Toolkit_2021.pdf (archived at https://perma.cc/FL5X-YACL)

8

Robber barons feel assured... and overshoot

Becoming captains of blockchain industry

We have seen how Big Tech quietly but zealously raced to master blockchain technology. We have seen how they filed patent after patent, poured a fortune into blockchain companies and partnered across the value chain, all to intrude deep into banking territory. We have seen how quick they are to change tack, as when AWS did a brutal 180 on blockchain in the cloud and within record time became the major BaaS platform.

In fact, the only thing we did not see was tech titans embracing cryptocurrencies. Both Google Ads and Facebook Ads even explicitly banned advertisements for cryptos and wallets on their platforms up until late 2021. In China, Ant Financial and Tencent unsurprisingly steered clear of them too since the government forbade any dealings with cryptocurrencies.

Yet speculation that Big Tech would enter the space abounded. Companies are at their strongest when they control multiple layers of the supply chain. And they are most profitable when they control the customer interface. So why focus on the protocol layer, shut-off blockchains that make finance more efficient, rather than on bitcoin and Ethereum that excite end-customers? Each nod in that direction, regardless of how small, was eyed very closely. When in 2017 Amazon secured three crypto-domains (AmazonEthereum.com, AmazonCryptocurrency.com and AmazonCryptocurrencies.com) the blockchain world held its collective breath (Zafar, 2021). And it kept holding it for a long time, because the e-commerce titan from Seattle made no more hints towards the crypto-space for years.

Catching the crypto bug

Those with the longest breath lived to see the inflection point. At the end of 2021 Amazon published a job advert looking to hire a 'Head of Digital Currency and Blockchain'. The ad made clear that the candidate would not only spearhead Amazon's centralized blockchain efforts but also its crypto adoption. It included building up an entire team and a roadmap (Cag, 2021). Whether this means Amazon will soon accept crypto-payment on its platform or build its own native token remains to be seen.

Amazon also proved it believes in crypto-assets by investing in Dibbs, a blockchain-based marketplace for sports memorabilia. Collectors can send sports cards to the company's vault. Then, an NFT is generated, fractionalized and sold to numerous investors (Cag, 2021). The Chinese tech juggernauts started building NFT marketplaces even before that. Tencent was the pioneer with its Huanhe platform, and Alibaba was quick to follow suit with Blockchain Digital Copyright and Asset-Trade, an auction marketplace where artists and creators can sell the copyrights to their products.

Alphabet also caught the crypto bug in 2021, though its strategy was slightly more cautious and mainly meant removing from Google's blacklist crypto-credit cards issued by exchanges. Holders of a virtual card issued by Gemini (since April 2021) and Coinbase (since June 2021) could finally use it with Google Pay and Apple Pay. In October Google partnered in a similar way with the crypto marketplace and custodian Bakkt. Tellingly, the payments are still converted to fiat money in the background. Bakkt, Visa, Google Pay – so much for eliminating the middlemen.

But once those first steps into the crypto-world were made, it was clear there was no going back. An email was leaked to Bloomberg that showed Alphabet was preparing to launch a new unit called Labs that would bundle visionary technologies such as the blockchain. Shivakumar

Venkataraman, a seasoned and high-ranking Google Vice President, was about to take the lead (Berg, 2022). Around the same time Google had also hired a former PayPal executive to rebuild its payment division, with cryptocurrencies being a major building block in a range of financial services.

Blockchain banks with a licence

The Big Five and its Chinese counterparts are tightening their grip on blockchain technology on all levels. They run the infrastructure layer. They invest a fortune in challenger firms. They collaborate with banks to build permissioned blockchains. And now they are even endorsing crypto – as a means in their payment app, as validator nodes and as BaaS providers for distributed apps. Is there any more evidence needed that they are using the blockchain to seriously attack banking?

There is one more foray that makes it as explicit as it gets. In 2019 Tencent's Fusion Bank received the green light from the Hong Kong regulator to form a blockchain-based virtual bank (Pan, 2019). It thus has a banking licence and does not even have to leave the financial plumbing to traditional banking institutes anymore. Fusion Bank is a joint venture of Tencent, the Industrial and Commerce Bank of China (ICBC), and two other institutional investors based in Hong Kong. Though it still collaborates with banks, Tencent now has access to all the expertise and knowledge needed to run a fully fledged bank. It is taking the same line as Ant Financial's MyBank, a licensed digital bank that will increasingly profit from Ant's blockchain initiatives. After all, the company has already used distributed ledgers to let migrant workers cheaply send money back home, to improve trade financing and even to track donations. At the moment it is also working on using the technology for asset management.

One tech giant chooses another path

You might have noticed that one tech titan is markedly absent from the discussions on blockchain: Apple. This is astonishing at first.

From a strategic standpoint the colossus from Cupertino would have a lot to gain by mastering blockchain technology. With its iPhone it runs the mobile hardware layer. Its iOS and App Store control what is happening on the software layer. The Apple wallet is a powerful gatekeeper for the mobile payment interface. And it owns not just the smartphone channel, but an entire ecosystem. Think Apple TV, Apple Watch, the iPad and the MacBook. They all intertwine seamlessly. Apple is a master of vertical product and horizontal supply chain integration. So why not cover the financial backend process yourself?

It is not that Apple is not interested in the finance world. Apple Pay is the best proof for that. It was a project of utmost strategic priority. Even as initial customer scepticism and sobering adoption rates threatened to turn the project into a failure the company kept going at it. The desire to capture the store checkout and the generated payment data was that central.

Yet when it comes to blockchain Apple has made headlines only once. A patent filed in 2017 fuelled speculation (US Patent and Trademark Office, 2017). The patent established a method for creating and checking digital timestamps. Three scenarios were described, of which one involved the use of blockchain technology. No further steps in that direction have been taken since and today the patent is yesterday's news.

Apple's attitude towards cryptocurrency was similar to that of other technology giants: forbidding at first, then slowly turning to sceptical consideration. At least the iPhone now allows for crypto-wallets, and credit cards issued by exchanges can be used with Apple Pay. In November 2021 Apple's boss Tim Cook even admitted that he held cryptocurrencies in his private portfolio, while quickly adding that Apple as a company would not invest in them (de la Merced, 2021).

Apple is not a cloud heavyweight like Amazon or Alphabet. It doesn't own the social connections like Facebook. And it does not have the software gravitas of Microsoft. Apple's major assets are hardware and branding. This might not make the company an instant fit for blockchain technology, but these are not the reasons it has shied away from it.

Apple and the open-network worldview

The entire blockchain idea – centralized or decentralized – is antithetical to Apple's nature. As a technology the blockchain is open source by ethos. And as an industry finance is interoperable by necessity. If you want to merge those two you must make your service as easily accessible to as many people as possible. Regardless of whether the blockchain is controlled by an entity, there should be no discussion about the nature of its open access and its compatibility. Of course, I am not talking about applications such as trade finance, but when I want to send remittances to my family or trade a crypto-asset with a friend I shouldn't be limited by the hardware I use.

Apple has become the world's most profitable company by doing exactly the opposite, namely by driving platform lock-in to perfection. Just compare Microsoft's software to that of Apple. You can run Microsoft Office on pretty much every hardware and operating system. Whether you are using Windows or a macOS, you will be able to do your computations in Excel spreadsheets. Now compare that to the lock-in tactics that were highlighted during Apple's legal battle with Epic Games. For example, Apple refuses to make its popular iMessage app available on Android devices (Lamont, 2021).

It is one thing to have an incompatible charging or earphone port, but foregoing network effects on the mother of all network effects – communication – is a completely different ballpark.

Obtaining customer lock-in is just the first step of the strategy. Once customers' switching costs are too high, you can extract lofty rents from them. Third-party developers suffer from the same mechanism; the legal tussle with Epic Games is the best testament to it. This hampers the platform's attractivity and hence its innovation output. In a blockchain world every day a new groundbreaking application jumbles the market and such restrictions would be a platform killer.

Apple certainly has most of the key ingredients to become a benefactor of blockchain's promise, not least a gargantuan customer base willing to pay high premiums for its products. And maybe it is secretly working on a blockchain product that will stun us all. After all, it wouldn't be the first tech giant to do so. But it will have to shun its closed ecosystem mindset. Only when it understands the nature of distributed ledgers and financial services can it become a rival to its Big Tech peers. This can be a tricky thing to accomplish. Successful companies often fall prey to what management thinkers refer to as the 'Icarus Paradox' (Miller, 1990). It explains how companies that have become successful with a certain mindset, business model, or worldview blindly stick to it. What has worked in the past, they assume, must work in the future as well. They fail to understand that tomorrow's market might follow a different logic from yesterday's. This is particularly true when a technology sets off a new techno-economic paradigm.

Apple might be the most obvious example, but the Icarus Paradox is relevant for every company entering the blockchain age. The new technology will alter the rules of competition, so whether tech giant or bank, it is important to check if the current strategy and mindset are still fit for it. Regardless of how successful the past has been, it is no indicator of how well a company is equipped for the future.

The hubristic dream of a modern Libra

As the 19th-century Californian Gold Rush gathered pace, the shiny metal flooded the continent. To store the gold and turn bullion into coins the San Francisco Mint was opened in 1854. Only 20 years into its existence, it had to move to a bigger building, today known as the Old San Francisco Mint. The mint grew into a vital liquidity generator and at the beginning of the 20th century the building held as much as a third of all US gold reserves. Though the Old San Francisco Mint is not churning out gold coins anymore, in June 2019 it became the epicentre of an announcement that shook global finance.

From the podium in the neoclassical granite building David Marcus, a high-ranking Facebook executive and former PayPal president, thundered that the financial system was about to be fundamentally rewired. The driver of this revolution was a Facebook-led initiative the public had never heard about: a new blockchain-based coin called Libra. The name of the project showed the scale of the ambition. It was a reference to the most basic unit of weight in Ancient Rome; the libra was used as the standard to weight gold and silver and to mint coins. Facebook's Libra would let unbanked people around the world send and store money without a bank account and at close to no cost. Libra would enable micro-transactions on a large scale. Libra would eliminate the power of central and commercial banks and put it in the hands of... Big Tech. Marcus did not actually say the last sentence, but the message was crystal clear from the setup of the protocol and its governance.

The Libra coin was to be managed by a global alliance initiated and headed by Facebook and supported by 27 partners such as Uber, PayPal and eBay. Each of them had to pay $10 million for a seat at the table, which included the option to become a validator node of the network. The goal was to have 100 members before the launch at the Mint (Popper and Isaac, 2019).

Libra was to be built on a centralized blockchain and not to be confused with cryptocurrencies that had an independent exchange rate. Libra would be a classic stablecoin with its value bound to a basket of fiat currencies involving the US dollar (50 per cent), the euro (18 per cent), the British pound (14 per cent), the yen (11 per cent) and the Singapore dollar (7 per cent). Markedly missing in this composition was the Chinese yuan (Bartz, 2019).

A conspicuous absence also characterized the roster of partner companies. Obviously, none of Facebook's Big Tech rivals had joined the alliance, but neither did any banks. Despite the centralized governance of the chain and banks' readiness to pay for tech platform market power in the past – see Google Pay and Apple Pay – not one institution supported the initiative.

Their instincts proved right. Regulators, legislators and central bankers lunged at Libra and publicly dismantled Facebook's idea. They worried about global financial stability, data privacy, market monopolies, dollarization of smaller currencies, money laundering, tax evasion and the circumvention of sanctions. It is a long and heavy list. So, less than half a year after the announcement, all payment heavyweights that had initially joined Libra quit the alliance: Visa, Mastercard, PayPal and Stripe. Their departure, the *Wall*

Street Journal surmised, had deprived Facebook of the clout it would have taken to realize its ambitious project (Andriotis and Rudegeair, 2019).

The business model behind Libra

But Facebook didn't let go. David Marcus in particular did not tire of convincing the public that these were just temporary setbacks and Libra was truly revolutionary. So, what was it that kept Facebook pouring so much money and talent into this project? How was the social media giant supposed to make money out of a coin that could not significantly appreciate in value and whose operation was run by a consortium of companies?

The business model behind the initiative was one of the most debated mysteries. The revenue driver couldn't be the miniscule money transfer fees. They were set only high enough to prevent attackers from overburdening the system but so low as not to bother any user. One way every Libra stakeholder would benefit was the free capital users pumped into the system. To get access to Libra, users were meant to deposit fiat and get Libra coins in return. They could send and receive those coins, as well as purchase goods.

The fiat that people deposited was designated as collateral. Users could get this fiat back only by swapping back their Libra. This is how the asset-backing of the coin would be kept in balance. As users don't earn interest on the fiat they deposit, Libra Alliance members have access to free capital. It is somewhat comparable to Jack Ma's Yu'e Bao, the micro savings tool we discussed in Chapter 1. At hyperspeed it became the world's largest money market fund simply by the sheer size of its user base.

But what benefit did Facebook in particular gain by grabbing the steering wheel of the project? It all comes down to the customer interface, the cockpit by which Libra can be managed: Calibra. Facebook launched the subsidiary Calibra to offer a digital wallet of the same name. Calibra was conceived as a smartphone application that enabled users to save, send and spend the virtual money. Note the criticality of the gateway layer that we discussed in Chapter 6 when talking about DeFi. Though Libra is not an example of decentralized finance, it shows that wallets are the place to own the customer relationship.

Wallets are where the data flywheel is powered. Financial transactions are the most important of all data modules that can help to target ads better and sell them at a higher price. Yet Facebook (2019) explicitly pledged that Calibra would be logically separated from other applications such as Facebook Messenger and WhatsApp. No data would be exchanged and no information on money movement would be used to polish ad targeting. Legislators on both sides of the aisle flaunted their serious doubts about this claim when they grilled Mark Zuckerberg in a seven-hour Congressional Hearing on Libra (*Washington Post*, 2019).

But even in Facebook's official Libra narrative, ads play a role. Zuckerberg admitted to Congress that the goal of Libra was to boost ad revenues. It would do so not by more accurate targeting but rather by snatching e-commerce activity from competitors (*Washington Post*, 2019). Libra was some kind of lock-in mechanism because users couldn't take their coins to platforms that were not part of the alliance, say Amazon or Google. The ease and low costs of Libra purchases would stimulate shopping activity on the websites of Facebook and its allies. And it would bring more of the value chain under its control. No longer would somebody who sees an ad on the social network have to leave the Facebook universe to complete the purchase. It is the classic techfin approach of including financial services to bolster the core platform.

But this was just the opening gambit. Facebook had its eyes set on the very core of financial services: loans. Calibra's VP Kevin Weil (2019) openly pondered providing loans to customers and businesses. This could be done in two ways: either with Facebook acting as a broker and earning fees for connecting lenders and loan seekers, or it could issue the loans by itself. In a more distant future, it could also be imagined that the Libra alliance could target a fractional reserve banking model. Instead of having a 100 per cent backing of the coin with fiat, why not provide more credit than available in the reserves? In a nutshell, challenging and replacing banks might be a long and multi-step process, but Big Tech is aware of the ideal game plan. At the very least there should be no doubt as to whether tech titans really plan to transcend payments.

Geopolitics

Facebook is not just any company. Finance is not just any industry. And the US dollar is not just any currency. So, Libra quickly became a matter not just of financial stability but geopolitical strategy. After all, Facebook had almost 2.5 billion monthly active users in 2019, a number that climbed up to close to 3 billion in 2022 (Statista, 2022).

Much of the United States' economic, political and financial hegemony stems from the unique status of the dollar. The greenback is the undisputed regent of global finance. It is the currency that makes up around two-thirds of the world's reserves. The dollar is involved in 88 per cent of global currency trades, 79 per cent of international trade invoices and 60 per cent of international banking liabilities. More than 65 countries have their local currencies directly linked to the value of the dollar. And in the SWIFT system that coordinates more than half of global cross-border transactions, the dollar secures the US and its allies control over national and international monetary flows. This dollar dominance translates to hard power across the world. The US can unilaterally leverage biting sanctions against countries, companies and individuals. Russia was immediately cut off from the financial system following its invasion of Ukraine. The US can write and check compliance rules almost at will and hence effectively monitor most global monetary movements. The dollar's special position also hands the US government and its firms decisive economic advantages by keeping the cost of capital low as the US can easily issue low-interest debt (Sung and Thomas, 2022).

Could a currency like Libra challenge the dollar's hegemony?

All these privileges are at stake should the greenback face a challenger that is sufficiently trusted and much more potent as a means of international trade. But would Libra actually challenge the dollar or would it enhance its appeal? Opinions on it are divided. Bank of England governor Mark Carney sees it as a means to end unilateral dollar dominance. He even laid out a plan for a new financial system based on a Libra-like reserve currency (Swint, 2019).

Mark Zuckerberg, on the other hand, argues exactly the opposite, claiming that Libra is a bulwark against China's global aspirations. This comes after he did a brutal 180 on China. Zuckerberg reportedly approached Xi Jinping to ask whether his child could have an honorary Chinese name, worked on a Facebook censorship tool to enter the Chinese market and built a Facebook innovation hub in China. When the social media giant remained barred from the other side of the Great Firewall it changed tack. Libra was talked up as a torchbearer of US financial leadership and democratic values. The argument became that those two things would be threatened if Libra didn't go live before a Chinese digital currency (Glaser, 2019).

Whatever you might think of this flip-flopping on China, Libra was not threatening the Fed's money monopoly. At least not once it gave up on the idea of a currency basket peg. Libra was renamed Diem and the plan changed to providing several coins, each linked to one currency. Insiders told the *Financial Times* that Diem would start with the dollar-coin before moving to others (Murphy, 2020). Pivoting away from the currency basket idea was a prerequisite to keeping the project alive. If Facebook hadn't, Libra would effectively have been a supranational monetary actor which, by changing the composition of the basket, could wreak havoc even across large economies.

As the monetary economist George Selgin (2022) explains, there is little justification for the fear that Diem could erode the dollar's dominance: money must be thought of as a network economy. It is always the most popular, i.e. widely used, exchange medium that prevails, not the most widely held asset. While Facebook might have a large network of users for other services, that does not automatically translate to a large currency network. It wouldn't have turned into a money behemoth in a flash.

The lesson here is pretty straightforward: whoever wants to mint the big coin of tomorrow must equip it with such a clear benefit that not only will people use it, but they will also switch the majority of their financial dealings onto the new coin. A user base in another segment, say communication, will not be enough on its own.

Selgin also challenges the notion that Diem would have been a bad thing. As long as it was pegged only to the US dollar and not, as initially conceived, to a basket of currencies, Diem would have made the dollar more popular, not less so. Of course, rules would be needed on things such as reserve assets, a proper disclosure or redemption procedures, but the sheer size of Facebook should not automatically preclude it from issuing a stablecoin. The Fed wouldn't be out of business; on the contrary, the easier it becomes to use the US dollar, the more popular it gets. After all, this is how the greenback has grown into the world's number one currency in the past. In the words of Selgin (2022): 'Private US dollar innovation makes the dollar strong. That's what we should be focusing on.'

National champions: danger or force for good?

If you didn't have national tech champions, you would have to build them. This is what the EU has been trying to do for years. French President Macron, for example, envisioned 10 European tech giants by 2030 that are worth €100 billion or more. To achieve this vision, he initiated the Scale-Up Europe initiative (Kayali, 2021).

There is no doubt private enterprises are the source of a country's prosperity, but Facebook's argument for Libra went further. In his opening address to the House Financial Services Committee on Project Libra, Mark Zuckerberg (2019) claimed that it is in the United States' strategic interest to have a US company rather than a Chinese one issue the first global digital currency. Never mind that the coin was to be issued by an alliance headquartered in Switzerland and composed of up to 100 companies. But indeed, foreign tech companies are frequently flagged as threats to national security. Just think of Google, Facebook and Twitter in China, or Huawei and ByteDance (the company behind TikTok) in the US. So, isn't there something to this argument that states should be putting their security at least partly into the hands of private companies?

Barry Lynn (2022) sums it up like this: 'The British East India Company was allowed to have an army, which at one point in time was even larger than that of the British state. But we don't do that in America. It's the government's job to keep us safe, not that of corporations. The government has a monopoly on security.' The influence via companies and private platforms is not a one-way street. They can just as well be used by adversaries to wield influence in their home countries: 'In fact, rather than being a protector of American interests, Facebook is a threat to national security by letting the propaganda of absolutist regimes shape the democratic discourse' (Lynn, 2022).

So what if Big Tech runs our financial system?

A study by Cornerstone Advisors (Shevlin, 2021) posed a decisive question: would customers be willing to entrust tech titans with banking services? Unfortunately, the study only surveyed Amazon Prime customers, but considering that 62 per cent of Americans have a Prime subscription it gives a good first picture of the customer sentiment. While people easily declare their interest in free products, it is impressive to see how many respondents said they would pay an extra $10 per year for an Amazon chequing account: GenZ, 42 per cent; Millennials, 48 per cent; GenX, 38 per cent; and Baby Boomers, 15 per cent. In each group, more than half of those who said they would take the offer also said they would make it their primary account. The most worrying figure for banks, however, should be that 90 per cent of those customers are not paying anything for their current chequing account (Shevlin, 2021).

That finding goes hand in hand with numerous brand trust studies that put tech brands at the pinnacle of the trust ladder. Morning Consult (2021), for example, ranks the top five like this: Google, PayPal, Microsoft, YouTube and Amazon. Visa is the only classic financial services company that makes the top 15.

So why are trust busters in the US and Europe – and more recently also in China – sceptical towards Big Tech's expansion? It is not like customers have seen the costs of payment rise due to Apple Pay or Google Pay. Neither have consumers in China. On the contrary, the foray of WeChat Pay or Alipay onto banking's turf has brought millions of unbanked rural Chinese into the financial system. The answer is simple: because the threat that their concentration of power poses extends beyond consumer welfare.

Barry Lynn can tell you about it. He spent 15 years at the New America Foundation, an influential Washington think tank, where he led the Open Markets Program. On 27 June 2017, however, his career took a turn. In a press release Lynn applauded the European Commission (EC) for levying a record €2.44 billion fine on Google for failing to give equal treatment to rivals in its Google search engine. In other words, the EC found that Google did not have a clear separation of its platform and its products and services. Following the events, Lynn and his entire team of 10 scholars had to leave New America. The *New York Times* (Vogel, 2017) reported that pressure from Google had led to Lynn's ousting. As an influential funder of the think tank, at that time Google was contributing some $21 million. New America reacted to the article, denying that Google had any say in their parting with Lynn's Open Markets Program (Slaughter, 2017).

Tech monopolies and antitrust

But Barry Lynn is also a luminary on monopolies, particularly tech monopolies. For more than two decades he has decisively shaped US understanding of antitrust. So, I decided to interview him for this book to find out whether Big Tech's entry into banking should concern only banks or society at large.

To understand the dangers of market concentration, you have to understand the reason antitrust exists in the first place. 'The original goal of antitrust law was to restrict capital from concentrating too much power, because capital uses the corporation to wield power in the real world' (Lynn, 2022). When I asked Lynn about the ultimate goal of antitrust, he described it as a hierarchy. 'At the top of the priority list is the protection of individual liberty from power, followed by the protection of democracy and the ability of people to stay in control of their communities. And then antitrust should also safeguard national security, foster innovation, and ensure efficiency and adequate pricing for consumers.' This stands in stark opposition to the consumer-welfare-driven approach preached by the Chicago school of economics and practised in the US since the 1980s. While under the Biden administration the pendulum is swinging back, the European Union's DG Competition is still primarily protecting consumers' pockets.

For finance in particular, how you think about the dangers of tech monopolies makes all the difference. If prices and innovation are all you care about, there is no reason to bar the Big Five from letting you pay with their app, holding your money in their accounts and financing your car. Free is their business model, so there's no need to fear they will extract higher rents than banks. And it would be hard to argue that the companies working on mobile payments and digital currencies are weakening innovation in an industry where customers have seen little change since the introduction of ATMs and credit cards.

See it as a matter of personal liberty and the picture changes. With every new line of application code, every new cloud server and every new device Big Tech puts in consumers' pockets, their power over them increases. Financial data is the most powerful kind of information. Just think how much credit bureaus charge banks to glimpse at a very limited set of data. Those survey respondents that were willing to pay for a chequing account from Amazon would basically lay bare much of their life to a corporation that already knows what they are buying (amazon.com), what they are watching (Amazon Prime) and what they are searching (Alexa).

Information gathered from corporate accounts is even more vital. The account provider can peek into them to extract the names of the enterprise's best customers, see which of them are paying late or not at all and deduce much of the commercial agreements with suppliers, customers and partners. Imagine if the bank, or whoever offers the chequing account, decided to compete in their corporate customers' industry. This invaluable intelligence would cause significant information asymmetries and effectively suspend vital free market mechanisms.

The special position of financial services

So whatever interpretation of antitrust prevails, there can be no doubt that banking is different to other industries due to its systemic relevance. The independence of banking is so important that in the US since the Civil War there has been a strict separation between commercial banks and corporations. The National Banking Acts of 1863 and 1864, and subsequent court interpretations of them, forbid national banks to invest in real estate or to operate a business. Banks and corporations have continually tried to blur the line between them, for example via bank holding companies. Congress and regulators fought back with legislation such as the Bank Holding Company Act of 1956, which prohibited such attempts to merge banking and non-banking activities (Shull, 1999).

The idea to separate banking and commerce particularly rose to prominence in the 1930s after the collapse of the banking system. But according to Selgin (2022), who has studied monetary history extensively, there is no convincing evidence that it was the mixing of commerce and banking that led to financial turmoil. In his view, merging banking and business would actually strengthen banks through diversification. And indeed, there are many countries around the world that don't have this strong separation, none of which have suffered problems because of it.

While other countries have more liberal rules that govern what banks can or cannot do, they all have special restrictions, rules and regulations about who can engage in banking activities and who can't. Loans and credit are regulated most harshly and restricted to banking licence holders. For payments, rules are much laxer. Yet considering the outsized value payment data has, obtaining it would also result in a strong power grab. The monopoly expert Lynn (2022) has a clear opinion on that: 'Whether it's loans or payments, tech giants shouldn't have their hand on anybody's money except their own.'

KEY TAKEAWAYS

- While US Big Tech gradually started to warm up to crypto, in China tech titans have reached for all segments of finance. They are already deploying the blockchain for remittance payments, trade finance, the tracking of donations, asset management and supply chain financing.
- Yet the most ambitious blockchain project came from Facebook when it announced its Libra initiative, a global mega-stablecoin pegged to a basket of fiat currencies. This would have turned Facebook and the Libra Alliance into a supranational monetary actor. Following a global regulatory backlash, the project was watered down and renamed Diem before being quashed completely in 2022.
- Libra lay bare Big Tech's ambition, the systemic dangers, the technology's potential and the geopolitical relevance of technology giants stepping into the money business. Facebook managers responsible for the Libra wallet, Calibra, publicly pondered entering the B2B and B2C lending business. Libra and its roadmap turned out to be a wake-up call for commercial and central banks.
- The fate of Libra shows that lawmakers and regulators will not accept stablecoins pegged to multiple currencies. The fate of those pegged only to one fiat currency is not so clear. Popular stablecoins can boost the underlying currency as it makes it easier to use, so regulators should harness private money innovation. At the same time, Big Tech-issued money entrenches tech monopolies and creates new non-financial risks (e.g. around data security).

References

Andriotis, A and Rudegeair, P (2019) Mastercard, Visa, eBay Drop Out of Facebook's Libra Payments Network, *Wall Street Journal*, 11 October, www.wsj.com/articles/mastercard-drops-out-of-facebook-s-libra-payments-network-11570824139 (archived at https://perma.cc/9HJW-6CKG)

Bartz, T (2019) Absicherung von Kryptogeld: Facebook verzichtet bei Libra auf chinesische Währung, *Der Spiegel*, 20 September, www.spiegel.de/wirtschaft/facebook-will-kryptowaehrung-libra-nicht-an-yuan-koppeln-a-1287853.html (archived at https://perma.cc/7GFY-SVRS)

Berg, M (2022) Google forms blockchain group under newly appointed executive, Bloomberg, 20 January, www.bloomberg.com/news/articles/2022-01-19/google-forms-blockchain-group-under-newly-appointed-executive (archived at https://perma.cc/9TAB-788V)

Cag, D (2021) Amazon to build blockchain and digital currency roadmap, *Fintech*, 1 November, https://fintechmagazine.com/financial-services-finserv/amazon-build-blockchain-and-digital-currency-roadmap (archived at https://perma.cc/SR8A-9CKK)

de la Merced, M (2021) Tim Cook has invested in cryptocurrency personally, but Apple has no plans to do so, *New York Times*, 11 November, www.nytimes.com/2021/11/09/business/dealbook/tim-cook-cryptocurrency-apple.html (archived at https://perma.cc/H4EQ-MNVL)

Facebook (2019) Coming in 2020: Calibra, Press Release, 18 June, https://about.fb.com/news/2019/06/coming-in-2020-calibra/ (archived at https://perma.cc/X43M-6FFK)

Glaser, A (2019) Why Mark Zuckerberg keeps saying Facebook needs to win against China, Slate, 23 October, https://slate.com/technology/2019/10/mark-zuckerberg-facebook-libra-cryptocurrency-china-free-speech.html (archived at https://perma.cc/J6ZZ-4Z34)

Kayali, L (2021) Macron aims for 10 European tech giants valued at €100B by 2030, Politico, 15 June, www.politico.eu/article/macron-aims-for-10-european-tech-giants-valued-at-e100b-by-2030/ (archived at https://perma.cc/VGA5-C5EF)

Lamont, J (2021) Apple used iMessage exclusivity to maintain platform lock-in, MobileSyrup, 9 April, https://mobilesyrup.com/2021/04/09/apple-imessage-exclusivity-platform-lock-in/ (archived at https://perma.cc/YFN8-65UJ)

Lynn, B (2017) Open Markets applauds the European Commission's finding against Google for abuse of dominance, New America press release, 27 June, www.newamerica.org/open-markets/press-releases/open-markets-applauds-european-commissions-finding-against-google-abuse-dominance/ (archived at https://perma.cc/ZP5X-X64U)

Lynn, B (2022) Personal interview, 5 April

Miller, D (1990) *The Icarus Paradox: How exceptional companies bring about their own downfall*, Harper Business, New York

Morning Consult (2021) Most Trusted Brands 2021, https://morningconsult.com/most-trusted-brands-2021/ (archived at https://perma.cc/EXW6-2WC6)

Murphy, H (2020) Facebook's Libra currency to launch next year in limited format, *Financial Times*, 27 November, www.ft.com/content/cfe4ca11-139a-4d4e-8a65-b3be3a0166be (archived at https://perma.cc/Z5KJ-RSCZ)

Pan, D (2019) Tencent to build virtual bank after Hong Kong regulator approves license, CoinDesk, 8 November, www.coindesk.com/markets/2019/11/08/tencent-to-build-virtual-bank-after-hong-kong-regulator-approves-license/ (archived at https://perma.cc/69YU-MB98)

Popper, N and Isaac, M (2019) Facebook plans global financial system based on cryptocurrency, *New York Times*, 18 June, www.nytimes.com/2019/06/18/technology/facebook-cryptocurrency-libra.html (archived at https://perma.cc/2JGL-4FKZ)

Selgin, G (2022) Personal interview, 28 April

Shevlin, R (2021) When will Amazon offer a checking account? *Forbes*, 14 June, www.forbes.com/sites/ronshevlin/2021/06/14/when-will-amazon-offer-a-checking-account/?sh=4dc4ca9e7312 (archived at https://perma.cc/XFX2-A34Y)

Shull, B (2021) The separation of banking and commerce in the United States: an examination of principal issues, *OCC Economics Working Paper 1999–1*, www.occ.gov/publications-and-resources/publications/economics/working-papers-archived/pub-econ-working-paper-1999-1.pdf (archived at https://perma.cc/XZJ4-F5HS)

Slaughter, A (2017) New America's response to the *New York Times*, New America press release, 30 August, www.newamerica.org/new-america/press-releases/new-americas-response-new-york-times/ (archived at https://perma.cc/Z56F-STAU)

Statista (2022) Number of monthly active Facebook users worldwide as of 1st quarter 2022, dynamic list, www.statista.com/statistics/264810/number-of-monthly-active-facebook-users-worldwide/ (archived at https://perma.cc/UR94-KDTJ)

Sung, M and Thomas, C (2022) The innovator's dilemma and U.S. adoption of a digital dollar, Brookings Institute, 24 March, www.brookings.edu/techstream/the-innovators-dilemma-and-u-s-adoption-of-a-digital-dollar/ (archived at https://perma.cc/N57A-CX6Y)

Swint, B (2019) Carney urges Libra-like reserve currency to end U.S. dollar dominance, Bloomberg, 23 August, www.bloomberg.com/news/articles/2019-08-23/carney-urges-libra-like-reserve-currency-to-end-dollar-dominance (archived at https://perma.cc/2TGU-3DSU)

US Patent and Trademark Office (2017) Obtaining and using time information on a secure element (SE), Database, 7 December, https://patents.google.com/patent/US20170353320A1/en (archived at https://perma.cc/KU4B-BLGA)

Vogel, K (2017) Google critic ousted from think tank funded by the tech giant, *New York Times*, 30 August, www.nytimes.com/2017/08/30/us/politics/eric-schmidt-google-new-america.html?_r=0 (archived at https://perma.cc/VER8-3YBT)

Washington Post (2019) Watch live: Facebook CEO Zuckerberg is grilled in Congress on cryptocurrency, 2020 election, YouTube recording, 23 October, www.youtube.com/watch?v=wLOBd45OGG4 (archived at https://perma.cc/L47R-H2UQ)

Weil, K (2019) An interview with Kevin Weil and Dante Disparte about Libra and Calibra, Stratechery, 26 June, https://stratechery.com/2019/an-interview-with-kevin-weil-and-dante-disparte-about-libra-and-calibra/ (archived at https://perma.cc/Z5WF-9UHD)

Zafar, T (2021) Amazon could be the first among FAAMG to launch a crypto token, FX Empire, 23 December, www.fxempire.com/forecasts/article/amazon-could-be-the-first-among-faamg-to-launch-a-crypto-token-849008 (archived at https://perma.cc/Z88A-CG2Q)

Zuckerberg, M (2019) Opening Statement to the House Financial Services Committee on Project Libra, *American Rhetoric Online Speech Bank*, 23 October, https://www.americanrhetoric.com/speeches/markzuckberglibraprojectcongress.htm (archived at https://perma.cc/8G7Q-Q25Y)

9

The sheriffs come to town: regulation bends the trajectory

Libra backlash

The immediate outpouring of rejection of Libra was overwhelming. Testifying before the House Financial Services Committee on Facebook's plan the Federal Reserve Chairman Jerome Powell made his scepticism clear, voicing concerns on everything from money laundering to the stability of the financial system, as well as privacy and consumer protection. He warned that these concerns must be addressed before a go-live. President Trump's tweet was more direct: Facebook could not become a bank without becoming subject to all banking regulations (both quoted in Jimenez, 2019). Internationally Libra was greeted with similar hostility. While the Bank of England tried to keep an open mind, countries such as France, Germany, China and India all made clear they would block Libra (Mearian, 2019).

The headwind the project received became too strong. Diem withdrew its application for a payment system licence with the Swiss regulator FINMA and instead partnered with Silverbank, a Californian state-chartered bank. In this new setup Diem would be issued by Silverbank, so no special licence was needed (Diem, 2021). But even the watered-down proposal (giving up the peg), the name change (Diem) and moving the Diem Association from Switzerland to the United States did not appease lawmakers. In 2022 Facebook had to officially call it quits as it became clear from talks with regulators that the project could not go live. Eventually, Silverbank bought the Diem assets for $200 million (Diem, 2022).

It is also unclear whether Facebook and its partners would have succeeded commercially. While focusing on the unbanked has worked very well for mobile network operators in Africa and WeChat Pay and Alipay in China, it would have been much tougher in the West. The US and Europe boast highly mature payment systems with cutthroat competition. Whether it is credit cards, instant payments via bank account or the likes of PayPal – transactions between individuals and shops within a country are quick, easy and mostly free.

Unleashing a regulatory mania

But Facebook's foray did have a long-term impact: it kicked regulation on Big Tech and the crypto-world into high gear. Governments around the world had already been sceptical about the power of tech titans, but through Libra/Diem they started realizing how dangerous those could really become if given a free hand.

The 'Keep Big Tech Out Of Finance Act' (116th Congress, 2019) was the most direct rebuttal of projects like Diem. It basically carries its simple contents in its name: no large technology company shall offer financial services, neither licensed nor unlicensed. The proposal also explicitly prohibits any involvement with cryptocurrencies, as well as any partnerships between tech behemoths and banks. The bill was never passed, but it was a foretaste of what was to come.

The pressure to crack down on Big Tech also rose from the private sector. Banks urged regulators to toughen their stance on tech giants. Banking trade groups unanimously complained about technology companies providing the same financial services as banks but not being regulated the same way, eventually hurting consumers and competition (Berry, 2021). In the US a rare bipartisan consensus emerged on the issue. More than a dozen tech-focused bills were introduced to Congress in the year before Diem gave up (*The Economist*, 2021).

On the other side of the Pacific Chinese regulators were cracking down on Big Tech too, only with much more zeal. IPOs were thwarted, companies shut down and market valuations slashed (Yuan, 2022). To be sure, Diem had never been designed to be available in China, but the sheer ambition of the project called attention to how quickly a tech giant could try to rewrite the financial system. The power of national champions had to be curbed before they could accumulate too much influence and become uncontrollable.

The impact on crypto-rules – meet the EU's MiCA

Lawmakers and regulators did not only take aim at Big Tech, but also at the crypto-sphere. China banned all mining, crypto-trading and derivatives on virtual currencies. Bitcoin and ICOs had been prohibited for years, but in 2021 the government joined forces with the central bank (PBoC), the commercial banks and the Big Techs to eliminate any possibility of dealings with crypto-assets. Social media accounts promoting cryptocurrencies were banned and foreign exchanges were forbidden to serve Chinese nationals.

Germany pioneered a more moderate way. A law for regulating the crypto-sphere came into effect in January 2020 (Deutscher Bundestag, 2020). At its core the law elevates the custody and trading with crypto-assets to the status of financial services, which makes it mandatory to have a BaFin licence. But while the BaFin (Federal Financial Supervisory Authority) is also the financial regulator that oversees banks, the law requires a strict segregation of banking activities and crypto-assets. Banks cannot directly offer cryptocurrencies nor stablecoins (though it might be possible via a subsidiary).

The EU lived up to its epithet of a regulatory superpower and was among the first to come up with a comprehensive framework. The Markets in Crypto-Assets proposal – MiCA – defines everything that cannot be answered by the existing financial market regulation such as the second Payment Services Directive (PSD2) or the Markets in Financial Instruments Directive (MiFID) (European Commission, 2020a; see also the significantly extended update in Council of the European Union, 2021). It is supposed to prevent a state-by-state patchwork approach and thus needs no separate implementation in national legislation. MiCA is not yet signed into law, but even the publication of such a detailed draft helps the industry to understand where regulation is going in the future.

MiCA defines crypto-assets as a new investment class. Blockchain-based money will become a licensed business and so MiCA will end the Wild West status that crypto-projects have enjoyed for a long time. Crypto custodians and traders will require a crypto-licence that can be transferred to other states via passporting, similar to the existing banking licence.

The European Banking Authority (EBA) and the European Securities and Markets Authority get significant supervisory authority, while the ECB can issue opinions. Crypto-issuers must have an office in one of the member states and must officially submit a white-paper and go through an approval process. This goes hand in hand with the harsher liability of issuers and enhanced investor protection. For example, individuals buying crypto-assets can rescind the purchase up to 14 days later.

MiCA was obviously drafted with Big Tech in mind. Most of the regulation applies only to issuers and projects above a certain threshold. A focal element of the proposal is stablecoins, in particular those pegged to a *basket* of other assets (which MiCA calls asset-referenced tokens). If a stablecoin reaches a certain daily trading volume or number of transactions, additional safeguards are mandated. Issuers need to suspend emitting new coins until the volume falls below the threshold again. Stablecoins too need to be authorized by regulatory institutions. This authorization can be revoked based on multiple grounds, which drives up the operational risk for any would-be issuer. This would effectively bar initiatives such as Diem, but probably also other popular privately issued stablecoins such as the DAI. Algorithmic stablecoins like the collapsed Terra would be forbidden anyhow. Moreover, collecting interest on stablecoins is also prohibited, thus impacting DeFi models such as staking.

MiCA also shows the mammoth task of putting in place effective crypto-regulation. Though the 2021 draft had grown to over 400 pages it had not fully addressed even major use cases such as crypto-lending. With all the innovative explosion outpacing the regulatory process – think DeFi, DAO and NFT – it will be an eternal game of catch-up.

The UK and US step into a similar direction

The UK's approach is very much in line with MiCA. As of January 2021, all UK crypto-asset firms must be registered with the Financial Conduct Authority (FCA) and must comply with guidelines such as AML, sanctions, tax evasion and so on (FCA, 2022).

The US has been more cautious of a sweeping framework, with many authorities such as the Securities and Exchange Commission (SEC) or The Commodities Futures Trading Commission (CFTC) weighing in with their (often-differing) views. While the trend is clear to regulate crypto-assets mostly as securities and to subject them to similar rules as other financial assets, many questions such as the legality of DAOs have been left to the individual states. In an Executive Order, however, President Biden sketched out a cryptocurrency regulatory framework designed to bring clarity and uniformity to six crypto-asset priorities (Biden, 2022). In the US too stablecoins are a matter of special attention. The President's Working Group on Financial Markets made a number of recommendations to curb the risks of stablecoins (US Department of the Treasury, 2021).

Regulatory rodeo

Though the last word has not yet been spoken on regulating crypto-assets and stablecoins, the broad strokes are becoming visible. At the same time the difficulties of regulation are also becoming painfully clear. One is the extreme pace with which the industry is evolving. Whereas current regulatory attempts are wrestling with basic concepts such as cryptocurrency, advances like DAOs, NFTs and DeFi lending are mushrooming in record time. Crypto-innovation cycles get shorter and it is increasingly difficult to identify the risks they might bring with them.

While legislators might groan under the innovative pressure, this is a highly welcomed trend. Indeed, keeping the innovative explosion going is a major goal and poses the second challenge for lawmakers: how to balance the mission to eliminate risk and keep innovation alive. Only with a light-touch approach and little bureaucracy can innovation occur. The more government intrusion, the fewer breakthroughs. The formula is simple but to find the right spot is tricky, as the British government can tell you. It almost made a fatal step in this tightrope walk between security and progress. The regulations set up to follow MiCA were seen as too tight by the crypto-sphere and quickly led to an exodus of blockchain start-ups. Ergo the government changed its stance on stablecoins. Stablecoins are considered so central that this change of tack is supposed to turn the UK into a global hub for crypto-assets. The government has also announced it will create incentives by setting up sandboxes, issuing DeFi loan legislation and addressing DLT in finance more broadly (UK Government, 2022).

Obviously, when you ban cryptocurrencies or stablecoins, innovation will grind to a standstill. But overburdening compliance requirements can suffocate innovation just as much as a straight ban. The European Commission (2020b) did an impact analysis on MiCA and concluded that the costs for a whitepaper would rise from almost zero to between €35,000 and €75,000. Other compliance costs are in the millions. Investor protection might put an end to scams and uncertainty, but it might do the same to the Cambrian explosion of blockchain-run challengers.

Finally, regulation is always a theoretical assessment. Measures taken often don't yield the intended effect. Sometimes they cause the exact opposite. Take the open banking mandates that have targeted an unbundling of financial services. Banks have to make their APIs accessible to competitors and this would, so the reasoning goes, enable new challengers to focus on specific parts of the value chain. Economies of scale and scope would no longer pose an entry barrier. Eventually this would lead to more diversity and competition in the market and hence more innovation and lower prices. To some extent this has indeed happened, but open banking has also allowed Big Tech to reverse this unbundling of financial services. As masters of the platform economy, they are benefitting from the standardization and utilizing their scale to consolidate the value chain again.

The difficulty of regulating Big Tech

We have seen that Big Tech is silent about its ambitions in finance all the way to a big bang announcement. Think Libra or Apple Pay. Due to their unparalleled consumer access, their financial resources and technological know-how these forays can soar to a systemic financial risk overnight. And due to Big Tech's nature of global and cross-industry operations this risk could spread through the world economy like wildfire.

The Financial Stability Board (FSB, 2019) points to a number of systemic financial risks specific to Big Tech. One is their aforementioned speed to scale. Another is the strong interwovenness with traditional financial players. A problem such as a system outage or a liquidity shortage at the technology company might easily infect the traditional financial system at large. Two tech titans run the vast majority of cloud infrastructure, which today is a vital part of the finance value chain. This concentration is not exactly making the system more resilient.

These unique new risks must determine how competition is structured. Most regulation is based on the principle of 'same activity, same risk, same regulations' – but this is not an adequate approach for Big Tech according to Tobias Adrian (2021) from the IMF. Governments have the choice between activity-based (e.g. payments) and entity-based (e.g. banks or insurances) regulation. Regardless of their size, tech companies are currently controlled by what they are doing, not by who they are. If they engage in payments, they have to stick to the AML and data privacy rules. There will be no specific guidelines on what corporate governance they must set up and they will not have to report financial figures to the authorities.

In this activity-based model compliance is ensured by levying fines, whereas disregarding regulation in an entity-based model can cost the company their licence to operate. In an entity-based approach licensed companies engage in regulated activities. Rules are imposed on the level of the organization. Think capital requirements for banks. There is a continuous engagement with and supervision by the authorities. The idea of governing activities rather than companies is supposed to stimulate competition, but the drawback is that it is hard to get a complete picture of the risks involved, especially of cross-border and cross-sectoral activities. In short, the current handling of tech titans hinders comprehensive oversight and might turn them into shadow banks with risks inherent in their business model.

Moreover, Big Tech would be at an advantage compared to banks, which are also regulated as entities and not solely by what they do. This is unfair competition because banks have higher compliance costs and less flexibility in business models, pricing and the like. It is not just unfair, but endangering financial stability. The competition from Big Tech might diminish banks' resilience towards financial shocks. On the one hand, the free or low pricing slashes profitability and hence shrinks the buffer for bad times. On the other it might weaken banks' funding stability.

Moving away from activity-based regulation

This is why the IMF (Adrian, 2021) has been advocating a hybrid approach to Big Tech ever since 2014. The basis would be regulation on the entity level but the specific requirements would be different for every tech giant depending on which activities they engage in. This hinges primarily on tech giants' home countries. China has already shown a willingness to apply such rules to its own giants. The EU has expectedly taken a host-country stance with the Digital Services Act and the Digital Markets Act, which means all will ultimately depend on Washington DC. It is critical to designate Big Tech companies as systemically important infrastructure providers, if not for their cloud computing dominance, then at least once they enter the financial arena.

The Bank for International Settlement (BIS, 2021) is also advocating a recalibration of the entity-based and activity-based regulation. Activity-based rules can only be a supplement, not a substitute for regulating systemically important organizations. The modus operandi of data giants corroborates the fear that solely regulating activities might be too little. None of the Western tech titans has a banking licence – though Ant Financial and Tencent do. They are, however, very active in payments. Amazon and Facebook have payment licences within their corporate group in the US, UK and EU. Google has its own licence within the group *plus* a partnership with an established financial institution in all three of those markets. Apple has the same model in the US, yet in the UK and EU it does not run licensed businesses but resorts to partnerships. Amazon and Facebook pursue the latter strategy with regards to credit licences (BIS, 2021).

This rank growth of different legal standings leaves an activity-based approach vulnerable to blind spots and serious interconnected risks. Those risks will be turbocharged when Big Tech enters the DeFi realm. DeFi only unfolds its true potential when its building bricks are combined. It is hard to imagine that Big Tech will stop at enabling their customers to buy and hold crypto-assets. Instead, crypto-assets will be staked, insured, used as collateral in loans or linked to derivatives. Regulating solely on an activity basis will monitor only risks within silos and this might have catastrophic effects.

Certainty lures settlers

Whatever the concrete rules said, the newly found certainty ultimately made corporate and banking giants move into the space of decentralized blockchains, albeit cautiously. Many questions remain and it is hard to set enduring rules when the technology is evolving at such a rapid pace. But the introduction of laws and provisions signals a general seal of approval for the industry. And this has made investing in it easier. Firms such as Tesla, Square and Coinbase have already purchased large quantities of bitcoins (Graves and Phillips, 2021) and as we will see in Chapter 11, so have banks.

Buying cryptocurrency is one thing, but it is another to offer investment services for them. After all, this comes with a host of rules and licence requirements that need to be followed in many jurisdictions. Yet even the cautious banks have started to make small moves in that direction. Whereas digital-native banks such as Revolut have offered crypto-trading since 2017, big banking pioneers only started getting into the arena in 2021. In January 2021, Spanish BBVA launched its first bitcoin transaction and custody service in Switzerland (Dolghier, 2021). Two months later Morgan Stanley became the first major US bank to offer its customers access to bitcoin investment. Goldman Sachs and others followed with similar announcements. Those offerings were timid; Morgan Stanley had a $2 million threshold in place (Son, 2021), and Goldman Sachs restricted trading to its private wealth clients worth more than $25 million (Hale, 2021).

These thresholds and limitations are likely to get looser over time, but the fact that the offering is on the table illustrates a mind shift. In October 2021 the first futures-based bitcoin ETF started trading in the United States. For the first time it let main street investors speculate on the future price of the cryptocurrency. And some months later Goldman Sachs even accepted bitcoin as collateral for a cash loan (Yang, 2022). Things can move very fast once that initial step into the crypto-sphere is taken. In fact, according to research by *Forbes*, 8 out of the 10 largest publicly traded companies were crypto-bulls. Warren Buffet (Berkshire Hathaway) and Tim Cook (Apple) are the only ones not interested in cryptos. Apple's silence on blockchain especially is seen as 'most surprising' (del Castillo, 2021).

And the battlefield once more is payments

The pendulum is even swinging back to where the blockchain started out: the transfer of money. Unsurprisingly payment giant Visa kept looking at how to enhance settlement via the blockchain. The best way to do so, it decided, was by utilizing stablecoins. When credit card users pay for something in cryptocurrency (in this case via a partnership with crypto.com), Visa needs to exchange that currency for fiat money in the settlement process. Visa chose USD Coin (USDC) for the pilot, but in future the setup could be easily expanded to other types of stablecoins (Visa, 2021).

Moreover, increasing regulatory clarity made many payment companies give crypto-purchases another look. Stripe, the largest privately held fintech, worth some $95 billion, was an early champion of bitcoin payments until it quit offering them in 2018 due to their volatility and fund transfer inefficiency. Four years and a regulatory wave later, Stripe got back into the crypto business, even expanding its offering. It now allows Twitter users to be paid via the USDC stablecoin. Furthermore, Stripe does not rule out accepting bitcoin as a means of payment at a later stage. Besides Visa and Stripe, other processors including PayPal and Mastercard have made or announced similar moves recently (Browne, 2022).

And it is not just payment processors. Tesla had actually accepted bitcoins as a means of payment for new cars from March to May 2021. It stopped when Tesla's boss Elon Musk found out that the cryptocurrency had an energy problem – not the best association for an electric vehicle manufacturer. But in an SEC filing at the end of that year the company explicitly mentioned it might pick up cryptocurrency transactions again (Tesla, 2021).

Another company joined the fray: a tech giant that had burned its fingers on digital currencies and had set in motion the entire regulatory frenzy in the first place – Meta. The name of the company might have changed since David Marcus announced the Libra initiative from that podium at the Old San Francisco Mint; its ambition had not. Despite its recent setback, Meta squandered no time but started working on another attempt to muscle its way into finance. Its persistence to climb to the apex of blockchain for finance is the ultimate testament to the fact that whoever wins the blockchain race will be at the helm of global finance.

At the heart of Meta's new strategy is once more payment – this time called Meta Pay – but the social media giant swapped the stablecoin idea for the more mainstream crypto-approach. Meta filed five trademark applications (USPTO, 2022). They let us peek into the company's future strategy. Meta Pay is designed as a wallet to hold crypto and fiat assets of all kinds, ranging from NFTs, stablecoins and cryptocurrencies to pounds and dollars. What has happened was that Meta redefined the layer it seeks to dominate. Banned by regulators from the asset level it turned its focus to the layer above: gateways.

We have discussed the massive importance of gateways in the form of wallets in Chapter 6. Whoever controls the gateway, controls the customer interface. Ergo, moving money is just the first step. From the texts of the trademark applications, it seems that Meta Pay will also have a crypto exchange function, and later might offer lending and investment services; the next tussle with lawmakers and regulators is guaranteed.

Placing your wallet as the central hub for users' finances is the key to rule end-customer finance. For Meta it is even more than that. The wallet is a vital component in another effort, which is as large as its push into finance: the metaverse economy. But before we enter this new virtual world, we must look at who will fill the vacuum on the asset layer left after Diem's demise. After all, the assets are foundational to the applications and gateways sitting on top.

KEY TAKEAWAYS

- The Libra/Diem project triggered a regulatory backlash across the world. Lawmakers made it more difficult for Big Tech to enter finance. Moreover, regulation like MiCA brought clarity to the entire cryptosphere. Companies and banks now have a better understanding of which activities are permitted and which licensing criteria apply.
- Clear laws made the first banks and companies invest in cryptocurrencies, offer crypto trading services, and accept cryptos as means of payment. The competition for tomorrow's finance is once more happening on the level of payments.
- The most striking example of this trend is Meta Pay. This future project is a move of Meta away from what it tried to do with Libra (i.e. run the asset layer) towards grabbing for the gateway layer. Whoever controls the gateway, controls the customer interface.
- At the same time regulators will have to yield their activity-based approach to Big Tech in finance as it leaves the system vulnerable to blind spots and serious interconnected risks. Rather, rules must also be imposed on the level of the organization as Big Techs are systemically important infrastructure providers.

References

116th Congress (2019) H.R.4813 – Keep Big Tech Out Of Finance Act, 23 October, www.congress.gov/bill/116th-congress/house-bill/4813/text

Adrian, T (2021) BigTech in Financial Services, International Monetary Fund, 16 June, www.imf.org/en/News/Articles/2021/06/16/sp061721-bigtech-in-financial-services (archived at https://perma.cc/M4ML-8Q6B)

Berry, K (2021) Banks get behind CFPB's tough approach to tech giants, American Banker, 9 December, www.americanbanker.com/news/banks-get-behind-cfpbs-tough-approach-to-tech-giants (archived at https://perma.cc/Q95H-JF2P)

Biden, J (2022) Executive Order on Ensuring Responsible Development of Digital Assets, 9 March, www.whitehouse.gov/briefing-room/presidential-actions/2022/03/09/executive-order-on-ensuring-responsible-development-of-digital-assets (archived at https://perma.cc/PFQ2-AUAJ)

BIS (2021) Big techs in finance: regulatory approaches and policy options, FSI Briefs, March, www.bis.org/fsi/fsibriefs12.pdf (archived at https://perma.cc/WA3T-6XTL)

Browne, R (2022) CNBC DISRUPTOR 50: Fintech giant Stripe jumps into crypto with a feature that lets Twitter users get paid in stablecoin, *CNBC*, 22 April, www.cnbc.com/2022/04/22/stripe-launches-crypto-payments-feature-with-twitter-as-first-client.html (archived at https://perma.cc/AJF3-95VP)

Council of the European Union (2021) Proposal for a Regulation of the European Parliament and of the Council on Markets in Crypto-assets, and amending Directive (EU) 2019/1937, 19 November, www.consilium.europa.eu/media/53105/st14067-en21.pdf (archived at https://perma.cc/CE3Y-64U2)

Del Castillo, M (2021) Warren Buffett and Tim Cook snub blockchain as corporate giants embrace, *Forbes*, 13 May, www.forbes.com/sites/michaeldelcastillo/2021/05/13/warren-buffett-and-tim-cook-snub-blockchain-as-corporate-giants-embrace/?sh=7e220fe6bd5c (archived at https://perma.cc/H9SQ-M6Y6)

Deutscher Bundestag (2020) Gesetz zur Umsetzung der Änderungsrichtlinie zur Vierten EU-Geldwäscherichtlinie, 1 January, https://dip.bundestag.de/vorgang/.../251728 (archived at https://perma.cc/4G36-HCLF)

Diem (2021) Diem announces partnership with Silvergate and strategic shift to the United States, Press Release, 12 May, www.diem.com/en-us/updates/diem-silvergate-partnership/ (archived at https://perma.cc/NY2A-62TD)

Diem (2022) Statement by Diem CEO Stuart Levey on the sale of the Diem Group's assets to Silvergate, Press Release, 31 January, www.prnewswire.com/news-releases/statement-by-diem-ceo-stuart-levey-on-the-sale-of-the-diem-groups-assets-to-silvergate-301471997.html (archived at https://perma.cc/VZ3T-QG2Q)

Dolghier, C (2021) BBVA's goal is to provide our customers with access to new digital asset markets, The Tokenizer, 25 January, https://thetokenizer.io/2021/01/25/bbvas-goal-is-to-provide-our-customers-with-access-to-new-digital-asset-markets/ (archived at https://perma.cc/6ELF-7ZHD)

European Commission (2020a) Proposal for a Regulation of the European Parliament and of the Council on Markets in Crypto-assets, and amending Directive (EU) 2019/1937, 24 September, https://eur-lex.europa.eu/legal-content/EN/TXT/?uri=CELEX%3A52020PC0593 (archived at https://perma.cc/NW3G-GKVF)

European Commission (2020b) Commission staff working document impact assessment: Accompanying the document. Proposal for a Regulation of the European Parliament and of the Council on Markets in Crypto-assets and amending Directive (EU), 24 September, https://eur-lex.europa.eu/legal-content/EN/TXT/PDF/?uri=CELEX:52020SC0380&from=EN (archived at https://perma.cc/S692-RRKX)

FCA (2022) Cryptoassets, 23 May, www.fca.org.uk/consumers/cryptoassets (archived at https://perma.cc/4TAM-B5AV)

FSB (2019) BigTech in finance: Market developments and potential financial stability implications, 9 December, www.fsb.org/2019/12/bigtech-in-finance-market-developments-and-potential-financial-stability-implications/ (archived at https://perma.cc/LW5D-FJKY)

Graves, S and Phillips, D (2021) The 10 public companies with the biggest bitcoin portfolios, Decrypt, 30 December, https://decrypt.co/47061/public-companies-biggest-bitcoin-portfolios (archived at https://perma.cc/SLZ2-V3K4)

Hale, K (2021) Goldman Sachs cryptocurrency endorsement boosts wealth management, *Forbes*, 5 April, www.forbes.com/sites/korihale/2021/04/05/goldman-sachs-cryptocurrency-endorsement-boosts-wealth-management/?sh=311bfc4461cb (archived at https://perma.cc/9W9X-RSWU)

Jimenez, G (2019) Donald Trump blasts Bitcoin, Facebook's Libra in Twitter tirade, Decrypt, 12 July, https://decrypt.co/7848/donald-trump-blasts-bitcoin-facebooks-libra-twitter-tirade (archived at https://perma.cc/LW7U-BG7D)

Mearian, L (2019) Why France and Germany fear Facebook's cryptocurrency – and plan to block it, Computerworld, 18 September, www.computerworld.com/article/3439436/why-france-and-germany-fear-facebooks-cryptocurrency-and-plan-to-block-it.html (archived at https://perma.cc/4ZA5-A2WX)

Son, H (2021) Morgan Stanley becomes the first big U.S. bank to offer its wealthy clients access to bitcoin funds, *CNBC*, 17 March, www.cnbc.com/2021/03/17/bitcoin-morgan-stanley-is-the-first-big-us-bank-to-offer-wealthy-clients-access-to-bitcoin-funds.html (archived at https://perma.cc/R2RM-CKVH)

Tesla (2021) Quarterly Report Pursuant to Section 13 or 15(D) of the Securities Exchange Act of 1934, *United States Securities and Exchange Commission –*

Form 10-Q, for the quarterly period ended September 30, www.sec.gov/Archives/edgar/data/1318605/000095017021002253/tsla-20210930.htm (archived at https://perma.cc/J8QQ-NQU2)

The Economist (2021) Joe Biden's tech policy is becoming clearer, 27 December, www.economist.com/united-states/2021/11/27/joe-bidens-tech-policy-is-becoming-clearer (archived at https://perma.cc/N4CF-AKWQ)

UK Government (2022) Government sets out plan to make UK a global cryptoasset technology hub, News Story, 4 April, https://bit.ly/3Ov2zGO (archived at https://perma.cc/Q6NA-6XMP)

US Department of Treasury (2021) President's Working Group on Financial Markets Releases Report and Recommendations on Stablecoins, Press Release, 1 November, https://home.treasury.gov/news/press-releases/jy0454 (archived at https://perma.cc/K42G-SY2W)

USPTO (2022) Trademark/Service Mark Application, Principal Register, Serial Number: 97409240, 13 May, https://tsdrsec.uspto.gov/ts/cd/casedoc/sn97409240/APP20220517095918/1/webcontent?scale=1 (archived at https://perma.cc/QQ49-6QER)

Visa (2021) Digital currency comes to Visa's settlement platform, *The Visa Blog Newsletter*, 29 March, https://usa.visa.com/visa-everywhere/blog/bdp/2021/03/26/digital-currency-comes-1616782388876.html (archived at https://perma.cc/E9VY-XCMN)

Yang, Y (2022) Goldman offers its first bitcoin-backed loan in crypto push, Bloomberg, 28 April, www.bloomberg.com/news/articles/2022-04-28/goldman-offers-its-first-bitcoin-backed-loan-in-crypto-push#xj4y7vzkg (archived at https://perma.cc/QZ8A-KP7T)

Yuan, L (2022) As Beijing takes control, Chinese tech companies lose jobs and hope, *New York Times*, 5 January, www.nytimes.com/2022/01/05/technology/china-tech-internet-crackdown-layoffs.html (archived at https://perma.cc/BX7U-GVDK)

10

Dawn of a new era: central bank digital currencies vs private stablecoins

Why create new central bank money?

Facebook's Libra was a watershed moment not only for legislators and regulators, but also for central banks. They have been playing with the idea of a central bank-issued digital currency for quite some time. Yet only when they realized how sudden and real Big Tech's threat to their monetary monopoly could be did they kick their efforts into high gear. Instead of solely barring new players from issuing systemically relevant stablecoins, central banks realized the potential and got into the arena themselves. The Bank for International Settlement found that 86 per cent of central banks – representing 95 per cent of the global GDP – are actively looking into blockchain-powered currencies (BIS, 2021). More than 50 countries are already in an advanced phase, meaning development, pilot or launch. The Bahamas were the first country to issue a digital version of their currency (sand dollar). The East Caribbean (dCash) and Nigeria (e-naira) followed suit (Atlantic Council, 2022).

This form of blockchain money is known as CBDC or central bank digital currency. CBDCs are a third form of central bank money next to cash or reserve money. They are a particular type of stablecoin. Just like other stablecoins they are pegged 1:1 to the country's fiat currency, but the decisive difference is that CBDCs are centralized.

The central bank has full authority over the network and that is why the coins they issue on the blockchain are issued with the same authority as coins and bills. At the same time CBDCs are more than just a digital representation of a dollar or a pound, because they have all the advantages of the underlying distributed ledger technology. A CBDC is smart-contract-enabled, meaning that you can program money in a way previously impossible. CBDCs benefit from immutability, so history cannot be rewritten. Moreover, the network is more resilient due to its distributed nature.

CBDCs are wedding the benefits of blockchain with those of fiat currencies. First, CBDCs eliminate price volatility and enable a widespread use of digital assets. Second, CBDCs enable the central bank to adjust money supply and exchange rates to the economic conditions. Note that this is antithetical to the initial crypto-idealism that saw inflation as one of the great evils of monetary policy – and this is antithetical to the initial crypto idea. And third, CBDCs are actually an efficient form of payment. There is an institution of trust managing the supply and flow of this new money, hence there is no need for cumbersome decentralized consensus mechanisms. CBDCs can reach unprecedented transaction capacities. Bitcoin can handle seven to eight transactions per second; the Chinese CBDC pilot handles 300,000 transactions in the same time (Tonkovska, 2022). And Project Hamilton – a centralized system built by the Boston Fed and MIT's Digital Currency Initiative – handles a staggering 1.7 million transactions per second (Federal Reserve Bank of Boston, 2022).

Arguments for CBDCs

So CBDCs are a more efficient form of blockchain money. But why do we need them? Just as Jack Ma framed the discussion on techfins around financial inclusion, so too governments like to talk about making financial services accessible. Holding, receiving and sending CBDCs via a smartphone wallet does not require a banking infrastructure and works even in the most far-flung places. Emerging economies could thus leapfrog credit cards and bank accounts altogether. It is no wonder that seven out of eight central banks successfully looking into CBDCs are from emerging economies (BIS, 2021). But why would countries such as the UK or Canada which have a mature payment infrastructure work on CBDC initiatives?

One explanation offered is domestic and cross-border payment efficiency. But CBDCs' impact on it is largely exaggerated. Disintermediation would only occur if CBDCs were to materialize in their most radical form, which in most countries they will not. There are two competing CBDC models. In the extreme retail approach central banks would issue CBDCs directly to the citizens. People could choose to hold their money in central bank accounts, which would remove commercial banks from the equation. This is unlikely to happen for a number of reasons. Central banks would deprive themselves of powerful monetary instruments. Moreover, they would have to deal with customers directly, which no central bank is keen on doing. In fact, the spiralling global inflation of 2022 has been attributed exactly to central banks performing too many tasks outside of their core perimeter instead of focusing on inflation (e.g. *The Economist*, 2022). Thus, a wholesale approach is the likeliest scenario. Central banks will mint new CBDC but it will be the commercial banks who are the link to the citizens.

With the sanctions against Russia for invading Ukraine, another argument has taken centre stage, namely that CBDCs can help governments to punish bad actors. Sanctions could be levied easily by adding new rules to the CBDC blockchain, and the fight against money laundering or terrorism financing would become easier. This is a frail argument. CBDCs or not, you can't use your MasterCard or Visa in North Korea and you can't wire a payment to your local drug dealer. Even today sanctions can be imposed very quickly. Whether it is the SWIFT network, payment processors or payment apps, there are many levers to pull (see also Pejic, 2022).

A more convincing argument for CBDCs is the financial hegemony reasoning. On the one hand they could be a defensive measure against sanctions. Countries that fear they could become the target of international isolation can build their own CBDCs to have an efficient transaction system without relying on primarily US firms and infrastructure. More important, however, is the offensive use of CBDCs whereby the issuer country gains influence in other territories, for example by being used in cross-border transactions. This has been a motivation for China in particular.

China seeks to turn the yuan into a major reserve currency. It is a big lender to other countries, who owe it some $5 trillion (Lee, 2019) but these loans are predominantly issued on a USD basis, not in yuan. In fact, the dollar makes up more than 60 per cent of the world's reserves, the euro more than 20 per cent and the yuan languishes behind even the pound and the yen (Statista, 2021).

How could a Chinese CBDC alter that ratio? It is hard to believe that anybody in the West would start to use yuan for transactions, but it could easily spread to the South-East Asian economies that are considered part of the Chinese techno-sphere. And this is where Big Tech comes in once more. After all, they are part of the digital yuan's pilot just as much as the country's big banks. Piggybacking on giants like Alipay or WeChat Pay, who have a massive footprint in many Asian countries, could indeed make the digital yuan attractive.

Paving the way for an autonomous economy

All of the arguments in favour of introducing CBDCs rely on one crucial assumption: that they will be used by the population. If nobody is using a digital pound for transactions, then sanctions deployed on it won't bite and any efficiency gains will be in vain. So why should people and companies use it?

CBDCs are more than just a digital representation of fiat; this exists already. They equip fiat money with the capabilities of (advanced) blockchains, above all smart contracts. This leads to a programmability of payments and value exchange more broadly. All kinds of scenarios can be built in which money is automatically moved, whether I want shares to be sold or collateral for a loan released. On such scale this can neither be done via today's fiat money, nor via bitcoin. Most such automatic transfer rules resort to stablecoins, but a CBDC eliminates the step of having to swap the desired asset for a stablecoin and back.

This eliminates risks of private stablecoin issuers and the benefit adds up. In tomorrow's digitalized economy money must be issued and transferred seamlessly between people, corporations, banks, governments and machines. The last point is frequently forgotten but the internet of things (IoT), also known as the autonomous machine economy, will connect 24 billion devices by 2030 (Hatton, 2020). The IoT is a network of connected computing devices (i.e. computing chips in all types of physical objects – 'things') which communicate autonomously without the need for human intervention. Those devices need an automatic way to exchange value. CBDCs, alongside private stablecoins, today look like the best way to do so. Equally critical to machines communicating with each other is machines transacting with each other. Machine-to-machine transactions and pay-per-use models both require payments to be programmable. And often they also require micro-payments. The frequently invoked fridge that autonomously orders milk might sell the data of that transaction to an AI company. The value of such information would be only a fraction of a cent. Blockchain-based fiat could also handle such miniscule amounts.

According to an analysis by the German Bundesbank (Deutsche Bundesbank, 2020) no other network can be as efficient an underpinning for the machine economy as CBDCs. Conventional fiat and classic crypto tokens don't offer the smart contract capability. Privately issued coins with smart contract capability could provide programmable payments, but the German Bundesbank concludes that three factors preclude it from being a viable alternative to CBDCs:

1 Volatility: CBDCs have their value pegged to fiat.
2 Legal certainty: the rules for using central bank money are well established.
3 Interoperability: having only one stablecoin (if alternative products are forbidden) or even one stablecoin with preferential treatment would preclude the market from splintering off into multiple popular coins (i.e. formats).

In my view, only interoperability is a (partly) valid argument as points 1 and 2 can be easily remedied. Volatility could easily be countered by having privately issued stablecoins with the value pegged to fiat. Legal certainty on stablecoins will be achieved soon with all the movement as we have seen in the last chapter. The interoperability argument is indeed a powerful one. A CBDC would set a de facto standard, which would help the coin reach scale quickly, whereas private stablecoins would have to win gruelling format wars first. On the other hand, open competition would ensure the most potent application ends up on top. There is an approach that combines both of those scenarios, namely what the German Bundesbank calls 'tokenized commercial bank money', which is nothing other than privately issued stablecoin by banks. It would be a middle ground as the number of banks able to pull off a stablecoin is limited, yet unlike with a CBDC there is competition, which ultimately incentivizes the banks to work on a superior coin.

Regardless of whether CBDCs or privately issued stablecoins take centre stage, automating the machine economy will drive GDP. The Bank of England (Barrdear and Kumhof, 2016) found that replacing a portion of payments with a digital currency could boost global GDP by 3 per cent permanently, lower barriers to financial inclusion and empower consumers.

Big Tech as the bridge

If there is anybody besides central banks and commercial banks that can issue a stablecoin and recruit a userbase strong enough to sustain it, it is Big Tech. Libra foundered on the backlash of legislators and regulators, but this is not to say that future projects will meet the same fate. Amazon, Google and Apple are all faring better on trust surveys than Facebook (e.g. Seitz, 2021). And any new project will have learned from Libra's mistakes, primarily trying to peg the value to a basket of currencies and headquartering the initiative outside the US.

Yet even if the data giants do not go full-in themselves, they will be a vital enabler for CBDCs. The payment apps and wallets they have built over the last few years are channels through which digital fiat can be distributed to end-users. This is already happening in China. Alibaba's MyBank has joined the e-CNY project (*CNBC*, 2021) as have WeChat Pay and Alipay (Kharpal, 2022). In that regard China's tech titans are performing the same function as commercial banks – they are making central bank money accessible to vast amounts of users.

The equivalents of Alibaba and WeChat are preparing to go the very same way. Amazon (Cag, 2021) published a job advertorial looking to hire a 'Head of Digital Currency and Blockchain' to build the company's roadmap, especially focusing on crypto acceptance on various platforms. Very interestingly, the job ad also required knowledge on CBDCs. Even if Big Tech does not capture the asset layer directly, it will be a vital player underpinning the autonomous economy.

Worries of a super-state

The Wild West was a space of liberty, free of any government intervention. But as the frontier closed the state moved into the vast space and became more powerful. The introduction of CBDCs marks a similar development in the crypto-space. While regulation is coming to the industry step by step, CBDCs are a monopolistic endeavour that completely pushes out private actors. Crypto-enthusiasts' visceral reaction comes as no surprise, as bitcoin was the antithesis of central bank-issued money. At the same time there is a more mainstream outcry about governmental overreach and the death of privacy.

CBDCs are private blockchains, meaning that only the nodes who run them see the transactions. But employees at the central bank could access the CBDC ledger, which would show all transactions done with the digital fiat. Today banks see your transactions, credit card companies have an overview of your purchases, processors like PayPal know what you bought online and so on. If those transactions used a CBDC, they would all be visible on the ledger. And more information would be pooled there. Central banks would also see who gets credit. If governments want to hand out cheques to the needy – say as a form of Covid relief – then this kind of information would also appear in the ledger. Also, when you have the information on monetary flows in one place, why not monitor them for AML, CTF and other noble purposes? Why not let advanced analytics run through them to improve compliance protocols and analyses for the future? Consider also that even if people do not actively opt for CBDC usage, they still might be used in the background, for example as a stablecoin bridge between fiat and cryptocurrencies.

A CBDC would likely turn central banks into financial super-surveillance institutions. This new power would once more diffuse the focus of central banks, whose primary purpose is to keep inflation under control and unemployment low. Second, it would endanger the independence of central banks. Even today politicians are exerting pressure to impact monetary policy. Just think of the plea to central bankers to lift interest rates in order to curb the inflation caused by the war in Ukraine. Now imagine what would happen if there was an institution that with a click could access a near-omniscient ledger. For crypto-maximalists all centralization is automatically suspicious. Yet it is a different thing if companies offer centralized solutions than if states do so. As Selgin (2022) explains, 'We have a choice with private firms. Nobody *has* to use Facebook or Amazon to make payments. In this regard private firms pose less of a risk than states do of abusing data. A CBDC will not improve a currency's status as an international reserve currency, but it will expand the control by letting them snoop on its citizens.'

Privacy and competing in the CBDC race

The privacy discussion is so elementary that it has so far determined who will be ahead in the CBDC race. Of all the major economies, the People's Bank of China (PBoC) is by a long way the most advanced central bank in its CBDC project. While the US, UK and EU are mired in discussions on whether any public actor should get that kind of power, the promise of immense centralized control seemed to be a catalyst in China. The digital yuan named e-CNY (earlier known as DC/EP or Digital Currency Electronic Payment) was piloted as early as April 2020. At the Winter Olympics in February 2022 the wallet was already live in 11 regions, plus it was available to visitors to the Games. By that time more than 260 million wallets, including many corporate ones, had been opened. Citizens were incentivized via a lottery to use it and the e-CNY was accessible through the country's large payment channels such as Alipay and WeChat Pay (Atlantic Council, 2022).

Meanwhile the European Central Bank (ECB, 2021a) undertook a public consultation in which it asked citizens and professionals about their view of a digital euro. By far the largest concern was privacy. Forty-three per cent of the respondents said it was crucial to them, compared to 18 per cent who worried about the second-ranked security aspect. Thus, more than twice as many people are concerned whether officials will be able to see their transactions than are afraid they might actually lose money. Merchants and other companies that were part of the study had similar concerns. After all, trade secrets can be extracted from transaction data.

Together with the Bank of Japan, the ECB has been working on project Stella, a CBDC proof of concept to be the basis for a digital euro, which is supposed to launch by the mid-2020s. To address privacy concerns, the ECB (2021b) envisions anonymity vouchers that hide the identity of the counterparty. Those vouchers are handed out by the AML authority to citizens. They are non-transferrable, low value and only valid for a limited time. The privacy-enhancing techniques are to be deployed on top of the CBDC, not as an integral part of it. It is likely that anonymity vouchers will find their way into many Western CBDCs, which would make them easily digestible for users – of course assuming they have the basic trust that the central bank will create such vouchers without leaving open any backdoors. What thresholds to set, what techniques to use, which information to hide – these questions will ultimately be determined in the democratic discourse, but the technological possibility to preserve privacy is there. So, whether CBDCs are a tool to foster democracy or authoritarianism eventually depends on a country's institutions and people.

Are CBDCs sounding the death knell for private stablecoins?

Whether a state takes an outsized role with CBDCs is not only a matter of privacy, it is also a matter of future innovative potency. The Chinese CBDC effort is admired by many experts around the world. But what the government and the central bank actually did was monopolize a market that was efficiently supplied by more than one actor. Such governmental overreaches suppress innovation in a market, because public actors don't feel the pressure to innovate. Monetary history is littered with examples of *private* innovation, such as the invention of Europe's first paper money in 17th-century Sweden. 'That is why we need competition in money, including competition of all substitutes for official government fiat' (Selgin, 2022).

The innovative power of the private financial sector has been particularly visible in recent decades. Credit cards and ATMs were developed without governmental input, not even to mention the Cambrian explosion of private money innovation in the fintech era.

Thus, forbidding private stablecoins is definitively the wrong way to go. But how can we trust that private stablecoin issuers will not endanger monetary stability? How can we be sure that a coin that reaches mainstream adaption and becomes a vital cog in our economy does not collapse the way Terra and Luna did? When the stablecoin TerraUSD lost its peg to the dollar it killed off a major part of the crypto-world's market value. Such a cataclysmic effect cannot be allowed to spill over to the off-chain economy. To prevent such a scenario the first thing to do is to set a cap on the size of *algorithmic* stablecoins or to forbid them altogether. Algorithmic stablecoins are pegged to fiat like any other stablecoin, but the peg and thus the entire coin is much more fragile. They hold their value solely by adjusting supply and demand of two virtual tokens they issue. So, there is no hard backing with real-life fiat. An algorithmic stablecoin issuer might theoretically hold zero US dollars in reserves and still peg the coin to the currency. If, however, the algorithm has insufficiencies in the code or fails to adjust quickly enough the value will de-peg and a precipitous plunge will follow. There is no question that a viable CBDC alternative must be backed by sufficient funds and regulated properly.

There are two ways in which an actual or prospective stablecoin issuer might convince regulators that their coins don't pose any systemic risk. First, the issuer could become a fully fledged, FDIC (Federal Deposit Insurance Corporation)-insured bank. This is a pretty straightforward route, tried and tested and legally solid. Also, deposits are insured, so customers will trust the offer more easily. However, this is a strenuous process that many stablecoin issuers aren't prepared to go through. Hence, insisting on it could mean not having a competitive and innovative stablecoin industry.

The second possibility is that the Fed allows uninsured private stablecoin issuers to have master accounts at the central bank. This is the safest way of keeping genuine fiat money reserves. The very least the Fed should consider doing is allowing stablecoin issuers to keep 100 per cent reserves with it as an alternative to having to insure their coins. This is what Selgin (2022) calls a 'narrow stablecoin' option. The concept is analogous to the narrow banking idea that has been proposed as an alternative to deposit insurance for ordinary banks. Other countries have taken a similar approach already. The Bank of England opened its settlement accounts to fintechs back in 2017. The IMF (Adrian, 2019) has proposed a somewhat similar approach which it dubbed 'synthetic CBDC'. The advantage for the central bank is also that it can outsource costs and risks. Technological choices, customer management or compliance monitoring – all are done by the partners so that central bankers can focus on their core duties.

Granting stablecoin issuers the right to hold accounts at the central bank would also have another benefit: it would make them part of the settlement system and thus vastly enhance the efficiency of their coins. They could settle transactions with other account holders just the way debit card and check transactions are settled today.

Moreover, stablecoin issuers would not be operating from outside of the banking system. They would no longer depend on opening accounts at a correspondent bank. As long as they are at the mercy of correspondent banks, they not only pay considerable fees, but more importantly the banks can impose their conditions. So far, in most cases that has meant they rejected serving stablecoin issuers altogether (Selgin, 2022).

Can CBDCs and private stablecoins co-exist?

If private issuers of stablecoins are regulated adequately and perhaps even allowed to keep their balances at the central bank, then does it matter that they co-exist with CBDCs? It does. The sole licence to operate does not level the playing field.

Powerful central banks by nature cannot fairly compete with private suppliers. They can regulate their rivals and they can subsidize their own products. Above all, 'They cannot fail, and if you can't fail in a commercial sense, you are not really competing' (Selgin, 2022).

If central banks issue CBDCs to compete with private stablecoin issuers, this will inevitably discourage private entry, thereby curbing innovation. Nobody can tell which novelties this would preclude, says Selgin (2022): 'We have not yet heard the last word on digital currency tech. Had we banned cryptocurrencies, no one would be talking about CBDCs today. They wouldn't exist. Entrepreneurs have challenged the status quo and that is why the crypto-space has seen so much innovation.'

For central banks it is a difficult balancing act of how much to get involved. By giving up on CBDCs they would forgo many benefits. Perhaps one of the largest is the opportunity to set a standard for their digital fiat variant. Pure private supplier competition would take some time until converging around the best standard and monopolistic tendencies would be hard to avoid. One way to merge the advantages of private sector competition and central bank-mandated unity would be the described synthetic CBDC concept proposed by the IMF. In this public-private partnership the central bank would provide the trust, while private actors take care of innovation and customer management. In this scenario the private partners would have to be highly regulated firms, preferably with competencies in financial services, and of a size to be able to handle the compliance requirements. So whichever way the stablecoin arena evolves, banks and technology giants will be squaring off with each other over the future of finance.

KEY TAKEAWAYS

- CBDCs – or central bank digital currencies – are a form of central bank money just like cash or reserve money. They are blockchain-based, centralized stablecoins pegged to the country's fiat.
- Eighty-six per cent of central banks are working on CBDCs, with some projects already live. The PBoC is the most advanced of all the major economies in this. Privacy concerns in particular are holding back the EU, UK and US.
- CBDCs are set to become major settlement assets, with multiple benefits such as currency stability, programmability, resilience and interoperability. Ergo, the question is how to handle private stablecoins. As private competition has been the driver of much innovation in money, it is wise to keep the market open to non-central bank competitors and also to enable them to operate from within the banking system.
- Big Tech is an enabler for CBDCs in that it helps with distributing the new money to users. This is an involvement of Big Tech unseen with other forms of central bank money. It is yet another front at which tech titans are entering into direct competition with commercial banks. Owners of the customer relationship will have an edge.

References

Adrian, T (2019) Stablecoins, central bank digital currencies, and cross-border payments: a new look at the international monetary system, *Remarks by Tobias Adrian at the IMF-Swiss National Bank Conference, Zurich*, 14 May, www.imf.org/en/News/Articles/2019/05/13/sp051419-stablecoins-central-bank-digital-currencies-and-cross-border-payments (archived at https://perma.cc/25VV-BHNZ)

Atlantic Council (2022) Top 100 Central Bank Digital Currency Tracker, dynamic list, www.atlanticcouncil.org/cbdctracker/ (archived at https://perma.cc/H3KB-V2RA)

Barrdear, J and Kumhof, M (2016) The macroeconomics of central bank issued digital currencies, *Bank of England Staff Working Paper No. 605*, July, www.bankofengland.co.uk/-/media/boe/files/working-paper/2016/the-macroeconomics-of-central-bank-issued-digital-currencies.pdf?la=en&hash=341B602838707E5D6FC26884588C912A721B1DC1 (archived at https://perma.cc/Y6QU-7SVB)

BIS (2021) Ready, steady, go? – Results of the third BIS survey on central bank digital currency, *BIS Papers No 114*, January, www.bis.org/publ/bppdf/bispap114.pdf (archived at https://perma.cc/RN34-CDHF)

Cag, D (2021) Amazon to build blockchain and digital currency roadmap, *Fintech*, 1 November, https://fintechmagazine.com/financial-services-finserv/amazon-build-blockchain-and-digital-currency-roadmap (archived at https://perma.cc/4WKC-57V4)

CNBC (2021) Online bank backed by Alibaba's Ant Group joins China's digital yuan pilot, 22 February, www.cnbc.com/2021/02/23/mybank-backed-by-alibabas-ant-group-joins-chinas-digital-yuan-pilot.html (archived at https://perma.cc/7DPU-88YA)

Deutsche Bundesbank (2020) Money in programmable applications: Cross-sector perspectives from the German economy, 21 December, www.bundesbank.de/resource/blob/855148/ebaab681009124d4331e8e327cfaf97c/mL/2020-12-21-programmierbare-zahlung-anlage-data.pdf (archived at https://perma.cc/J4GQ-2W27)

ECB (2021a) ECB publishes the results of the public consultation on a digital euro, Press Release, 14 April, www.ecb.europa.eu/press/pr/date/2021/html/ecb.pr210414~ca3013c852.en.html (archived at https://perma.cc/L7LP-NA7P)

ECB (2021b) Appendix: The Eurosystem's analysis of privacy-enhancing techniques in central bank digital currencies, www.ecb.europa.eu/pub/pdf/annex/ecb.sp210414_1_annex~43eee6196e.en.pdf (archived at https://perma.cc/5B6F-99TX)

Federal Reserve Bank of Boston (2022) Project Hamilton Phase 1 Executive Summary, 3 February, www.bostonfed.org/publications/one-time-pubs/project-hamilton-phase-1-executive-summary.aspx (archived at https://perma.cc/E9ZG-B8KZ)

Hatton, M (2020) The IoT in 2030: 24 billion connected things generating $1.5 trillion, IoT Business News, 20 May, https://iotbusinessnews.com/2020/05/20/03177-the-iot-in-2030-24-billion-connected-things-generating-1-5-trillion/ (archived at https://perma.cc/TXH5-ATPV)

Kharpal, A (2022) China's digital currency comes to its biggest messaging app WeChat, which has over a billion users, *CNBC*, 6 January, www.cnbc.com/2022/01/06/chinas-digital-currency-comes-to-tencents-wechat-in-expansion-push.html (archived at https://perma.cc/UA46-ZPX6)

Lee, A (2019) China's loans to rest of the world worth US$5 trillion, 6 per cent of global economy, new study reveals, *South China Morning Post*, 9 July, www.scmp.com/economy/china-economy/article/3017902/chinas-loans-rest-world-worth-us5-trillion-6-cent-global (archived at https://perma.cc/Z98K-GZQS)

Pejic, I (2022) How effective are payment system sanctions really? The New Frontier, 1 March, https://igorpejic.substack.com/p/how-effective-are-payment-system (archived at https://perma.cc/E83E-X4HM)

Seitz, P (2021) Survey reveals which tech companies consumers trust the most, *Investor's Business Daily*, 2 August

Selgin, G (2022) Personal interview, 28 April

Statista (2021) Share of currencies held in global foreign exchange reserves from 1st quarter 1999 to 4th quarter 2020, www.statista.com/statistics/233674/distribution-of-global-currency-reserves/ (archived at https://perma.cc/5C4U-PXPK)

The Economist (2022) The danger of excessive distraction, 20 April, www.economist.com/special-report/2022/04/20/the-danger-of-excessive-distraction (archived at https://perma.cc/WYX5-TJDE)

Tonkovska, K (2022) Digital Yuan – the financial revolution of the East, Industria, 9 February, www.industria.tech/blog/digital-yuan-the-financial-revolution-of-the-east/#:~:text=The%20digital%20yuan%20has%20a,new%20system%20should%20reflect%20this (archived at https://perma.cc/T8SF-9XYD)

11

Commercial banks and the frontier experience

Still centralized, yet transformed

It should be clear by now that over recent years technology has put unprecedent pressure on banking. It has led to new regulation, increased customer demands, a heightened price sensitivity and, above all, to the entry of Big Tech into banking. The reaction of banks has been twofold: protect their turf but at the same time leverage the technology to improve their existing processes.

No story tells this as well as the fate of Google's ambitious Plex project. In November 2019 Google unveiled its vision of mobile bank accounts under the banner of financial inclusion. The accounts would include features leveraging other Google products. Users would be able to hit buttons dubbed 'Get gas' and 'Get food' and the app would display the nearest gas station or restaurant. Purchases could be made automatically from the account. According to the *Wall Street Journal* (Rudegeair, Benoit and Ackerman, 2021) 400,000 people had signed up to the Plex waiting list, making it all the more surprising that Google abandoned the project 12 months later. Google said it ended the project due to a shift in strategy. It no longer wanted to serve the end-customers but rather provide digital enablement for financial institutions. In other words: it will be a supplier for banks rather than offer its own B2C accounts. But where had this change of heart come from all of a sudden?

A Google executive hinted at the fact that some banks were not amused about the new competitor, which has led some (e.g. Shevlin, 2021) to speculate that the search giant had to back down due to pressure from some big players such as JPMorgan Chase, Wells Fargo and Bank of America. But why does their opinion have such clout? While banks might be competitors, first and foremost they are major customers *and* essential partners for Google's parent company Alphabet. The giant's core services are advertisement, cloud computing and AI – all components where banks are crucial customers. At the same time, it would be very hard to offset any lost business with the new revenue generated by banking services. On the one hand it takes time to build up a *profitable* business, and on the other, cooperation with banks in some form is necessary. The latter is particularly true for the US where business and finance are strictly separated. Even Plex was supposed to be powered by Citibank. Hence, turning banks into open enemies is currently not an option.

Unlike when Apple Pay came along, banks are starting to respond forcefully to some Big Tech initiatives to ringfence their core business. This is, however, just the first step needed to fight off the tech onslaught. The second is to leverage new technology to expand it.

Are banks missing the point of blockchain?

We have seen in Chapter 2 the multitude of blockchain projects that the likes of JP Morgan Chase are pursuing. In Chapter 6 I described how big banks are also joining forces, for instance when funding the fintech R3. R3's Corda blockchain has become the dominant smart contract platform in the world of finance. And we have also seen how banks are linking arms with each other, as well as logistics and tech companies, in blockchain-based trade finance consortia. Banks have been all but idle when it comes to deploying the new technology, and today they are amongst those players with the highest blockchain expertise.

Finance incumbents have started with the most straightforward use cases involving cross-border payments, syndicated loans or asset management. And as we will see, they are not even shying away from decentralized finance applications anymore. Banks are, however, still a bastion of centralization. Their own blockchain efforts are either built on centralized blockchains or they use decentralized blockchains with some sort of layer that gives them control over what is happening. Just look at JP Morgan's launch of Quorum, which is a permissioned application on top of the permissionless Ethereum protocol (see Chapter 2).

And whenever banks are giving their customers access to decentralized finance, they are shrouding it in their own centralized construct: investing in bitcoin might only be possible via Exchange Traded Funds (ETFs), i.e. via pools of crypto-related assets sold on traditional exchanges. Obviously DAOs can be partners at best, not subsidiaries. Banks don't ever deploy blockchains that everybody can read or edit without permission. And smart contracts are treated like an IT asset to make existing processes more efficient rather than a tool to outsource control to an open protocol.

The crypto-sphere routinely proclaims that this is either because banks do not understand the disruptive potential of the blockchain or because they shun self-cannibalization. Neither is true. Banks, as well as Big Techs for that matter, understand that money is subject to what I (2019) have called the 'institutional imperative of money'. While you can decentralize and automatize large chunks of the finance value chain, there will always be a vital role to be played by institutions of trust. A system run by a leaderless DAO might handle mono-dimensional tasks such as locking crypto-assets as collateral in a digital vault. But it cannot recognize systemic risk, which is only multiplying with the possibilities offered by DeFi. It cannot let central banks take drastic monetary policy measures needed during crises and economic shocks. It prevents governments from punishing rogue states and sanctioning illicit transactions on the web. And finally, there is no accountability if things go bad, whether it be due to weak code or systemic failures.

It is no secret anymore that centralized blockchains have been a boon for commercial and central banks, as well as corporations of all hues. Yet paradoxically, even DeFi might end up bolstering the importance of centralized institutions. The higher the micro- and macro-economic risks, the more centralized and regulated organizations are needed. Those with the deepest expertise in decentralized technology will be sought after most. Banks are getting there, but so is Big Tech. While technology giants are struggling with the regulation part, banks wrestle with their IT systems.

Putting legacy into the museum

Before the power of blockchain can be unleashed, though, banks must bring to heel their legacy systems. Old IT infrastructure and bad software code are rampant throughout the economy. In Europe and the US, the average IT system is 32 years old; in China it is only seven or eight years of age (Zhu, 2014). But banks in particular are crippled by technical debt and monolithic core banking systems. Thanks to the pioneering role of banking in the mass deployment of computing, many IT systems were built in the middle of the 20th century, and unfortunately they have never been completely replaced. As PwC Luxembourg (2022) highlights, 75 per cent of banks' IT budgets are spent on keeping the lights on instead of working on new products and features.

This is one of the major differences to tech titans, who are continuously refining their systems. While banks often have four or fewer IT releases per year, Amazon sometimes adapts its systems five times per second (McComb, 2018). Ant Financial, for example, does not only pursue cloud computing, artificial intelligence and blockchain with a rare zeal, it also trashes its entire infrastructure every three to four years (Skinner, 2018).

Sluggish legacy systems are a heavy drag on corporate performance. Systems are frequently down, workarounds are costly and crucial resources cannot be used to develop new products. Compatibility with new tech is hampered. Coders are getting more expensive and harder to find. And the more money companies pour into old systems, the stronger the lock-in.

And often legacy systems are straight-out dangerous. Examples abound in which old software and missing security updates left doors wide open to hackers, resulting in large-scale customer data theft or the complete paralysis of companies. The Equifax hack is the most prominent case. Equifax is one of the largest credit-tracking firms worldwide, so it was all the more devastating when in 2017 attackers managed to steal from it some of the most sensitive data of 148 million customers (US House of Representatives Committee on Oversight and Government Reform, 2018).

While cardinal mistakes of IT security such as storing passwords in plain text exacerbated the situation, it was really down to a legacy-infused mess in the company's backend systems. Critical security patches were not implemented, intrusion detection certificates had not been updated for 19 months and so on. The legacy systems had gotten so complex nobody in the company had an overview of who was responsible for which database. Additionally, fewer and fewer employees had been around long enough to really understand the antiquated systems and how to change them. One of the drivers behind Equifax's legacy proliferation was the aggressive growth strategy that resulted in the acquisition of no less than 18 companies since 2005 (US House of Representatives Committee on Oversight and Government Reform, 2018). Rampant acquisitions, a lack of staff versed in old coding languages and a slow reaction to critical security holes – Equifax is a paragon of what can go wrong when the grip of legacy gets too tight.

As the global financial crisis of the late 2000s shows, old IT systems can be even more devastating. Among the many causes of the cataclysmic collapse, one has been the prevalence of legacy systems in banking. Despite finance giants spending more money on IT than any other industry – $500 billion globally in 2009 (*The Economist*, 2009) – its infrastructure was incapable of timely performance of critical functions. The fragmented IT landscape made it exceedingly difficult to track a bank's overall risk exposure before and during the crisis. While new tech would have allowed aggregate risk to be shown in real time, decision makers were seeing fresh figures once a day. Those were useless for seeing the crisis coming, let alone containing it.

Why is legacy so prevalent and what exactly is it?

Nobody doubts the danger of legacy systems. But their growth is often an inescapable result of solid business decisions, or rather the aggregation thereof. Vivid merger and acquisition activities, the imperative of backward compatibility and local, fragmented decisions all lead to rank growth of legacy systems. What is often forgotten is that old tech sometimes has specific advantages. COBOL, a fossil among the programming languages, reaches incredible processing speed with its batch system. But above all, existing systems work reliably. Forty-six per cent of banks consider any kind of tinkering with the core system a significant operational risk (Bloomberg, 2015).

Is every old system legacy? And how old is 'old'? Heritage systems are so hard to define because they are pervasive in the entire economy. Letters of credit in trade finance are largely sent via fax. Ariane 5 Flight 501, a European Space Agency rocket, exploded right after take-off because old software turned out to be incompatible with new architecture (Hein, 2014). And according to a Congressional Report from 2016, the US Department of Defense uses eight-inch floppy disks to coordinate the nation's nuclear forces (United States Government Accountability Office, 2016). Legacy systems have existed for thousands of years in machinery, processes, employees, customers and mindsets.

There is no cut-off date when a system solidifies into legacy structure. Instead, many factors have to be considered: Are there enough programmers? Can it be scaled and plugged into more modern applications? Has the soft- or hardware reached its end of life?

Another crucial indicator is the speed with which complexity grows. Complexity in a company's systems is the main cost driver and agility inhibitor. Dependencies grow exponentially with each new software package, each new feature and each new workaround. Eventually every new unit costs more, not less. Economies-of-scale advantages are reversed.

Proliferating complexity also leads to what is known as legacy lock-in. It is a vicious spiral that makes you more dependent on your systems and your providers every time you think you are taking a step forward. Major inventions of the past such as ERP or relational databases were supposed to improve complexity, but actually made it worse (McComb, 2018). The banking world is touting agility, but if it is to be a corporate characteristic rather than just a way of working, legacy systems need to be reined in.

Business complexity is always linked to costs, not just linearly but exponentially. Most large projects are delayed, cost a multiple of what was budgeted and in the end many of them are abandoned altogether. But the real dangers are the hidden costs. Two out of three CFOs say they don't have the time for strategic tasks because they are overburdened by chores such as assembling data and solving inconsistencies (BCG, 2017). CMOs and other executives suffer from similar problems.

The opportunity costs in terms of money and new functionalities are even harder to estimate, while the consequences are no less dire. The danger of missing out on future markets or competitive advantages tops the threat list. Lagging product features and external interfaces inhibit competitiveness and profitability. McKinsey (2015) found that executives attach to new IT more potential to bring in new revenues than to fix expenses. The same executives, however, also admit companies don't act accordingly.

Technical and technological debt

Despite all the dangers and drawbacks, building legacy can be a good strategy. Doesn't make sense? Please focus on the word *can* for a moment. In 1992 Ward Cunningham coined the term *technical debt*, explaining how companies creating their first code accept its imperfections in return for a speedy market entry. Just like financial debt, it enables rapid growth in the beginning, but slows down the debtor later when interest accrues. If ignored, it leads to bankruptcy.

Indeed, in many cases flaws are never ironed out. Companies spend lavishly and accumulate more debt due to liquidity shortages, which in this case is programmers' time. Accumulating debt can be a highly successful business strategy. In fact, most blitzscaling start-ups were able to grow quickly enough only because they were willing to accept imperfections in return for a quick launch and sustained hypergrowth (Hoffman and Yeh, 2018). The crucial thing, however, is to make design choices that will keep future costs of change manageable and ensure that you can use the latest available tech.

Cunningham used technical debt in a very narrow sense, namely to describe old and imperfect code. I suggest applying it more broadly to indicate the drag suffered by legacy systems in general, whether it be old and defunct code or an entire system that has been replaced by new innovation, say when chip cards replaced mag-stripe cards. Hence, banks should work with the broader term *technological debt*. This will enable them to get a full overview of where modernization in the enterprise will be necessary, what level of investment will be needed in the near and mid-term future and what downsides it will face if systems are not overhauled. In short, the concept of technological debt is a great tool for taking inventory and planning for organizational readiness.

Other forms of inherited trouble

Even more: heritage systems are a problem transcending the lines of code. Thinking of legacy solely as an IT operations topic is outdated. First, legacy can manifest itself on multiple levels, including machinery and people. Banks, for example, can have legacy customers that insist on going to a branch, rather than using online banking. Heritage thinking can be found in executives who had their formative years in the analogue world and never understood banking's digital transition. Or heritage problems could prevail in your marketing strategy, say if you are overpricing the wrong products to fatten your margins.

Combatting legacy systems

So what is the best game plan to recognize legacy? Which legacy to overthrow, which to modernize and which to accept? And how to execute the transformation? The best way is to have a scorecard that pinpoints where organizational legacy exists and which of those pain points to tackle first. For each functional area – IT, finance, marketing, HR, strategy – banks should identify the most common heritage problems and propose ways to get rid of them.

Ridding yourself of legacy is so much more than just exchanging an old technical system with a new one. Organizational changes are just as important. The first thing to do is to change the way of working, for instance by utilizing methods such as agile software development or Devops. Those working methods originated in software development but are lately spreading to other corporate areas as well. They feed primarily on the idea of a quick market entry followed by iterative improvements based on direct customer feedback.

Another suggestion is the creation of a new role called the Chief Digital Officer (CDO). Like the CFO, the CDO is more strategic and business-oriented than the Chief Information Officer (CIO) and the Chief Technical Officer (CTO), and can hence put technological legacy topics high up the organization's hierarchy. Also, it is a position with profit-and-loss responsibility and is well placed to make very hard decisions, such as whether and when to overhaul core systems.

Somewhat connected to this is the suggestion to report legacy as a liability on the balance sheet. This would force companies to keep their systems in order because investors could check the technological health of a company just like they can check the financial one.

Finally, legacy should be fought on the level of staff – e.g. recruiting and promoting risk takers with a dynamic skillset – and on the level of customers. For example, customers that still cling to bank branches shouldn't be the group at the top of your mind when striving for client satisfaction. Also, customers with old contractual conditions or unprofitable products should be migrated to more favourable ones. For more details on legacy systems and tools to manage them see Pejic (2022a, b and c).

Platformization – invading Big Tech territory

Overhauling old technological systems goes hand in hand with changing the business model to leverage platform economics. With the rise of APIs, open banking and a modular IT infrastructure banks can decouple their rigid core systems from the adaptable customer-facing IT modules. Hence, they can easily connect to the buoyant digital ecosystem around them. Today banks provide services for fees and capital for interest payments. This will always remain an integral part of banking, and with all the harsh banking regulation in place it is unlikely that banks will become data brokers who earn money from selling advertisements. But without emulating Big Tech's platform approach, banks stand little chance of competing with them in the long run. First, because platform orchestrators have been scientifically proven to be the most profitable companies (Libert, Beck and Wind, 2016). But even more importantly because platforms are where customers are spending their time. This is where long-term relationships are formed.

Bankers have realized the potential that platforms hold for their revenues. Kind of. According to a survey among German banks, 71 per cent of executives intend to operate a platform by themselves (PwC, 2021). And 9 out of 10 want to integrate non-banking services. So while players like PayPal or Revolut are vying to become financial super-apps, banks seek to go one step further. They want to rebuild their relevance in their customers' everyday lives. Big Tech has focused its ambush on the customer interface and tried to relegate incumbents to the invisible backend.

Building their own platforms by leveraging new technology is the way for banks to claw back. If customers look for real estate or shop for clothes via a platform run by their bank it will inevitably boost revenues on financial core products. This approach is called embedded finance, meaning that services such as payments or loans are offered to customers while their attention is on another product and therefore price sensitivity and the willingness to engage in comparisons are low. For this to work, however, banks will also have to change the way they segment customers. Platforms need to be built on domains of a customer's life, say mobility or education, rather than on socio-demographic segments.

But the aforementioned study also suggests that 43 per cent of banks will invest only €500,000 into the build-up of their digital ecosystem, whereas a quarter are looking to spend just up to €100,000. With this amount you might hire one developer. Not even a particularly good one, just one developer. Making a platform succeed is extremely expensive. While large banks have sufficiently deep pockets, it is difficult to make such a far-reaching investment decision. You can burn through large piles of cash quickly without a guarantee of success. One strategy out of this quagmire has a long history in banking: consortia, joint ventures, and other collaborations. Whether Visa, Mastercard or SWIFT, banks have frequently joined forces with competitors to leverage network effects. If at least some big players commit to such an initiative, it could slash the risk and at the same time limit the investment size.

The super money engine

The decisive question becomes why would customers use platforms run by banks rather than the Big Tech professionals? The key is payments. When paying offers added value to the customer, it can be a powerful glue that holds together seemingly unrelated fields. Banks will naturally pivot to platforms that revolve around things of material value, say a shopping or real estate portal rather than a pure networking site like Facebook. This means that competency around the movement of money takes centre stage. It needs to be easy, acceptable, secure, linked to the users' current systems, and it should seamlessly integrate other financial products such as loans or investments.

Whether it is Big Tech or Big Banking that will get to rule this system depends on the outcome of the DeFi battle we discussed in Chapter 6. To win at the checkout it will no longer be sufficient to have brand recognition and a functioning way to settle transfers. With the rise of DeFi, companies vie to dominate multiple layers of money, whether it is the settlements and asset layer (i.e. the underlying protocol and the tokens moved), the gateway and tools layer (i.e. wallets that let you access tokens and blockchain applications) or on-chain applications themselves.

All of the layers are equally important, yet what will make or break platforms is the gateway level. Moving money is already a highly complex affair, but in future it will require an exponentially more complex engine that can handle traditional as well as decentralized finance. It is what I call the *super money engine*. Operating dominant platforms in a decentralized world will only be possible with a super money engine. And this must be more than just a wallet that can hold balances of dollars and bitcoins. It must be capable of managing – which at least means holding, buying, selling, staking and swapping – all types of fiat and cryptocurrencies, private stablecoins, digital central bank money, as well as NFTs. A super money engine must also be able to build and execute smart contracts, as well as to integrate DApps. In short, it must be the one-stop shop for all things that have to do with money and assets. The user should not have to go to another marketplace to sell their NFT and then to an exchange to convert the Ether they received to dollars in order to buy stocks or securities. It should all work seamlessly in the super money engine.

FIGURE 11.1 The super money engine

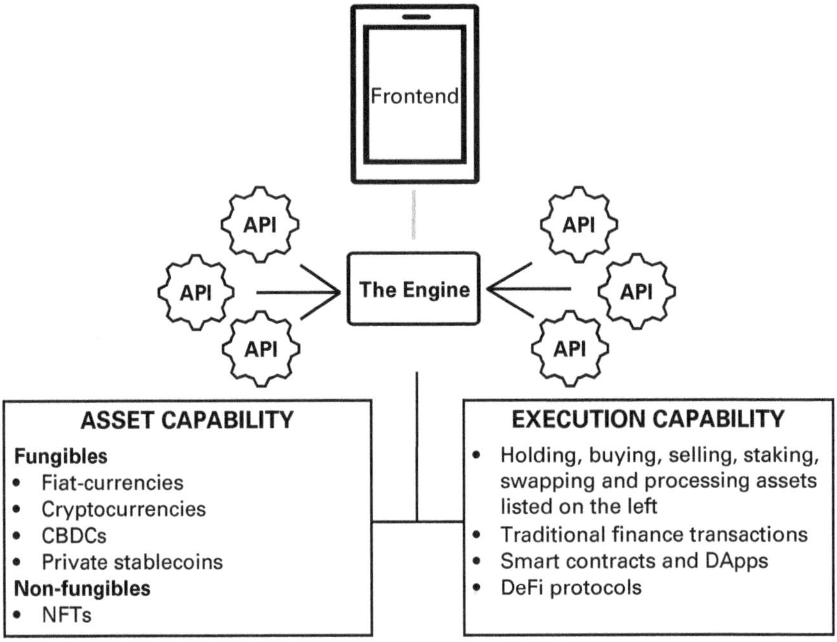

Today there are no simple white-label solutions that a bank or company could implement. Rather, having a super money engine will be a decisive competitive advantage. Whoever wants to realize it must build in-house blockchain expertise and applications compatible with powerful (i.e. smart contract and NFT-ready) and widely used protocols. Interoperability to both centralized and decentralized blockchain is vital if you want to reach full asset capability. Furthermore, the super money engine must not be a finite machine. New assets and new capabilities will be emerging continuously and the engine must be capable of incorporating them.

The possibilities of such an engine don't end there. The next logical step is that banks transcend their function as vaults for monetary value and also evolve into vaults for things such as personal data. Whether you safeguard digital security for bank account numbers, zip codes, health data or identities doesn't make a difference. If you have a trusted wallet, this is where you keep *all* things of value. This is your central hub for your entire digital life. In a world running on blockchain technology platform effects can turn out to be multiple times stronger than those of the internet age.

But it all hinges upon who can provide the best engine and who has the best integration of DeFi with traditional assets. As we will see in the next chapter, banks have already embarked on that journey. They are still at the beginning of what is possible, but it shows that an important realization has dawned and that tomorrow's finance arena will not be left without a fight.

Banks integrating DeFi

Coinbase going public in April 2021 was hailed by many as the first big step in integrating traditional finance with DeFi (Tepper, 2021). Indeed the move was unusual, because the company chose to go with a direct listing instead of an IPO. But Coinbase is a traditional, licensed company run by a clearly identifiable team. And Coinbase had an established business model: facilitating the trading of assets and taking a fee for it. It is far away from DAOs, non-custodial architectures and decentralized services. And it is far away from banking too. So, it didn't answer the question of whether centralized banks are compatible with decentralized services. DeFi is the LEGO of money; product modules can be combined with each other. But can they also be integrated with traditional banking services, or will DeFi continue to exist as an independent system?

Banks have been extremely hesitant to look into DeFi. Recently, however, the realization is dawning that they won't be able to ignore it in the long run. Yes, centrally run applications will remain the backbone of the economy, but DeFi is here to stay. It is not an alternative to classic banking, but an addition. And since banks vie to become potent platforms and aggregators of all financial services, they desperately need this addition.

Banks are taking notice

The first banks are already taking a serious look into advanced DeFi applications. ING performed an in-depth analysis of Aave (Meegan and Koens, 2021). Aave predominantly offers secured lending. It is a non-custodial liquidity protocol for earning interest on deposits and borrowing crypto-assets. Aave, like many other DeFi competitors, heavily relies on over-collateralization. You deposit $100 worth of crypto and can take a loan worth $75.

This is a fundamental difference from traditional banks, who are not simply taking funds from one customer and giving them to another. When banks issue credit it involves the creation of new money. The money loaned far exceeds the money deposited. This is known as leverage. In DeFi there is no such money creation. Not least this fundamental difference leads the authors to conclude there is a powerful complementarity between DeFi and banks, rather than competition (Meegan and Koens, 2021).

There is another pressing reason for banks to actively start getting hold of the DeFi space: the liability side. Due to its heavy use of stablecoins, DeFi could pump funding into banks' balance sheets. Stablecoins do not necessarily have to be pegged to fiat, but they can also hold certificates of deposits or commercial paper. If this happens and DeFi continues to grow at the rates it did in 2020 and 2021, a run on stablecoins could end in a funding shock for banks, say researchers from the BIS (Aramonte, Huang and Schrimpf, 2021).

One big bank has taken a step further than just looking at DeFi protocols and entered into cooperation with MakerDAO. Through its investment arm SG-Forge, Société Générale put real estate bonds onto the Ethereum blockchain. SG-Forge tokenizes those tokenized bonds and then locks them into MakerDAO's lending protocol. Using them as collateral, it borrows DAI worth $20 million against it (Carreras, 2022). DAI is MakerDAO's stablecoin, so SG-Forge will then swap those for fiat money. When the bonds mature, the banks will simply rewind the processes, meaning that it will use the fiat currency to buy DAI and unlock its on-chain bonds that have been serving as collateral. It is a prime example of how off-chain assets can be integrated into DeFi protocols.

But as much as banking will need DeFi, DeFi will also need traditional banking. DeFi can never reach the necessary liquidity by only handling crypto assets. It will have to tokenize assets from the physical world like houses, commercial property or commodities. This can only happen on a large scale by cooperating with banks. In the Société Générale example the MakerDAO protocol benefits not only from a boost to its traded volumes, but also by adding real-life assets to its reserves. This makes the protocol and the underlying DAI stablecoin more secure.

The bridge between a physical item and the digital token is legally tricky. Today, in many jurisdictions there needs to be a recognized (and centralized) agent such as a notary to verify that link. It is a role not foreseen in the original DeFi ecosystem.

Another issue is usability. The ease of use has improved massively in the DeFi space, but the products are far from understandable for mass-market customers. Comprehending them requires much time and effort which most people are unwilling to invest. The vast majority of people are struggling with basic financial concepts such as compound interest. Now imagine teaching them about staking and yield farming. It will require banks to 'translate' those new possibilities and ideally relegate blockchain and crypto speak to the backend.

This leads to a somewhat paradoxical situation. While in the past many a bank-fintech cooperation was born because fintechs enhanced the usability of financial products offered by banks, now this relationship gets reversed. DeFi challengers build the technical capabilities but to break into the mainstream it will require banks to present them to customers in an understandable way and to integrate them into the bank's product landscape. If the bank, for example, automatically deducts the capital gains tax on my crypto investments and also combines them with the gains and losses of my investment products, then this is not only a great added value, but it eases the entry of new users who otherwise wouldn't go through the trouble of managing all this by themselves. This is a major opportunity for banks and it is one they have to take since Big Tech is capable of offering the functionality and the user experience by itself. Whether the integration of DeFi offers succeeds will hinge on the fit to the other products offered by the bank. Integrating adequately requires a deep understanding of the potential and perils of the DeFi space.

First models of a deeper integration

Large banks have started with first investments into crypto-related firms. According to the BIS (Aramonte, Huang and Schrimpf, 2021) at the end of 2021 big financial players each held between $150 million and $380 million in crypto-equity. And research by BCG Platinion (2021) shows that 55 per cent of banks and insurances are assessing DeFi applications, while 23 per cent have already tested them. The study works with a broad definition of DeFi, but it demonstrates that crypto is gaining traction across financial companies.

Investments are the first step. Bridging the gap from on- to off-chain assets like Société Générale is the second. Yet banks' target must be to become a platform or a hub that connects all financial services. The perfectly suited place for that is the gateway layer. Ergo, banks must work towards developing potent wallets that can handle crypto assets, physical assets and all kinds of other financial services – the super money engine we discussed a couple of pages earlier. Those few banks and companies that succeed will stay the primary financial manager of their customers, get complete transaction data and can extract rents from providers that connect their apps to their platform.

Much of this is still theoretical, but some are venturing in that direction. An early example of what such a link between DeFi and traditional finance could look like is EQUIFI. It is a DeFi platform that is linked to a regulated and fully licensed bank called EQIBank. EQUIFI is a digital-first neobank and certainly built with global, crypto-affluent customers in mind, but its product portfolio shows what is possible. On the one hand EQUIFI offers classic banking services like a debit Mastercard, but on the other customers can securitize their loans with crypto-collateral. EQUIFI also offers a DeFi yield aggregator platform, which means that a protocol at the neobank automatically decides into which crypto assets customer deposits are invested.

EQUIFI also has its own governance token called EQX. It enables holders to vote on protocol changes, and everybody with more than 200,000 of them can even propose governance changes that the network must vote on. On top, the more tokens you own and stake, the more you earn.

An equally novel feature is a card NFT offered jointly with Polkacity. Polkacity is a blockchain-based gaming platform built on the Polkadot protocol, which allows you to transfer any type of asset across any type of blockchain (Polkadot, no date). We will look at NFTs in the next chapter; for now, let us simply define them as a digital original, something like a unique piece of digital art. In EQUIFI's case only 2,000 digital pieces (NFTs) of the card were minted. Purchasers of the card NFT get the proof of ownership for this digital original, but have other benefits too, which cleverly combine the on-chain as well as the off-chain world. Holders of the card NFT are eligible for a free bank account, a debit and credit card, and they get weekly crypto-rewards. As long as they don't sell the NFT, they earn rewards in the form of another type of token called POLC (Polkacity, 2021a).

On- and off-chain marketing is interwoven too. EQIBank will be placed as a virtual bank in Polkacity's upcoming 3D NFT game. You can imagine it like a traditional PlayStation or Nintendo game, only built on a blockchain. Instead of walking through the land of Super Mario or Grand Theft Auto, you walk through Polka City, a similar virtual space with one significant difference: it functions as its own economy in which you can spend and make money. Hence, a benefit of the partnership for EQUIFI and EQIBank is that they get featured in this economy prominently. Their brands and services will be advertised on in-game billboards. And holders of the card NFT will be able to unlock some game features and discounts (Polkacity, 2021b).

EQIBank is not a large retail bank and there are no signs it will challenge the likes of Bank of America or Barclay's. The reason it pays to look at such pioneers is that they show how a technology's potential can be translated to new services, new channels and new business models. They can also be great experiments for customer and regulatory acceptance. So, if other banks want to emulate EQIBank's DeFi-integration they could offer loans backed by crypto-collateral and DeFi yield aggregators, as well incentivize customers with NFTs that are not just marketing gags but have a real functionality such as voting on protocol changes and receiving weekly rewards.

So, what does all of this have to do with Big Tech? Why would Google or Facebook care if banks fight for the attention of nerdy gamers at some fringe frontline? Quite simple: because the fringes of today's frontier are the epicentre of tomorrow's.

KEY TAKEAWAYS

- Banks are using blockchain technology to become more efficient and ringfence their core business, but they will also have to rid themselves of legacy systems.
- Furthermore, banks will have to venture into tech territory, meaning that they will need to emulate their business models. Studies show that many bankers are now pondering platform approaches. Becoming go-to providers of blockchain-generated trust could put them at the heart of

digital ecosystems and thus on traditional Big Tech terrain. For platformization to work it will also require banks to embrace DeFi.

- Combating legacy, building centralized blockchains and integrating decentralized ones are the prerequisites to compete for the future of finance. Those companies that don't just want to compete but triumph will have to build what I have dubbed the super money engine. This is a hub that can handle all types of on- and off-chain assets, execute smart contracts and run complex decentralized apps. It merges a powerful asset capability with powerful execution capability. The super money engine will be the heart of every future platform as the world moves increasingly, but not exclusively, on-chain and thus into a multi-asset paradigm.

References

Aramonte, S, Huang, W and Schrimpf, A (2021) DeFi risks and the decentralisation illusion, *BIS Quarterly Review*, December, www.bis.org/publ/qtrpdf/r_qt2112b.pdf (archived at https://perma.cc/E6LK-J25E)

BCG (2017) The art of performance management, CFO Excellence Series, 30 April, www.bcg.com/publications/2017/finance-function-excellence-corporate-development-art-performance-management (archived at https://perma.cc/H4RX-T5ZW)

BCG Platinion (2021) quoted in Harrison, P J: Why traditional banks are embracing DeFi to catch up to challenger banks, *The Fintech Times*, 16 April, https://thefintechtimes.com/why-traditional-banks-are-embracing-defi-to-catch-challenger-banks/ (archived at https://perma.cc/9LUW-YZ69)

Bloomberg (2015) Banks too slow to modernize core systems, Bloomberg, 17 November, www.bloomberg.com/professional/blog/banks-too-slow-to-modernize-core-systems/ (archived at https://perma.cc/ZNL4-JUTH)

Carreras, T (2022) MakerDAO adds Société Générale to its vaults, Crypto Briefing, 14 July, https://cryptobriefing.com/makerdao-adds-societe-generale-to-its-user-list/ (archived at https://perma.cc/9BS4-RVGQ)

Cunningham, W (1992) The WyCash Portfolio Management System, *OOPSLA '92 Experience Report*, 26 March, http://c2.com/doc/oopsla92.html (archived at https://perma.cc/4G7L-5NBF)

Hein, A (2014) How to assess heritage systems in the early phases? *SECESA 2014,* 8–10 October, www.academia.edu/8441540/How_to_Assess_Heritage_Systems_in_the_Early_Phases (archived at https://perma.cc/8537-KLSZ)

Hoffman, R and Yeh, C (2018) *Blitzscaling: The lightening-fast path to building massively valuable companies*, Currency, New York

Libert, B, Beck, M and Wind, J (2016) Network revolution: Creating value through platforms, people, and technology, Knowledge at Wharton, 14 April, http://knowledge.wharton.upenn.edu/article/the-network-revolution-creating-value-through-platforms-people-and-digital-technology/ (archived at https://perma.cc/T6Y3-9L9C)

McComb, D (2018) *Software Wasteland: How the application-centric mindset is hobbling our enterprises, technics publications*, Basking Ridge, NJ

McKinsey (2015) Cracking the digital code, 1 September, www.mckinsey.com/business-functions/mckinsey-digital/our-insights/cracking-the-digital-code (archived at https://perma.cc/VT3W-R2A4)

Meegan, X and Koens, T (2021) Lessons learned from decentralised finance (DeFi), *ING Whitepaper*, www.ingwb.com/binaries/content/assets/insights/themes/distributed-ledger-technology/defi_white_paper_v2.0.pdf (archived at https://perma.cc/CWF8-RSZ3)

Pejic, I (2019) *Blockchain Babel: The crypto-craze and the challenge to business*, Kogan Page, London, New York, New Delhi

Pejic, I (2022a) Technological progress and the legacy trap, The New Frontier, 7 June, https://igorpejic.substack.com/p/technological-progress-and-the-legacy (archived at https://perma.cc/2KTK-S2CV)

Pejic, I (2022b) The three shades of legacy, The New Frontier, 5 July, https://igorpejic.substack.com/p/the-three-shades-of-legacy (archived at https://perma.cc/A93K-A9S4)

Pejic, I (2022c) 5 ways to cut the Gordian knot of technological debt, The New Frontier, 2 August, https://igorpejic.substack.com/p/5-ways-to-cut-the-gordian-knot-of (archived at https://perma.cc/E2A8-DL3H)

Polkadot (no date) A scalable, interoperable & secure network protocol for the next web, https://polkadot.network/technology/ (archived at https://perma.cc/WXE2-X72K)

Polkacity (2021a) EQIFI Bank NFT, Medium, 16 December, https://polkacity.medium.com/eqifi-bank-nft-5dbbbab1934a (archived at https://perma.cc/RUZ4-MP5T)

Polkacity (2021b) Polacity EQIFI partnership, Medium, 21 October, https://polkacity.medium.com/polkacity-eqifi-partnership-90dbb8ca67ed (archived at https://perma.cc/QUR9-WQ9W)

PwC (2021) Die neue Säule des Geschäftsmodells: Relevanz digitaler Ökosysteme für deutsche Banken – Befragung deutscher Bankentscheider, PwC Study, February, www.pwc.de/de/finanzdienstleistungen/studie-relevanz-digitaler-okosysteme.pdf (archived at https://perma.cc/QL25-S9TV)

PwC Luxembourg (2022) What are the hidden costs of legacy systems? Techsense, 2 May, https://techsense.lu/news/hidden-costs-legacy-systems-pwc (archived at https://perma.cc/6HSU-MRYV)

Rudegeair, P, Benoit, D and Ackerman, A (2021) Google is scrapping its plan to offer bank accounts to users, *Wall Street Journal*, 1 October, www.wsj.com/articles/google-is-scrapping-its-plan-to-offer-bank-accounts-to-users-11633104001 (archived at https://perma.cc/6YHB-WVZV)

Shevlin, R (2021) Google kills the Google Plex: It could have been a digital checking account killer app, *Forbes*, 1 October, www.forbes.com/sites/ronshevlin/2021/10/01/google-kills-the-google-plex-it-could-have-been-a-digital-checking-account-killer-app/?sh=211ffa6320d5 (archived at https://perma.cc/5QH5-LMXY)

Skinner, C (2018) *Digital Human: The fourth revolution of humanity includes everyone*, Wiley, Cornwall, UK

Tepper, T (2021) Coinbase IPO: Here's what you need to know, *Forbes,* 14 April, www.forbes.com/advisor/investing/cryptocurrency/coinbase-ipo-direct-listing/ (archived at https://perma.cc/GSY7-TBMV)

The Economist (2009) Silo but deadly: Messy IT systems are a neglected aspect of the financial crisis, 3 December, www.economist.com/finance-and-economics/2009/12/03/silo-but-deadly (archived at https://perma.cc/9DY5-TL7P)

United States Government Accountability Office (2016) Testimony Before the Committee on Oversight and Government Reform, House of Representatives, 26 May, www.gao.gov/assets/gao-16-696t.pdf (archived at https://perma.cc/29UU-C222)

US House of Representatives Committee on Oversight and Government Reform, (2018) The Equifax Data Breach, *Majority Staff Report 115th Congress*, December, https://republicans-oversight.house.gov/wp-content/uploads/2018/12/Equifax-Report.pdf (archived at https://perma.cc/BR92-VU3V)

Zhu, J (2014) *China Cloud Rising: China's journey towards technology supremacy*, Springer, Heidelberg/New York/London

12

Setting out for the next frontier: the metaverse and Web3

NFT-mania

In early 2021 a very unlikely actor created a stir in the blockchain world: the US auction house Christie's. Digital artist Beeple had just sold a collection entitled 'Everydays: The first 5,000 days' for a staggering $69 million. You might wonder why anybody would pay such a price for a digital picture that you cannot nail onto your wall; in fact visitors to the auction house's website (Christie's, 2021) can actually see and copy the picture at the click of a button. This question goes to the essence of why this moment was so crucial for the crypto-world. Beeple's digital picture was a unique copy of his work recorded on the Ethereum blockchain. While the picture indeed can be copied, only one person is registered as the owner of this particular token that represents Beeple's picture.

The vast majority of early blockchain applications were built around keeping track of who owns monetary value. Whether it was bitcoins or stablecoins, they all had a specific unit of measurement. Either they were directly linked to fiat currencies or they imitated their properties. As more people began racking their brains about what could be done with the new tech, all kinds of things moved onto the blockchain. Just think of the Basic Attention Token (BAT) we discussed earlier in the book and how it squeezed human attention into a token before eventually turning it into a neatly portioned asset on the blockchain.

A new type of token that enables non-fungible ownership

But Beeple's picture was yet another completely different type of asset. It is called an NFT, or non-fungible token. If something is fungible, it means that it can easily be swapped for something of the same kind. Dollars and pounds are fungible, as are bitcoins and ounces of gold. Each bitcoin is worth as much as any other bitcoin. Every dollar note buys the same value in a store. And so on. This is not the case for Beeple's picture. I cannot simply trade his collection for an NFT of the highly popular Bored Ape Yacht Club, just like I cannot simply swap the Mona Lisa for The Scream.

NFTs are immutable entries in a blockchain ledger used to track ownership, not of money, but of a digital artefact. These unique digital assets can be anything from pictures and concert tickets to virtual items in a computer game. Having proof of ownership of the token means you own a particular digital copy. Think of it as owning a rare postage stamp. You can trade it, sell it, negotiate for it, but you don't own the rights to copy it and make money from the design on it. And though commonly NFTs don't come with commercial rights, they could also be designed to represent exactly those.

Just like cryptocurrencies, NFTs are based on blockchain technology to solve the double-spend problem, which means they are both digital asset classes that cannot be copied. The crucial difference is that with NFTs there is no like-for-like swapping.

NFT popularity exploded. Beeple was just the peak of the iceberg. Some exemplars of pixelated collectibles called CryptoPunks were sold for eight-figure sums. Companies like Visa, museums like the Albertina and soccer clubs like Juventus Turin were quick to mint their own NFTs. The media brimmed with enthusiasm and those long enough in the crypto-game had deja-vu, taking them back to a time when ICOs started to muscle their way onto the crypto-stage. The value of art NFTs sold in September 2021 soared to $844 million from a meagre $38 million just two months earlier. Yet it plummeted as quickly as it had climbed. In March 2022 investments into art NFTs were back to $37 million a month (Statista, 2022). There was no doubt the hype was over. Most NFTs weren't worth the hard drive space they are stored on. And certainly not the carbon emitted while minting and transferring them.

In search of a utility value for digital originals

Jack Dorsey, Twitter's boss, minted an NFT representing his first tweet and sold it for $2.9 million. When Sina Estavi, the man who had bought it, was asked why he invested so much, he compared it to the Mona Lisa. It was a unique historic artefact that would multiply in value, he was convinced. After a year Estavi decided to test his hypothesis and tried to auction away the NFT for an asking price of $48 million. The highest offer he received: 2 ETH, which at that time was the equivalent to $6,800 (Reuters, 2022). Unlike with blue-chip cryptocurrencies there was no inherent value in those digital originals. Art NFTs turned out to be a purely speculative asset class.

But why would we be discussing an innovation at such length, if it is just a means of monetizing empty investor expectations? Moreover, this book is about finance, so why write about art and collectibles? Because what started as a way for artists to sell digital pictures will be the building blocks of a digital world in which NFTs fulfil a utility function. Emma Todd (2022) pointedly calls the first tweet NFT the 'emperor has no clothes moment'. That does not invalidate all NFTs, however. While some NFTs make no real utility sense and their value is just artificially inflated, other contexts benefit largely from having a digital original (Todd, 2022).

Utility NFTs hold enormous promise. They could, for instance, be used to trade and manage exploitation rights. Just like the picture NFT can be a unique asset, so can intellectual property. Copyrights, drilling rights and all kinds of other non-fungible assets that are recorded in a company's balance sheets could be easily deployed or traded if put onto a blockchain. Utility NFTs can be used in internet domain names that are resistant to censorship, in computer gaming artefacts that power up your character, or in incorruptible land registries. User imagination is the only limit.

But the most game-changing NFT impact will be somewhere else: a completely new virtual world that transcends everything we have seen with regard to online technology. Enter the metaverse. And NFTs are the bricks from which this land is built.

Fake real estate or the next generation of social media?

At the end of 2021 a real estate purchase made headlines. A pseudonymous investor had paid $450,000 for a plot of land next to the mansion of the rapper Snoop Dogg. The catch: the property was not located in California, but in a metaverse game called The Sandbox. Many home buyers pay similar sums for a brick-and-mortar house including the land on which it stands. In this case the buyer received an NFT whose sole purpose is to record the ownership of a pixelated piece of virtual land on a blockchain.

The purchase was no isolated incident. The list of high-profile investors includes companies like Adidas, Samsung and PwC Hong Kong, and celebrities like Paris Hilton and Justin Bieber. Barbados became the first country to open an embassy in Decentraland, another leading metaverse. Big venture capitalists are storming the new market and even banks started pouring money into it. JP Morgan Chase purchased a plot of land in a prestigious location in Decentraland to open its Onyx Lounge. This is a nod to the bank's suite of blockchain products of the same name. Typical for early metaverse appearances, JP Morgan is using its presence for purely promotional and educational purposes. People can listen to a message from Jamie Dimon, the bank's CEO, examine the Onyx suite of products and attend some lectures on cryptocurrencies. While most of the investment goes to four metaverses – The Sandbox, Decentraland, Cryptovoxels and Somnium – there are hundreds of different universes that today exist independent of each other (Birch, 2022).

But what is the metaverse anyway? Isn't it just a hyped online computer game? No. The metaverse is a fully immersive, 3D version of the internet. But it is so much more than just an engaging place to play video games and socialize with other people's avatars. The metaverse is a fully fledged economy in which possessions are built, traded and used to generate income. For example, you can own an NFT entitling you to run a factory or a theme park in the metaverse and charge people to use or visit it. This business model would generate value in the form of crypto-tokens that you can exchange for fiat currency.

If you are now thinking that this sounds like something out of a science-fiction movie, you are wrong. It actually originated from a sci-fi novel called *Snow Crash* (Stephenson, 1992). And science fiction is pretty much where the idea had remained for almost 30 years until in October 2021 Mark Zuckerberg announced that from now on his company would put its entire weight behind the metaverse idea. He would create a holding company for his social media platforms Facebook, Instagram and WhatsApp. The name of the company: Meta. Within five years the goal for Meta was to have at least 10,000 people working in metaverse-related positions within the EU alone (Clegg and Olivan, 2021). To achieve that, Meta quickly started poaching engineers from Microsoft (Tilley, 2022) and Apple (Gurman, 2021).

Facebook finds new land – meet the metaverse

Facebook had just come out of a public relations nightmare. Its mega-project Diem was dying after being torn apart by regulators around the world in live-streamed Congressional hearings. The whistle-blower Frances Haugen had released tens of thousands of harmful documents about the platform's role in driving polarization and extremism, as well as its prioritization of profits over security (Waterson and Milmo, 2021). So, when Zuckerberg announced the rebranding, most pundits saw in it an attempt to divert public attention from the devastating news cycle.

Yet the metaverse idea proved remarkably persistent. Rather than fizzling out, it has whipped up the enthusiasm of entrepreneurs, journalists and even some bankers. A Citibank study (Citi, 2022) estimated the metaverse's broadly addressable market at 5 billion users, which translates to a monetary value of \$8–13 trillion by 2030. Van Rijmenam (2022) puts the estimate even higher at \$15–20 trillion. The underlying thinking: today's top 10 internet companies alone are worth north of that and the metaverse will be bigger than the internet. The independent digital asset strategist Armando Aguilar (2022) notes that neither of these projections takes into account the derivatives of the creator economy and that the real added value will be exponentially higher. If metaverse believers turn out to be even remotely right, then the impact NFTs will have on the metaverse economy will eclipse the value they have for art and all other areas.

Blockchain and DeFi as the big metaverse enablers

With such sky-high promises it is not surprising that the metaverse is controversial. The *New York Post* (Hope, 2022) ran a title calling it 'fake real estate' while Mark Zuckerberg (2021) sees in it the next evolutionary step of the web. In his view, the revolutionary thing is that you are not looking at a reality projected on a screen, but you are part of this reality. And in this reality, you can meet people from anywhere around the world. It is akin to the next generation of social media.

But what has made the metaverse idea spread so quickly from the pages of a novel to the agendas of many corporate boards? It can't be the renaming of Facebook to Meta alone. The short answer is that a series of rapid technological breakthroughs occurred in parallel, all of them in different domains but all crucial to the metaverse. Extended reality and immersive interfaces enable us to experience digital life, not just look at a screen to kill time. Donning smart glasses is not the same as typing on your computer keyboard. The rise of 5G networks makes it possible to seamlessly stream this new virtual world without the hourglass icon interrupting your every action. Thanks to powerful cloud datacentres the new universe can be entered by everybody at the same time and is not limited to a couple of hundred players like today's highly popular online games. And AI helps to populate the world with automatized characters.

Yet all of these advances would have just made gaming more performant and engaging had it not been for a host of blockchain breakthroughs to turn it into a functioning economy. NFTs are the building blocks. They allow people to own things in the metaverse, whether it is virtual plots of land, jeans and T-shirts for avatars, digital paintings or commercial rights within a metaverse. DAOs allow large-scale automatic management of those assets. Cryptocurrencies and stablecoins underpin the new universe with a monetary system that is compatible with the physical world but shuns middlemen and sometimes centralized institutions altogether. Finally, the rise of DeFi is enriching this virtual financial system with elaborate financial products. And as we have seen in the previous chapter the link between on-chain and off-chain finance will mean that all sorts of assets will be interwoven. Thus, whoever eventually turns out running money in the metaverse will also shape the future of money outside of it.

Being successful in the metaverse

Tokens.com is a publicly traded metaverse incubator which through its subsidiary Metaverse Group invests millions in digital land. It purchases plots in multiple metaverses, develops them and rents them out to tenants. When I asked their CEO Andrew Kiguel what made him bet big on the metaverse, he boiled it down to two words: 'digital scarcity'. Coming from the bitcoin mining industry, Kiguel immediately drew the parallel: 'A finite amount of something meets an increasing demand. Just like the number of bitcoins is capped at 21 million, the number of parcels in Decentraland cannot exceed 45,000 (Kiguel, 2022).

The importance of a new monetary system as the underpinning of the metaverse cannot be overestimated. In an interview Mark Zuckerberg made it unmistakably clear that the metaverse is in some way a continuation of the Libra/Diem project, proclaiming that Facebook has been the most advanced of the Big Techs when it comes to DAOs and smart contracts (Heath, 2021). Had it been successful, Diem would have handed an unparalleled advantage to the social media giant. Dominating the settlement and asset layers means having an edge even over companies that dominate metaverse hard- and software. Yet with Diem failed, the gates are open to competition.

Targeting the settlement and asset layer will prove too ambitious for most companies, and selling interface equipment to enter it is only an option for a narrow group of companies. Yet there is still plenty of opportunity to benefit from the metaverse. The first is through investments in virtual land and simply showing presence there, perhaps even offering basic services. Cleverly utilizing metaverse applications might not only provide companies with an additional revenue potential, but let them occupy high ground for later when the metaverse user base grows.

There is a tsunami of metaverse-native enterprises entering the arena. Their core products are in the founding protocols, virtual investments or metaverse applications. But those are complimentary. More worrying for Meta should be the moves of its Big Tech rivals.

Other Big Tech players in the meta-economy

With the new frontier Meta is trying to bounce back onto the blockchain stage after it had to bury Diem. But another tech titan will benefit just as much from the metaverse. You might remember from Chapter 6 that Microsoft had been one of the blockchain cloud leaders until it announced it would stop its Azure blockchain service. In a metaverse world it has all the cards to roar back. It is a heavyweight in gaming, owning the Xbox gaming console. Just as important as its stronghold on hard- and software are Microsoft's advances with interfaces. Its HoloLens virtual reality glasses are predestined as a gate to the metaverse. Add to this Microsoft's cloud heft, a highly developed B2B business, and deep blockchain knowledge and the metaverse emerges as the place where it could bundle its core competencies. Microsoft's investments tell a similar story. In 2022 it invested heavily in the Ethereum-expert ConsenSys and purchased the game-maker Activision. Whereas Microsoft used to be a leader in the B2B blockchain realm, the metaverse will let it tackle B2C customers as well.

Alphabet too is eyeing the new space. Google Cloud struck a deal with the Canadian blockchain studio Dapper Labs to move the NFT development to Google data centres. Dapper Labs is a specialist for NFTs and boasts high-visibility projects such as CryptoKitties and NBA Top Shots, as well as other metaverse-ready games and apps. Also, it runs the fourth-largest NFT marketplace by sales volume and its Flow blockchain is an alternative to the seemingly omnipresent Ethereum and its ERC-721 token standard for NFTs (Del Castillo and Bambysheva, 2021). Google Cloud will be a network operator that provides the necessary infrastructure for Flow. Its move marks a clear challenge to Amazon Web Services, whose blockchain-friendly cloud tools have given it an edge with blockchain developers.

Google Cloud doubled down on its metaverse efforts a couple of months after the Dapper Labs deal, announcing it would build a Web3 team. The product and engineering group will be led by James Tromans, a former executive at Citigroup. This is yet another tell-tale sign that success in the metaverse is inextricably linked with the future of money. Alphabet seems to have picked up the original open nature of the metaverse. According to the head of Google's Cloud unit, its tools work in other environments too, say on Amazon's cloud (Novet, 2022).

Amazon has been bickering with Meta over the metaverse idea, proclaiming that it prefers to focus on the real world instead of a fantasy (Clark, 2022). At the same time it has released a metaverse-like game titled AWS Cloud Quest and it remains a central infrastructure backbone of most of today's blockchain applications, in particular those running on Ethereum. On top, AWS has started hiring technical product managers for the metaverse (Choudhary, 2022).

Amazon is still quiet about its ambitions though. When a trove of tech companies including Meta, Google and Microsoft formed the Metaverse Standards Forum, a body that shall ensure a joint standard and hence interoperable metaverse applications, neither Amazon nor its subsidiary AWS participated (Paul, 2022). Close observers of the company's communication strategy will be reminded of the time when AWS introduced the blockchain-as-a-service model and became a leader overnight, after first denouncing the blockchain idea (see Chapter 6).

More telling is the absence of Apple from the Metaverse Standards Forum. As I argued in Chapter 8, the colossus from Cupertino has an ethos fundamentally at odds with the open and interoperable blockchain idea. This is why it struggles with DeFi and this is why it will struggle with the metaverse. Apple prefers closed ecosystems over which it has absolute control. Asked at an all-hands meeting about Apple and its role in the metaverse, Mark Zuckerberg (quoted in Heath, 2022) made no secret about seeing the hardware giant as a competitor, but added that it has a different worldview. He sees a struggle between open and closed ecosystems and adds that the approach that has worked for the iPhone in the past might not work in the metaverse. However, Zuckerberg seems to believe that Apple too is about to compete in the new arena. If this is really so, it will be via its VR or AR headsets and possibly a connected app store. The levels closer to money in the metaverse – say protocols and applications – are likely to be run by its peers.

China's tech juggernauts and the metaverse

For Chinese tech giants the metaverse is all but an easily accessible frontier given the strict laws on crypto-assets. NFTs are considered highly speculative and are therefore prohibited. Yet Ant Financial and Tencent are reportedly finding creative ways to circumvent the ban. They are dropping the word 'token' in the Chinese translation of 'non-fungible tokens' and they are shunning the Ethereum network. Instead, the tech giants are minting their version of NFTs on their own hybrid, semi-centralized blockchains. They are very cautious not to overstep the line. Alibaba banned its NFT re-sales upon realizing that one NFT fetched a price 1,000 times its original value. The goal is to keep the projects low-profile (Yang, 2021).

That Tencent and Alibaba are finding ways to work on the metaverse is not surprising. After all, they both have deep blockchain expertise and Tencent is a gaming goliath. What is more surprising is the breadth of metaverse activity of Chinese companies. In total they have filed more than 16,000 trademark applications relating to the metaverse (Sundararajan, 2022). How does this square with a regulation designed to counter decentralized technologies? The answer is that there are two fundamentally distinct ways in which the metaverse can be built.

The difference between Web2, Web3 and the metaverse

In Ernest Cline's novel *Ready Player One* (2011) inhabitants of a dystopian world in the year 2045 are retreating into a kind of metaverse called OASIS. Just like Meta's vision, it is a place where people socialize, work, go to school and do all other things that could be done in the real world. Its native currency is the most stable in the world. So far, so good. But OASIS is run by the company of its creator and the novel revolves around gaining control over the deceased founder's legacy. This means that one person or company can effectively decide how the metaverse is run, who can participate in it, who earns money through ads and basically all other rules of this world.

This is not the kind of metaverse that Andrew Kiguel (2022) envisions or that he has invested in. 'Metaverses like Minecraft and Roblox are the most successful ones today, but in the end Roblox is a digital prison. I can buy the in-game currency Robux with fiat but then I am trapped. I can't use those coins outside. I can't trade them. I don't own them.' Worlds like The Sandbox and Decentraland, on the other hand, have fully fledged cryptocurrencies called SAND and MANA. They can be bought, sold and traded outside their universe just as well as NFTs – say a pair of sneakers for my avatar or my entire identity.

Web3 is about infrastructure and the underlying economics

Both OASIS and Decentraland are metaverses, but they each have a fundamentally different worldview at their core. To understand this dichotomy and the terminological confusion it has caused, we have to look at the history of the internet. In the Web1 generation you owned your data, your servers, your emails and so on. Then suddenly there were companies that made it easy to sell stuff – Amazon – companies that made it easy to build websites – WordPress – companies that made it easy to host stuff – cloud providers – you get the point. This became known as Web2. The big question is whether the metaverse will go down the road of centralization and thereby let Big Tech run our lives even tighter, or whether business will use the blank canvas of Web3 to create a decentralized web again (Van Rijmenam, 2022).

Web3 (short for Web 3.0) was a term coined by the co-founder of Ethereum, Gavin Wood, back in 2014. It denotes the third generation of the internet and a return to its decentralized and more democratic roots. In his view, it means reversing the concentration trend in the hands of Big Tech thanks to the technical possibilities of trustless protocols enabled by the blockchain. This does not mean that the likes of Meta or Microsoft are doomed, but that monopolies are preempted by having multiple, interoperable systems (Kharpal, 2022).

Web3 as a concept is at least as important as the metaverse and probably even more so. The term is often confused with the metaverse, but the distinction is crucial. 'Web3 is infrastructure. The metaverse is built on top of an infrastructure, which can be Web3, but it can also be Web2. If it is built on Web2 then we have the same scenario as now: walled gardens and no interoperability. If the basis is Web3 you have ownership of assets, identity, and data' (Van Rijmenam, 2022).

In other words, the metaverse is an immersive internet that is replicating and extending our lives in an extremely accessible and seamless way. Web3 is about the underlying technology and economics. It revolves around self-sovereignty of identities and assets. I can create, hold and take my identities and belongings to different metaverses and to the real world. No centralized authority that runs one of these worlds is able to take my possessions or delete my avatar. It is decentralized and this is why the blockchain is the foundation of Web3.

Table 12.1 summarizes the core distinctions between a metaverse based on Web2 and one based on Web3. Neither of them exists in its purest form, especially not Web3. The race to rule the metaverse will be decided on a time horizon of decades. Van Rijmenam (2022) eventually sees companies with a Web3 mindset coming out on top. That does not necessarily mean they will be DAOs. Some of those new companies will be start-ups with a conventional corporate setup. Though DAOs will play a vital role in the metaverse, platforms cannot start as DAOs. Some start-ups might turn into DAOs along the way, while others might aspire to become the next generation of Big Tech.

For banks and financial services companies, on the other hand, the conclusion is pretty clear: whoever wants to run finance in the future must be able to handle assets, payments and financial products *native to both world views*. Integration in a super money engine (see Chapter 11) is the winning formula.

TABLE 12.1 Metaverse infrastructure: Web2 vs Web3

	WEB2	WEB3
PLATFORM CHARACTERISTICS		
Governance and ownership	• Centrally owned and governed • Dominated by Big Tech	• Owned and governed by active participants of the blockchain network • DAOs
Data storage	Centralized servers	Decentralized nodes
Access via	PC, console, VR/AR hardware, mobile/app	Generally equal to Web2, but particular focus on immersive tech (e.g. AR/VR)
USER CHARACTERISTICS		
Identity	In-platform avatars at the mercy of platform's owner	• Self-sovereign and interoperable identities • Identities are private-key-based and pseudonymous
Roles	Passive consumers	Consumers, value extractors, sometimes code contributors
FINANCIAL CHARACTERISTICS		
Asset ownership	• Locked within platform • Little value outside	• Transferable • Immutable • Can be utilized to generate new value • Can become part of financial services (e.g. loan collateral)
Payments	Traditional (e.g. credit cards)	Cryptocurrencies, stablecoins
Business model	• Fees and purchases from users and developers flow to platforms • Ad revenue	Value creation through asset sale, trading, utilization
EXAMPLES	Second Life, Roblox, Fornite, World of Warcraft	Decentraland, The Sandbox, Somnium Space, Cryptovoxels

Adapted from JP Morgan Chase, 2022

Governance in Web3 – a utopia or dystopia?

Announcing the rebranding to Meta, Mark Zuckerberg (2021) has stressed that the metaverse needs to be safe and private from day one. Van Rijmenam (2022), a metaverse expert and entrepreneur, is sceptical on whether Meta will deliver on these promises: 'Zuckerberg says all the right things. We need privacy, security, interoperability, but I don't trust Facebook. Gen Z and Gen Alpha don't trust Facebook. I think it will not succeed.' He admits that Meta early on recognized that the metaverse will be a big topic, but they take the wrong approach. They see the metaverse as another tool for value extraction, rather than value creation. Eventually, it will leave them uncompetitive (Van Rijmenam, 2022).

Opinions are divided over whether Meta can succeed. Vitalik Buterin (2022) tweeted that anything will misfire that is created now, as we still don't know what people want. Aguilar (2022) points to Meta's mishandling of data in the past and its declining community engagement. He suggests it would be best to deploy the capital through ventures. Others like Kiguel (2022) say you should never count Meta out. Many in the crypto-community dislike it but it will produce a competitive metaverse. 'Meta has deep pockets. It can hire the best people in the world. Moreover, Zuckerberg is astute and has subscribed to a Web3 vision of its metaverse.'

But even if Web3 companies end up on top, will it lead to the democratic utopia its proponents suggest? Not if you believe Twitter founder Jack Dorsey (2021). He made it clear that Web3 might not be owned directly by companies, but in the end it is venture capitalists running the show and hence it is still centralized.

This is a tweet that triggered a principal debate on Web3 amongst the who's who of the digital age. Elon Musk sided with Dorsey; Marc Andreessen did not. Andreessen's VC company owns a stake in the Web3 DeFi protocols Compound and Uniswap. In these two protocols the top 1 per cent of token holders own 95 per cent of all governance tokens, and according to Pitchbook data made available to the *New York Times*, venture capitalists and exchanges such as Coinbase or FTX were indeed the largest investors in Web3 (Livni, 2022).

The problem with the Web3 utopia is similar to the problem we discussed in Chapter 7 about the governance of cryptocurrencies. Regardless of whether the network is sustained by Proof-of-Work, Proof-of-Stake or any other consensus mechanism, some form of investment or buy-in into the chain will be necessary to participate in its governance. The same applies to DAOs. Ergo, even in a fully decentralized metaverse Big Banking and Big Tech will have good cards to call the shots thanks to their massive capital reserves.

Centralization is not only inevitable on the level of investment and governance, but also driven by users. In the words of Kiguel (2022), 'Everything eventually becomes centralized. We have even seen it with bitcoin and Ethereum.' Most people invest in cryptos via an ETF or other proxies. When they buy them directly, they do so via centralized exchanges like Kraken and Coinbase. And after the purchase many keep holding the keys in custodial wallets. 'Centralization makes things easily accessible and enables large-scale adoption. Moreover, people trust centrally run entities. This is why they go to the likes of Wells Fargo' (Kiguel, 2022).

It is still a long way towards decentralization. According to Van Rijmenam (2022) a hybrid version of the metaverse will rule the next two decades. In this transition Web3 infrastructure will be used for control and ownership of assets and identities. Yet all of this data will be streamed via centralized Web2 technologies. Even Web2 technology will struggle with the performance requirements, though it is multiple times more performant than Web3 infrastructure.

Whoever controls the foundational protocols of the metaverse, whether it is Web2 or Web3, will write the rules of the financial system. Which DeFi services are offered? Who can offer them? Are there rules and regulations within this world to follow? Equally important, these actors will also have a say in which underlying settlement asset(s) will be used.

MetaFi – money in the metaverse

Personally, I had been intrigued with a blockchain-built metaverse from the day Facebook announced its rebranding to Meta. I was convinced it was in some way a continuation of the Diem ambition and thus a reach into the banking world. But it wasn't until I read an announcement on LinkedIn by Umar Farooq (2022), the CEO of JP Morgan's blockchain suite Onyx, that I had my theoretical ruminations confirmed. The bank was opening up a lounge in Decentraland, thus becoming the first major US bank to establish a presence in the metaverse. The fight for the future of money had just been expanded to a new, fancy arena.

Other financial incumbents have shown interest in the metaverse too. HSBC revealed plans to purchase land in The Sandbox as it seeks to gain a foothold in the e-sports and gaming community. American Express is filing patents that hint at metaverse plans (Crosman, 2022). In metaverse-friendly South Korea one of the largest financial institutes – Kookmin Bank – has developed an entire financial town. They have opened up truly functional bank branches with clerks that can perform remittances. Employee avatars will also hold consultations with clients (Zelealem, 2021).

Those forays are trying to copy existing models of banking into the metaverse. One might wonder who would visit a bank branch in the metaverse, when most people shun them in the physical world. It might be counterintuitive, but doing those things is still important. Not only does it put the metaverse on banks' agendas, but these efforts also signal presence. After all, not everybody would expect to meet their house bank in the new digital world. It is like a big publicity campaign.

Yet the bulk of bank business will be migrating to so-called MetaFi. Our avatars have different capabilities than we do, and so does their money. Enter TerraZero Technologies, a company that provides mortgages for buying virtual land in Decentraland. It works similarly to a common real-estate loan, just that the logic is recorded and automatically executed on a blockchain. A customer borrows money to purchase a parcel of digital land. TerraZero provides the financing but stays the rightful owner of the land until the loan is paid back. The collateral is the land, i.e. the NFT (Rosen, 2022). A DeFi protocol specifies the rules when the NFT changes hands and when the customer defaults. This is a prime example of on-chain finance handling metaverse assets.

Some challenger banks are also working on bridging on-chain and off-chain finance. Zelf has built its banking businesses around the metaverse (Zelf, 2022). Customers get an FDIC-insured deposit account and a classic Visa card. If they are short on cash, they can load the account with a payday loan they received for locking up their metaverse assets, say a game token or cryptocurrency. NFTs can be displayed in Apple and Google Pay. And game loot can be sold for fiat money. DAOs are also trying to bridge the physical and digital worlds. Using Boson Protocol users can turn physical assets into NFTs and use them in DeFi transactions in the metaverse. This realm of merging physical and digital worlds is sometimes referred to as the omniverse (Kamin, 2021).

The next level of DeFi

'MetaFi is the next level of DeFi. The great thing is that NFTs and fungible tokens can collaborate' (Van Rijmenam, 2022). What this means is that you can have also digital originals such as an NFT denoting the property rights for metaverse land and you can use it as collateral in a mortgage. Or you can tokenize the copyrights and exploitation rights for movies, songs or books and put them in a fund. It has even become possible to fractionalize these tokens, meaning that you can split the ownership of highly expensive (virtual) real estate such as an office building into many parts and let retail investors put their money behind it.

Applications such as MetaFi loans will be an arena of intense competition. Equally important, if not more so, is which underlying assets and which settlement protocols are used. The money masters of the metaverse will be those that can combine all those layers in one engine.

Most transactions in the metaverses are done via native currencies. In Decentraland you pay for land or unique avatar names with MANA. NFTs in The Sandbox change hands via transferring SAND tokens. So far, no preferred cross-metaverse currency of exchange has crystallized. Rather, a multi-token trend is taking hold. And while SAND and MANA are both built on Ethereum's blockchain and its ERC-20 token standard, competing chains are gaining a foothold in the metaverse. Hence, we are headed not only towards a multi-token but a multi-chain paradigm. Over the coming years the competition is set to become more, rather than less. As soon as big economy central banks issue their first live CBDCs those will join the roster too. And once the status of privately issued stablecoins is clarified in the US, EU and UK, another powerful contender group will emerge.

Yet in the long run I believe we will see a weakening of the multi-token and multi-chain paradigm. As is the case in all format wars, the market converges around a handful of formats, sometimes even around only a single one. Whether it was the .pdf format for opening documents or Windows for operating PCs – provisioning interoperability is the key to capture a large user base. At the end of the day, currencies are also a kind of format and the US dollar has been the number one reserve and cross-border currency in history. I am convinced it will continue to dominate a global financial system on the blockchain, whether that be through a Fed-issued CBDC or a stablecoin issued by banks or corporations. The job freely floating cryptocurrencies are doing with regard to the three key functions of money (see Chapter 3) is simply too poor.

This format convergence will take some time though and will be decided by actual usage. In the short and medium term, resistance to government-issued money will fuel the importance of cryptocurrencies. Kiguel (2022) sees economics in the metaverse linked to fiat in some way, yet most of the metaverses will still have their own currencies for people to use. On why they would still be needed rather than directly resorting to CBDCs or some other fiat-backed stablecoins, he echoes the scepticism prevalent in much of the crypto-community: 'I am not a big fan of stablecoins, because ultimately they are controlled by the currencies' central banks and underlying countries, and usually governments don't make the best decisions regarding their currency.'

Banks are recognizing that multi-asset future. Citi (2022) concludes in its report that MetaFi can best be defined as a combination of decentralized finance (DeFi), traditional finance (TradFi) and centralized finance (CeFi). Centralized finance means that centrally run blockchains will be deployed by commercial banks, central banks and corporations to mimic the capacities of cryptocurrencies while still being run by institutions of trust. Those three strands – DeFi, TradFi, CeFi – will not only co-exist but they will merge to develop new products needed for the metaverse ecosystem.

JP Morgan (2022) has a similar vision and aims at provisioning interoperability. America's biggest bank sees the various metaverses as economies with their own inhabitants, GDPs, currencies and assets. In many ways this resembles the physical world, hence it can draw from its core competencies in cross-border payments, foreign exchange, asset custody and trading, as well as the creation of financial assets. JP Morgan aims to be the organizer of payments and financial transactions in the new generation of the web. To reach that, it points out how new capabilities must be built, stressing in particular tokenization and digital identity. It is a lesson applying to every bank.

This shows that the masters of MetaFi will be those companies with the fastest and best super money engines, as discussed in Chapter 11. Banks and tech companies are realizing this. It is no coincidence that both are cautiously warming up to handling cryptos. Google and Apple Pay can become dominant money engines if their capabilities are expanded. Meta Pay (see Chapter 9) is a clear effort to build an engine that can handle all types of on- and off-chain assets and will likely be equipped with crypto-exchange and DeFi capabilities. Industry insiders (e.g. Kiguel, 2022) don't expect Meta Pay to be choked off by regulators the way Diem was. What Meta will likely be proposing is a wallet and a cryptocurrency for its metaverse. In essence it is similar to what Decentraland or The Sandbox are doing, so it would be hard to justify separate treatment.

On-ramps and off-ramps

So, a super money engine must be able to handle all types of assets and execute DeFi logic. It ensures the seamless high-capacity financial infrastructure that is needed in the metaverse. On top of handling money and assets, the best engines will also become identity hubs. A complete engine that moves money has to perform all sorts of KYC, AML and other compliance checks without causing any friction or delay.

The way authorities fight money laundering in the crypto space is to mandate KYC checks when people are buying cryptocurrencies (on-ramps) and when they are selling them back for fiat (off-ramps). This way they can link the real-life identity of a person with a wallet address and circumvent blockchain's pseudonymity. Onboarding customers into a financial system is an area in which banks have long-standing expertise. Things such as account validation or sanctions screening are largely identical whether performed for the off-chain or the on-chain world. But the importance of identity management in the metaverse does not stop there.

On- and off-ramp identity checks usually require customers to upload a photo of their ID document, bank account slips and sometimes a video identification. While customers are prepared to do that occasionally, say when they register for an account at a crypto-exchange, they will not accept going through the procedures at multiple points in the metaverse. Also, customers are getting continuously more sensitive about their data privacy and they will object to multiple companies wanting to elicit, store and process their identity data. Herein lies the chance for banks.

It would be a selling point for every wallet if in addition to handling multiple assets it could become an identity tool for the metaverse. I could, for example, prove my identity when I am purchasing a parcel in a metaverse without actually having to reveal my personal data. I wouldn't have to upload my ID but I could simply prove that I have knowledge of my private keys. It is like a seal on a letter in the Middle Ages. Messenger and recipient would be convinced of the authenticity of the sender without having to open the letter and reveal the contents. The legal standing of the underlying technologies such as zero-knowledge proofs still needs to be clarified, but more and more institutions are using it.

While banks are in a favourable position to offer such a service, it is far from settled that they will be the metaverse's identity managers. Identity is another area where Big Tech can carve out large parts of the value chain. Microsoft has been working for years on a decentralized identity solution (DID) that is standardized and accepted but where users remain in control of their digital data. Identities work across different chains and ledgers. The identity attributes are safely stored off-chain in an identity hub and proof or access can be given by an individual's private keys (see whitepaper in Microsoft, 2018).

The showdown between Big Tech, Big Banking and Big Government

I started this book with Marc Andreessen's quote that software is eating the world. It so happens that Andreessen (Andreessen quoted in Fung, 2014) has also provided a fitting analysis for the outset of the last chapter. Speaking about the groundbreaking potential of bitcoin and the underlying technology, he explained its extreme dynamism across different actor groups: the decentralized technologies in the back enhance the power of people, the power of cooperation and the power of governments. At the same time each of those groups is very suspicious about how it escalates the power of the other groups. People worry about governments snooping on them. Governments are afraid that companies will flaunt financial rules and that individuals might escape their watchful control. And so on.

The metaverse puts this mechanism of power escalation under a magnifying glass. Plus, the panoply of companies vying for dominance is widening. There is a consensus that it will take decades until the metaverse comes into full swing, yet already now it is a highly competitive place. The reason: in the metaverse many different areas clash, all of which are considered home turf for different types of giants. It merges gaming, finance, identity management, as well as all layers of the digital technology stack. Each of these areas is dominated by titans and for each of them occupying high ground in the metaverse will be crucial not just to expand their reach, but to protect their core business.

What the metaverse will look like in 10 or 20 years nobody can tell. Even less so what money will look like. Will cryptocurrencies or CBDCs be the backbone of the metaverse economy? Can commercial banks transfer their position as masters of money into the new world? Or is it all playing into the hands of Big Tech? Can DAOs eliminate centralized institutions in general? And how much leeway will regulators allow for finance in the metaverse?

The answers will determine who will rule metaverse banking, but this is not the only thing to consider. The metaverse is blockchain-native, hence built around asset ownership. Even before actually making money in the metaverse, companies can use it as a laboratory to tinker with the possibilities of DeFi and its combination with traditional finance. It is a new virtual playground. All the more concerning are cries from some politicians who want to reverse the regulatory progress that has been made over the last couple of years.

Governments are well advised to take a light-touch approach

The basis for building a super money engine is the licence to handle all assets. Hence, even though you might take your business into a virtual metaverse, the rules of the game will still be written by physical authorities. This can be a confusing and sometimes contradictory matter. Consider the United States. The Fed, FDIC (Federal Deposit Insurance Corporation) and the OCC (Office of the Comptroller of the Currency) all have a say, while the latter was somewhat in the lead. The OCC had issued interpretative letters allowing banks to offer custody services for crypto assets, to hold reserves that back stablecoins and to use stablecoins and other blockchain technology for bank-to-bank payments.

In August 2022, however, a number of Democratic Senators including Elizabeth Warren and Bernie Sanders asked the OCC to take away the rights it had granted to the banks (De, 2022). Though there are currently no signs the OCC will rethink its openness to crypto, such demands are warning signals that some politicians will seek an outsized role for government. This in turn would hamper innovation in the financial services industry significantly while actually increasing the risks.

By barring highly regulated institutions from dealing with crypto-assets they are pushing the build-up of a new monetary system into unregulated territory. This is amplifying the hitherto unknown risks of new applications, especially since there are very few clear rules around crypto-assets at the moment. The second reason why locking banks out of cryptocurrencies and stablecoins is a terrible idea goes to the very essence of this book: the future of finance is a multi-asset world that runs on both on- and off-chain assets. Preventing banks from offering services within their core business would hand Meta and its peers on a silver plate the industry they have been eying for years. Not that there is anything inherently bad about Big Tech offering financial services, but each actor must have the same terms of competition. Otherwise, free market principles are suspended and innovation, financial stability and customer welfare will suffer. Governments should not be the ones picking winners and losers.

Prohibiting financial incumbents from participating in the crypto-economy will also leave their core business at risk. Aguilar (2022) describes an example where crypto-challengers have already snatched away the core business of financial incumbents. Mexico is the largest remittance market in the Americas and it used to be dominated by Western Union and MoneyGram. The crypto-exchange Bitso has turned this upside down in record time. 'Traditional finance institutions are seeing their revenues slashed. Their entire fee-based business model is being disrupted. That is why they are desperate to get into the new arena. Eventually technology and banking giants become adaptive' (Aguilar, 2022).

In the end, the customers will decide the future of finance

We have talked a lot about what Big Tech is doing to break into finance, what banks are doing to counter it and how governments are struggling to balance their urge to control with free market principles. We have also looked at how tinkerers and pioneers are pushing the limits of the technology and all the possible routes that are opening up. But which one we will take and which actors will end up on top will ultimately be decided by users and customers. After all, it is market demand that has shaped crypto-assets into their current form.

Had governments gotten their way with cryptocurrencies, bitcoin and others would have long been confined to the darkest corners of the dark web. But consumers purchased cryptos in ever-increasing numbers. This caught the attention of businesses, banks, entrepreneurs, investors and troves of world-class programmers. Cypherpunks might cringe when they hear about centralized blockchains, but the economy wishes for them, so businesses build them. Prowling the public ledger of bitcoin to link wallet addresses to identities is frowned upon by the crypto-crowd, yet compliance managers are loosening their purse strings, so analytics firms are mushrooming. Some retailers accept cryptocurrencies, but shoppers would rather spend dollars and pounds, so other retailers stay put.

Ultimately, market acceptance will surprise even the savviest mavens. Answer even one of the following questions differently than expected and you will get a completely different future: will people really spend so much time in the metaverse or will it fall short even of traditional gaming? Will people ever be comfortable with DAOs? Would users forgo their self-sovereignty for an easier login? Or a sign-up bonus perhaps?

It is one thing to ignite an initial following and capture headlines, but it is another to break into the mainstream. The big cryptocurrencies are only now on the verge of mass usage, so it will be a long time until the verdict is decided on the metaverse and Web3.

The transition to mainstream will also answer one question that will fundamentally decide the nature of money inside and outside of the metaverse: will people use stablecoins and if so, which ones? This more than anything else will shape the power relations between Big Tech, Big Banking and Big Government.

Technically CBDCs and private stablecoins are the most efficient solution in a multi-asset world. They combine the stability of fiat with blockchain characteristics such as programmability or immutability. It would be much easier to use them directly instead of resorting to private stablecoins or individual cryptocurrencies. But whether they live up to their potential will hinge on whether users prefer them to private variants. Their big drawback is privacy. Most people don't want the government to have direct access to their transactions, regardless of any self-imposed restrictions. And user preferences change over time, especially when the composition of user groups changes. 'The crypto-native crowd will never use CBDCs. They really care about pseudonymity and have an inbred distrust towards governments. But it really depends on whether one day they will be outnumbered by those users who don't really care,' says Armando Aguilar (2022).

The time of the consumer in crypto-assets has not yet come. True, we are seeing some early trends. People are holding digital assets with custodians rather than in paper wallets. They trust big institutions over small ones. And they invest mostly in tried-and-tested blue-chip assets. But overall, the space is still emerging and thus driven by tinkerers and trailblazers. Crypto-enthusiasts still make up most of the consumers. It is like in the early days of the Wild West: the first daredevil settlers are conquering the new land but it will be the later settlers that will eventually shape the way it looks and works.

KEY TAKEAWAYS

- Facebook rebranded its holding company in a nod to the metaverse, a gamified version of the web that will allow people to plug into a virtual, connected world and participate in its own functioning economy. Metaverses that run on Web3 infrastructure will be the next frontier for financial technology.
- Whereas Web2 stands for well-known virtual applications already in use, Web3 is a truly transformational world that runs completely on a blockchain layer. The technology enables digital scarcity and hence fully fledged ownership of identities and assets. They are traced as digital originals with a new type of blockchain asset called NFTs.

- Web3 is where fungible and non-fungible tokens work together, ergo it is the place Meta wants to pioneer its super money engine: Meta Pay. Signs abound that other Big Techs will follow suit. Banks must do the same if they want to power all sorts of transactions of money and assets in the metaverse and beyond.
- In the metaverse the coming multi-asset paradigm will spread first. The same is true for a completely new generation of financial products such as digital mortgages. In order not to suffocate the innovative potential, lawmakers and regulators must take a light-touch approach.

References

Aguilar, A (2022) Personal interview, 19 August

Andreessen, M quoted in B Fung (2014) Marc Andreessen: In 20 years, we'll talk about bitcoin like we talk about the Internet today, *The Washington Post*, 21 May, www.washingtonpost.com/news/the-switch/wp/2014/05/21/marc-andreessen-in-20-years-well-talk-about-bitcoin-like-we-talk-about-the-internet-today/ (archived at https://perma.cc/2PUX-LFM2)

Birch, K (2022) PwC, JP Morgan, Samsung – buying land in the metaverse, Business Chief, 19 February, https://businesschief.com/technology-and-ai/pwc-jp-morgan-samsung-buying-land-in-the-metaverse (archived at https://perma.cc/JG7K-PDKZ)

Buterin, V (2022) My critique is deeper than 'Metaverse Wikipedia will beat Metaverse Encyclopedia Britannica'. It's that we don't really know the definition of 'the metaverse' yet, it's far too early to know what people actually want. So anything Facebook creates now will misfire, Twitter, 31 July, https://bit.ly/3AUtEQ3 (archived at https://perma.cc/EU96-MFUN)

Choudhary, V (2022) Amazon is quietly hiring for the Metaverse, The Street, 18 February, www.thestreet.com/technology/amazon-is-quietly-hiring-for-the-metaverse (archived at https://perma.cc/K9HT-X69G)

Christie's (2021) 25 Feb–11 Mar 2021 | Online auction 20447 Beeple | the first 5000 days, 11 March, https://onlineonly.christies.com/s/beeple-first-5000-days/beeple-b-1981-1/112924 (archived at https://perma.cc/GG73-NQ4T)

Citi (2022) Metaverse and money: decrypting the future, Citi GPS, March, https://ir.citi.com/gps/x5%2BFQJT3BoHXVu9MsqVRoMdiws3RhL4yhF6Fr8us8oHaOe1W9smOy1%2B8aaAgT3SPuQVtwC5B2%2Fc%3D (archived at https://perma.cc/H7GK-UKN6)

Clark, M (2022) Amazon hardware exec takes another swipe at Zuckerberg's metaverse fantasy, *The Verge*, 20 May, www.theverge.com/2022/5/20/23131767/amazon-hardware-meta-metaverse-virtual-reality-vs-real-world (archived at https://perma.cc/BAA8-FA2U)

Clegg, N and Olivan, J (2021) Investing in European talent to help build the Metaverse, Meta, 17 October, https://about.fb.com/news/2021/10/creating-jobs-europe-metaverse/ (archived at https://perma.cc/3TUS-7STU)

Cline, E (2011) *Ready Player One*, Crown Publishing Group, United States

Crosman, P (2022) 4 ways banks are experimenting in the metaverse, American Banker, 21 March, www.americanbanker.com/list/4-ways-banks-are-experimenting-in-the-metaverse (archived at https://perma.cc/X2U3-TELR)

De, N (2022) US Senators Warren, Sanders ask key bank regulator to rescind crypto guidance, CoinDesk via yahoo!finance, 10 August, https://finance.yahoo.com/news/us-senators-warren-sanders-ask-171959792.html (archived at https://perma.cc/VSZ7-PFXB)

Del Castillo, M and Bambysheva, N (2021) Google takes giant step towards powering blockchain-based Web3, *Forbes*, 14 September, https://bit.ly/3PTlQlH (archived at https://perma.cc/HXK8-ZU3Y)

Dorsey, J (2021) You don't own 'web3.' The VCs and their LPs do. It will never escape their incentives. It's ultimately a centralized entity with a different label. Know what you're getting into… , Twitter, 21 December, https://twitter.com/jack/status/1473139010197508098?lang=de (archived at https://perma.cc/MU29-KTXC)

Farooq, U (2022) Another first by Onyx by J.P. Morgan! The first major bank in the #Metaverse Visit us at the Onyx by J.P. Morgan lounge at the Metajuku mall in Decentraland ! 🚀This wouldn't be possible without Christine Moy and Nicole Parina doing the heavy lifting to get us to the Metaverse #onwardsandupwards #dlt, LinkedIn, February, www.linkedin.com/posts/umarfarooq10_metaverse-onwardsandupwards-dlt-activity-6899407759394050048-VxHz/ (archived at https://perma.cc/6E65-JE88)

Gurman, M (2021) Apple aims to prevent defections to Meta with rare $180,000 bonuses for top talent, Bloomberg, 28 December, www.bloomberg.com/news/articles/2021-12-28/apple-pays-unusual-180-000-bonuses-to-retain-engineering-talent?sref=xRwgZENh#xj4y7vzkg (archived at https://perma.cc/8JEX-NJMK)

Heath, A (2021) Mark Zuckerberg on why Facebook is rebranding to Meta, *The Verge*, 28 October, www.theverge.com/22749919/mark-zuckerberg-facebook-meta-company-rebrand (archived at https://perma.cc/A7WX-JTYA)

Heath, A (2022) Zuckerberg says Meta and Apple are in 'very deep, philosophical competition' to build the metaverse, *The Verge*, 26 July, www.theverge.com/2022/7/26/23279478/meta-apple-mark-zuckerberg-metaverse-competition (archived at https://perma.cc/8ERD-JMSK)

Hope, A (2022) This is why New Yorkers are spending hundreds of millions on fake real estate, *New York Post*, 9 March, https://nypost.com/2022/03/09/this-is-why-new-yorkers-are-spending-hundreds-of-millions-on-fake-real-estate/ (archived at https://perma.cc/J5TY-A4D3)

JP Morgan Chase (2022) Opportunities in the metaverse: How businesses can explore the metaverse and navigate the hype vs. reality, JPM Onyx report, www.jpmorgan.com/content/dam/jpm/treasury-services/documents/opportunities-in-the-metaverse.pdf (archived at https://perma.cc/2NRF-8C2Q)

Kamin, D (2021) Investors snap up Metaverse real estate in a virtual land boom, *New York Times*, 30 November, www.nytimes.com/2021/11/30/business/metaverse-real-estate.html (archived at https://perma.cc/8M2B-KBTJ)

Kharpal, A (2022) What is 'Web3'? Here's the vision for the future of the internet from the man who coined the phrase, *CNBC*, 19 April, www.cnbc.com/2022/04/20/what-is-web3-gavin-wood-who-invented-the-word-gives-his-vision.html (archived at https://perma.cc/ZV53-EU9J)

Kiguel, A (2022) Personal interview, 17 August

Livni, E (2022) Tales from crypto: a billionaire meme feud threatens industry unity, *New York Times*, 18 January, www.nytimes.com/2022/01/18/business/dealbook/web3-venture-capital-andreessen.html (archived at https://perma.cc/QB4A-CD8X)

Microsoft (2018) Decentralized Identity: Own and control your identity, https://query.prod.cms.rt.microsoft.com/cms/api/am/binary/RE2DjfY (archived at https://perma.cc/937Y-KRWL)

Novet, J (2022) Google's cloud group forms Web3 team to capitalize on booming popularity of crypto, *CNBC*, 6 May, www.cnbc.com/2022/05/06/googles-cloud-group-forms-web3-product-and-engineering-team.html (archived at https://perma.cc/ER7C-3BV2)

Paul, K (2022) Meta and other tech giants form metaverse standards body, without Apple, Reuters, 21 June, www.reuters.com/technology/meta-other-tech-giants-form-metaverse-standards-body-without-apple-2022-06-21/ (archived at https://perma.cc/QT95-8ZSJ)

Reuters (2022) via the *Guardian*: Man who paid $2.9m for NFT of Jack Dorsey's first tweet set to lose almost $2.9m, *Guardian*, 14 April, www.theguardian.com/technology/2022/apr/14/twitter-nft-jack-dorsey-sina-estavi (archived at https://perma.cc/P68B-2GZS)

Rosen, P (2022) Metaverse mortgages are being issued to buy virtual land – and one of the first ever was just signed for a property in Decentraland, Markets Insider, 1 February, https://markets.businessinsider.com/news/currencies/metaverse-mortgage-terrazero-decentraland-virtual-land-real-estate-crypto-finance-2022-2 (archived at https://perma.cc/L86Y-W62L)

Statista (2022) Total value of sales involving a non-fungible token (NFT) in the art segment worldwide over the previous 30 days from April 15, 2021 to July 15, 2022, July, www.statista.com/statistics/1235263/nft-art-monthly-sales-value/ (archived at https://perma.cc/FR7A-4EE2)

Stephenson, N (1992) *Snow Crash*, Bentam Books, London/New York/Toronto/ Sidney/Auckland

Sundararajan, S (2022) Metaverse trademark applications reach 16,000 in China, yahoo!news, 22 February, https://yhoo.it/3CDCbrL (archived at https://perma.cc/T7U8-UFE7)

Tilley, A (2022) Microsoft hit by defections as tech giants battle for talent to build the Metaverse, *Wall Street Journal*, 10 January, www.wsj.com/articles/microsoft-hit-by-defections-as-tech-giants-battle-for-talent-to-build-the-metaverse-11641819601 (archived at https://perma.cc/6X45-HP3Q)

Todd, E (2022) Personal interview, 20 April

Van Rijmenam, M (2022) Personal interview, 25 April

Waterson, J and Milmo, D (2021) Facebook whistleblower Frances Haugen calls for urgent external regulation, *Guardian*, 25 October, www.theguardian.com/technology/2021/oct/25/facebook-whistleblower-frances-haugen-calls-for-urgent-external-regulation (archived at https://perma.cc/KL5C-6GGM)

Yang, Z (2021) Can NFTs happen in a crypto-less China? Amazingly, yes, protocol, 24 September, www.protocol.com/china/china-nft-crypto-workarounds (archived at https://perma.cc/HZ8W-RFTC)

Zelealem, F (2021) South Korea's KB Bank enters metaverse space, yahoo!finance, 30 November, https://finance.yahoo.com/news/south-korea-kb-bank-enters-121438920.html (archived at https://perma.cc/TRU5-2UBU)

Zelf (2022) Bank of the Metaverse, https://zelf.co/us/ (archived at https://perma.cc/8DA8-6GP3)

Zuckerberg, M (2021) Founder's Letter, 2021, Facebook News, 28 October, https://about.fb.com/news/2021/10/founders-letter/ (archived at https://perma.cc/ADD4-56WY)

Final remarks

At the beginning of the book I likened the blockchain to the development of the railroad in the Wild West. When the first tracks were laid throughout the continent, they made a vast new space accessible. Yet making the first locomotives steam through the great deserts and mountains was a mammoth task, only achievable by extraordinarily powerful corporations that only became more bloated by building the railroads. In order not to hinder them the government kept regulation loose. There were no safety standards, no efficient market, no checks and balances on the moguls controlling the business. Nobody challenged that. After all, the system had to grow. It took decades until the Interstate Commerce Commission drafted rules on things such as ticket prices and equal usage rights of the tracks. This, again, was a phase bedevilled by problems and only at the beginning of the 20th century did efficiency find its way into the system.

A similar situation is occurring with Big Tech in finance today. The five goliaths glide on the blockchain to new terrain as smoothly as a train through the great plains and prairies of the American frontier. Traditional banks are leashed by rules on capital requirements, corporate governance and reporting, as well as numerous restrictions on activities and exposures. The Big Five, on the other hand, can pick whatever part of the value chain fits their grand strategy and makes their data flywheels spin fastest. For KYC, AML and other invisible plumbing of the financial system they simply connect to financial institutes via APIs. It leaves the IT juggernauts free to offer cryptocurrencies in their wallets or buy NFT marketplaces without having to justify themselves. Instead of being berated as irresponsible, investors reward them for their courage and vision.

Tech giants have learned to skilfully tiptoe around hot-button areas, while hollowing out the banking business. Consider Apple Pay Later. What the initial Apple Pay offering did was to monetize the company's gatekeeper position. If banks wanted customers to use their card with the iPhone, they had to hand Apple a slice of the revenue pie. The subsequent move into the pay-later segment did not only mark an additional functionality, but Apple insourced much of the traditional banking value chain. Operations, risk management and even the credit checks are performed by its subsidiary Apple Financing LLC. The subsidiary holds a lending licence, though not a banking charter. Apple's partner Goldman Sachs is left with the mini-task of providing Mastercard payment credentials. Apple is reportedly also working on its own fraud checks and payment processing engine (Gurman, 2022).

The grip on finance will only get tighter. As we have seen throughout this book, all layers of the blockchain stack are up for grabs. Big Tech's cloud centres provide the infrastructure on which the distributed nodes run. Libra/Diem tried to conquer the asset and settlement layer. Wallets are being upgraded step by step to handle more assets and capture the gateway level. And there is little reason to doubt that companies such as Meta or Google could come up with the next killer app, this time on-chain.

The race will turn to creating the dominant super money engine – the heart of every future finance platform – as the world moves increasingly, but not exclusively, on-chain and thus into a multi-asset paradigm. The super money engine merges a powerful asset capability (including fiat currencies, cryptocurrencies, CBDCs, private stablecoins and NFTs) with powerful execution capability (including traditional finance transactions, smart contracts, DApps and DeFi).

When the first adventurers rode the new railroad connection the aggregate risks were negligible. Only when a critical mass of passengers boarded the trains regularly and made it a vital link within the US economy, did the potential perils start to bother regulators. As blockchain and crypto-usage reach the mainstream and more complex forms of the technology emerge, the new dangers have to be mitigated. The rise of DeFi in particular blows up risks exponentially. Not only that different applications are interwoven, but real-life assets are also becoming part of the picture. Big Techs are already at the brink of turning into shadow banks of systemic relevance with inherent cross-industry risks. And if they are honest about achieving their visions, say of building the metaverse, then they will inevitably have to put their weight behind DeFi as well. The speed displayed in their previous efforts combined with their heft could end in a cataclysmic chain reaction far away from the watchful eye of the regulators.

So what should lawmakers do? Just as we thought the frontier was closing with regulation on cryptocurrencies and distributed ledgers taking shape, new breakthroughs such as DeFi and Web3 shake things up again. True, those will require specific rules just as the first generation of cryptos did. Yet the more important thing is to look at the role of Big Tech more broadly. Legislators have already bared their trust-busting teeth. When a bipartisan consensus in Washington emerges these days, you can be sure a storm is brewing. On the other side of the Atlantic, London and Brussels are following suit. And Beijing has kept a close eye on its two tech champions for quite some time too. But how does that scepticism trickle down to concrete policies? Outlawing currency basket-pegged stablecoins is good policy; banning Big Tech titans from finance is not. Neither is breaking them up.

Data giants are innovation powerhouses and critical infrastructure providers, but they must not enjoy preferential treatment and they must not pile up systemic risks unnoticed. The balancing act can only succeed if today's activity-based approach yields to an entity-based one. All that technology goliaths have to fear from regulators are fines, whereas banks constantly fret for their very licences to operate. A 'We're sorry and we're working on a solution' shouldn't be an acceptable answer when dealing with data security and most certainly not when managing money.

The second thing that must be done is to put competition on an equal footing, allowing tech companies, banks and start-ups to compete fairly and make use of the promises of the new land. Laws cannot block one group from tinkering with crypto-assets, while allowing it to another. On- and off-chain assets will melt together, whether regulators like it or not. It is better to pen the rules early on than to sleepwalk into an inevitable future.

The new world of finance forces central banks to make some tough calls too. Not only because they are stewards of monetary stability, but also because of the geopolitical nature of the new tech. The question of which national currency will prevail, if any, is inextricably linked to the question of stablecoins and CBDCs. Should national banks really compete with private companies while regulating them at the same time?

The importance of regulators should not suggest that the future of Big Tech in finance will be determined by them alone. When targeting the flows of money Alphabet, Amazon, Meta, Apple and Microsoft will not meet passive resistance. Banks are determined to stay the masters of finance. Fintechs and DAOs are determined to get there. Whether they are carving out a profitable niche or building a super money engine, they will not fall over like incumbents in other industries that Big Tech has conquered in a blitz. Despite the breakneck speed with which blockchain technology is moving and markets are changing, the battle for finance will be raging on for a very long time.

Banks and businesses looking to traverse into this emerging world must take action now. Of all the advice that can be imparted on them one stands above all others: build deep expertise in the new technologies inside the organization. Specialized departments are imperative, but so are knowledgeable decision makers who drive and sign off corporate strategy. If the C-suite does not understand the latest breakthroughs and how they will shape the company's market, then the battle for tomorrow will certainly be lost. The same will be true if managers fail to grasp the urgency to act. The advances in blockchain technology are more dynamic than those of any other game-changing innovation in financial history.

Hence, the second critical recommendation is to watch the market closely and regularly. It is not only the technology that is moving quickly, but also the competition. Spotting small tell-tale signs of where the market is going can give you a crucial advantage. Is a Big

Tech running a job ad for CBDCs or filing a DeFi payment patent? How significant is the latest hack of a crypto-exchange? What is the new regulation draft saying about private stablecoins? The strength of the incumbents is one reason why the decision is not around the corner. Blockchain's trajectory as a technology is another. Some of the daredevils who ventured westwards in 19th-century America did so to find gold and earn riches, others looked to settle on cheap land, while yet another group were driven by their urge to explore. The same type of spirit gave us Bitcoin and the technology behind it. It continues to produce DeFi, autonomous organizations, Web3 and all of the breakthroughs yet to come. A technology that saw the light of the world only in 2009 has certainly not yet materialized in its final form.

Reference

Gurman, M (2022) Apple will handle lending itself with new pay later service, Bloomberg, 8 June, www.bloomberg.com/news/articles/2022-06-08/apple-will-handle-the-lending-itself-with-new-pay-later-service#xj4y7vzkg (archived at https://perma.cc/3WPR-YEWD)

GLOSSARY

Activity-based regulation: A regulatory approach that constrains individual corporate activities directly and on an isolated basis, not on an entity level. Activity-based regulation does not vary based on the other activities an entity performs. It is the opposite of entity-based regulation.

AI: Artificial intelligence is an umbrella term for different techniques that seek to make computers imitate human behaviour. Sub-disciplines include machine learning, artificial neural networks and deep learning.

Algorithmic stablecoins: A particular type of stablecoin that does not hold the peg to a stable asset such as fiat by having the necessary asset backing, i.e. it is uncollateralized. Instead it algorithmically adjusts the supply and demand of two types of token to hold the peg.

APIs: Application programming interfaces are a pre-defined way applications can access each other's functionality, i.e. communicate with each other.

Austrian School: An economic school of thought that emphasizes the actions of the individual and sees them as the driving force of social phenomena. It originated in the late 19th century in Vienna but spread throughout the world and saw renewed interest in the 1970s especially through the works of Friedrich Hayek. The idea of free banking particularly inspired the emergence of cryptocurrencies.

BaaS: Blockchain-as-a-Service refers to cloud service providers building, hosting and managing blockchain solutions on their cloud infrastructure. BaaS boosts blockchain adoption thanks to classic cloud benefits such as scalability and professional operations.

Big data: Collected data that serves as the fuel for AI algorithms. The difference to classic data analytics is that big data is characterized by 5Vs: value, veracity, volume, velocity (real-time updates) and variety (data structure). Classic data collection is usually restricted to value and veracity.

Big Iron: Term used to refer to banks' large mainframe computers that were used for mission-critical processing of large quantities of data.

Big Tech: Collective term for the five US tech titans: Alphabet (Google's parent company), Amazon, Meta Platforms (Facebook's parent company), Apple and Microsoft. China's Tencent and Alibaba display similar characteristics. The size, power and wealth of those companies transcends regions and industries in a way never before seen in history.

Bitcoin: The world's first fully fledged cryptocurrency and the first use case for blockchain technology. Up to this day, bitcoin holds the highest market capitalization of all cryptocurrencies.

Bitcoin Civil War: An episode of struggle in 2017 where different camps fought over the block size in bitcoin transactions in order to alleviate the scalability restrictions.

Blockchain: A specific version of distributed ledger technology that keeps track of token ownership in verified transactions recorded on distributed nodes. Transactions are recorded in blocks and each of those blocks is linked to the proceeding one, giving the history of transactions its eponymous shape. Any attempt to tamper with past transactions immediately breaks the chain and the link to all subsequent transactions. Blockchain legitimacy is cryptographically assured.

CBDC: Central bank digital currency stands for a stablecoin issued by the central banks and pegged 1:1 to the value of the fiat currency. It is a form of central bank money equal to cash or reserve money. CBDCs are a direct liability to the central bank. Most CBDCs are issued on centralized blockchains.

Centralization: Centralization is frequently mixed up with distribution. While distribution describes where data is stored and processed, centralization refers to the question of whether anybody can join the network as a validator node. In centralized (permissioned) blockchains only pre-approved nodes have editing rights, whereas in decentralized (permissionless) ones everybody can participate in the block verification.

Chicago School: A neo-classical, market-liberal economic school of thought particularly popular in free-market economies and often contrasted to Keynesian economics. At its core is the belief that market mechanisms are the best allocator of resources, hence government intrusion is to be limited to a minimum.

Chinese techno-sphere: China's technological sphere of influence over certain geographical regions, in particular over countries in South-East Asia. Often the term goes hand-in-hand with a strong local presence of Chinese Big Tech.

Cloud computing: A computing paradigm in which computer resources such as storage or processing can be rented on demand. Companies no longer require local data centres but can outsource IT infrastructure and the management thereof.

Coin market cap: The market capitalization of a digital coin calculated by multiplying the value of a coin with the number of coins in circulation.

Consensus: The consensus mechanism is the heart of every blockchain. A blockchain consensus protocol is necessary for the validator nodes to reach a common agreement (consensus) on the present data state of the ledger. Consensus mechanisms come in all shapes but the two most prevalent decentralized consensus mechanisms are Proof-of-Work (PoW) and Proof-of-Stake (PoS).

Core banking system: A bank's major backend system that processes financial transactions and updates other IT systems.

Cryptocurrencies: Digital assets issued on a blockchain that have their independent exchange rate. Technically, cryptocurrency could fulfil all three key functions of money: store of value, medium of exchange and unit of account. Practically, they have so far been inferior to fiat on all three dimensions. Hence, they resemble investment assets rather than currencies.

Cypherpunks: A group of pre-bitcoin cryptographers linking the heavy use of cryptography to political and social change. As advocates of free banking and libertarianism they came up with crucial technical concepts that set the stage for the invention of blockchain technology. The term is a blend of cypher (an encryption method) and cyberpunk (a dystopian sci-fi genre).

DApps: Decentralized applications that can do everything a regular application can, but that are built on top of blockchains. Thus, they benefit from properties such as immutability and programmability.

DAOs: Decentralized autonomous organizations are made up of smart contract code. They do not require staff or incorporation, yet are capable of performing tasks similar to those of corporations solely with software code. The difference to smart contracts is that DAOs also have their own funds, whereas smart contracts are the executing mechanisms.

Data flywheel effect: There is no one pot of data that powers data giants. Rather, data is fed from multiple sources. More data means better services because customers' preferences are better known. This in turn brings more customers and thus additional data, which in turn improves the product and so on. Whatever part of the flywheel is fed it accelerates business.

DeFi: Decentralized finance is an umbrella term for disruptive financial services based on decentralized blockchains. The most defining feature of DeFi is its composable architecture, which has earned it the nickname the 'LEGO of money'.

DEX: Decentralized exchanges are automatic and non-custodial alternatives to centralized crypto-exchanges. You can purchase and sell cryptocurrencies at a DEX without having to trust a company. Such exchanges are important building blocks of DeFi.

Digital assets: The term digital assets includes both fungible tokens (e.g. cryptocurrencies, digital currencies, CBDCs) and non-fungible tokens (e.g. NFTs representing digital land) that are recorded and transferred on a blockchain. Despite the name, digital assets may be considered securities, commodities, derivatives or other financial products.

Digital currencies: Digital currencies are money based on a blockchain. They are a broader category than cryptocurrencies as they also include private stablecoins and CBDCs.

DLT: Distributed ledger technology means that ledgers tracking the movement of assets are not stored and operated on a centralized server but on multiple dispersed nodes. The blockchain is a specific form of DLT since it boasts the characteristic form of blocks on a chain.

DMA: The EU's Digital Markets Act sets up rules targeted to prevent big technology platforms (e.g. search engines or social media companies) from abusing their market-dominant powers.

Double-spend problem: Describes the phenomenon that digital files are copied in the process of sending, which would have a catastrophic effect for everything of monetary value. The same money or asset could be spent multiple times online. The double-spend problem can either be solved via intermediaries or the blockchain mechanism.

DSA: Like the DMA, the EU's Digital Services Act seeks to limit the power of tech gatekeepers with a systemic role in the market. The goal is to protect users' rights and level the playing field among providers of digital services.

e-CNY: Also known as digital yuan or DC/EP initiative, this is a stablecoin issued by China's central bank (PBoC). It is the first digital currency issued by a major economy.

ECB: European Central Bank.

Ecosystem tokens: Also called utility, platform or primary token. This is the most important and fundamental type of token in a blockchain. Its movement is necessary in order to execute smart contracts and DApps that are run with secondary tokens. ETH is Ethereum's ecosystem token. When the movement of secondary tokens (e.g. BAT) is executed it also needs ETH to run the underlying machine.

Entity-based regulation: The focus of this regulatory approach is on preventing systemically relevant entities from failing so as to indirectly make core activities more resilient. Licences to operate are characteristic of entity-based regulation. It is the opposite of activity-based integration.

ETF: Exchange-traded funds are pooled securities that are linked to a particular index, commodity or other asset. ETFs are somewhat comparable to a mutual fund but can be traded on stock exchanges.

Ethereum: Turing-complete blockchain that can handle all types of assets and can execute smart contracts via its Ethereum Virtual Machine (EVM) that is sustained by its miners.

Exponential age: High-tech breakthroughs are occurring at an ever-faster speed and remodel the world so quickly that societies aren't capable of adjusting to it (as described by Azeem Azhar in his book of the same name).

Fed: Short for the Federal Reserve System (the US central banking system).

Fiat currencies: Currencies issued by the government but not backed by a hard asset such as gold.

Financial inclusion: The ideal state when people have access to basic financial services such as bank accounts or loans at affordable prices. When financial inclusion is high, the number of unbanked people is low.

Fintech: Companies trying to improve financial services by the use of new technology such as DLT or AI. Financial offerings are still at the core of the business model.

Free banking: A system in which central banks do not have the monopoly to issue currency. Banks can issue their own money and are not subject to special regulation. Market mechanisms will ultimately reward the best currency. Its most notable proponents include the economists Adam Smith, Friedrich Hayek and George Selgin. The free banking idea is most prominent in the libertarian worldview and inspired the cypherpunks.

Gas fees: Fees users have to pay if they want their smart contracts to be executed by the Ethereum network.

GDPR: General Data Protection Regulation that governs the collection and processing of personal data in member states of the European Union.

Gold standard: A monetary system in which the value of government-issued money is fixed to a specified amount of gold.

Governance token: A crypto-asset that grants holders the right to vote on protocol changes of a blockchain.

Hashing: Mathematical scrambling of input variables that generates a unique output (digital fingerprint) fixed in length. Hashing is a one-way function, meaning that computing backwards, i.e. deducing the right input variable solely from the output, is only possible with brute force.

Icarus Paradox: Theory that explains how companies that have become successful with a certain mindset, business model or worldview blindly stick to it. What has worked in the past, they assume, must work in the future as well. Often this rigidity leads to downfall, namely when technological progress alters the way competition works.

ICO: Initial coin offering – a process by which capital is raised through selling coins of a new cryptocurrency. Unlike in the eponymous IPO, there is no harsh regulation and the investments can be raised globally within minutes. At the same time ICOs lack investor protection and many were found to be scams.

IoT: The Internet of Things is a network of connected computing devices (i.e. computing chips in all types of physical objects – 'things') that communicate autonomously without the need for human intervention. These web-enabled smart devices exchange data, often gathered through sensors, with other devices and are present in all walks of life, from home appliances to industry applications.

Leapfrogging: The phenomenon when companies or nations immediately jump to the latest technologies skipping the traditional development path.

Legacy systems: Outdated soft- and hardware still in use. Legacy systems are often characterized by a lack of compatibility with new systems, lack of programmer know-how and lack of vendor support.

LEGO of money: *See* DeFi

Libertarianism: A political philosophy that strongly emphasizes individual freedom and private property and builds on classical liberal tradition as embodied by John Locke, David Hume and Adam Smith. Things like government regulation, wealth distribution or monitoring of individual communication are seen as unjustified coercion.

Libra/Diem: Led by Facebook and the Libra Alliance, Libra was a project that aimed to build a global blockchain-based currency pegged to a basket of fiat currencies. After facing strong regulatory headwinds, the Libra initiative was rebranded as Diem. This watered-down version gave up on the basket of currencies idea. Instead, Diem was supposed to have a dollar version, a pound version and so on. Eventually, the project was discontinued in 2022.

MetaFi: Short for finance in the metaverse, which can best be described as a combination of decentralized finance, centralized finance and traditional finance. MetaFi is particularly characterized by fungible and non-fungible tokens being highly intertwined.

Metaverse: Virtual world applications that are a fully immersive, 3D version of the internet. If built on Web3 infrastructure the metaverse is a fully fledged economy in which possessions are built, traded and used to generate income.

MiCA: The EU's Markets in Crypto Assets regulation proposal sets rules for crypto-assets currently not falling under any other EU regulation. It excludes non-fungible tokens and security tokens.

MiFID: The Markets in Financial Instruments Directive is an EU regulation that increases transparency and standardizes regulatory disclosures for companies operating on the financial markets of the European Union. The primary focus are stocks. Crypto-instruments such as security tokens also fall under MiFID rules.

Mining: Process by which many cryptocurrencies verify new transactions and thereby mint new coins.

Mobile payment: Term used to refer to physical POS payments with the smart phone, including a host of technologies such as NFC, SMS or QR codes.

Multi-chain paradigm: The co-existence of multiple different blockchains.

National champions (corporations): Private companies that have grown to such a size that they can foster a nation's interests (at home and abroad) and whose goals are thus not only regarded as maximizing shareholder value but also pursuing the common good of a nation. Policies often favour national champions, which is contrary to free market principles, but gives the country an advantage in strategically important sectors such as defence or technology.

NFT: Non-fungible tokens are a form of blockchain-recorded digital asset that cannot be traded on a like-for-like basis. NFTs constitute digital originals.

Node: Active participant to a blockchain network engaging in consensus and thus verifying transactions.

Open banking: A regulatory mandate that forces financial services providers to open up their APIs to other licensed third parties such as banks, fintechs or techfins.

Oracles: Third-party data feeds that serve as interfaces between the blockchain and data off-chain. In smart contracts oracles usually trigger the on-chain execution logic.

PBoC: The People's Bank of China (i.e. the central bank).

Permissioned vs permissionless: *See* Centralization

Productivity paradox: The phenomenon that novel technologies take a long time until they become more productive and profitable than their predecessors.

Project Hamilton: A centralized blockchain system conceived by the Boston Fed and the MIT's Digital Currency Initiative which is designed to handle up to 1.7 million transactions per second.

Project Stella: Joint project of the Bank of Japan and the ECB. This CBDC proof of concept should also serve as the basis for a digital euro, which is supposed to launch by the mid-2020s.

PSD2: The EU's second Payment Services Directive is a seminal legislative and regulatory foundation for open banking. Most notably it tries to level the playing field between financial services providers by forcing them to open up their APIs to competitors.

Reserve currency: Also referred to as anchor currency, the reserve currency is a foreign currency held by central banks and major financial institutions in large amounts to be used in international trade and transactions. Since the second half of the 20th century the US dollar is the world's unchallenged number one reserve currency.

Smart contracts: Algorithmically defined if-then scenarios on the blockchain. Smart contracts allow for on-chain transactions to be automatized. Not every blockchain is smart contract-ready. The concept was pioneered by Nick Szabo and popularized in the crypto-community by Ethereum.

Stablecoins: Unlike cryptocurrencies stablecoins are digital assets with a value pegged to a stable asset. In most cases the value is linked to fiat currencies or cryptocurrencies, but the value can be pegged to any stable asset like gold or oil, or even to a basket of stable assets.

Super apps: Powerful one-stop-shop smartphone apps that build an entirely new platform on top of mobile operating systems. Users can manage their finances, shop, book restaurants and much more without ever leaving the app. Super apps are dominant in Asia and de facto non-existent in the West.

Super money engine: A powerful hub that can handle all types of on- and off-chain assets, execute smart contracts and run complex decentralized apps. It merges a powerful asset capability (including fiat currencies, cryptocurrencies, CBDCs, private stablecoins and NFTs) with powerful execution capability (including traditional finance transactions, smart contracts, DApps and DeFi).

Synthetic CBDC (or sCBDC): This specific form of CBDC is a public-private partnership in which the central bank provides the trust, while private actors take care of innovation, technology and customer management.

Techfin: Term invented by Jack Ma to describe the entry of Big Tech into finance. While fintech uses technology to improve finance, techfin uses finance to improve technology. Techfin's underlying business models are platform improvement and data collection, not fees and interest payments.

Technical debt: Term coined by Ward Cunningham in 1992, describing how companies creating their first code accept its imperfections in return for a speedy market entry. Just like financial debt, it enables rapid growth in the beginning, but slows down the debtor later when interest accrues. If ignored, it leads to bankruptcy.

Technological debt: Broader than technical debt, as it refers to outdated and imperfect systems in general, not solely to software code.

Technology stack: Technology or tech stack refers to all technology components needed to run one application. The DeFi stack is a specific tech stack that includes multiple levels (e.g. infrastructure, assets) needed for decentralized finance application.

Telegram: An instant messaging service founded in 2013 with a distinct focus on privacy and independence from governments. Telegram became the de facto messaging channel for the crypto community.

Tier-two tech: Impressive tech companies with a market valuation north of $20 billion and sometimes even north of $100 billion. Tier-two tech includes all big tech companies except the five juggernauts collectively referred to as Big Tech.

Tokens: Tradable assets whose ownership transfer is recorded on a blockchain.

Tragedy of the Commons: Concept described by the ecologist Garrett Hardin in 1968 claiming that shared resources will ultimately become exhausted if they are unregulated. Individuals seek to maximize their own benefits, even if it is to the detriment of the common good. Hardin's thesis justifies the role of external governance in regulating scarce resources constituting a public good. Today *commons* also refers to technical infrastructure such as blockchain.

TVL: Stands for the total value locked in a DeFi application or the DeFi space in total. To calculate the TVL you multiply the number of tokens in a protocol with the token's value.

Utility tokens: *See* Ecosystem token

Wallet: Piece of software that allows users to manage specific assets recorded on the blockchain. There are custodial and non-custodial wallets. In the former a third party manages the private keys to the assets; in the latter the control lies solely with the user.

Web2: Denotes the second generation of the internet, which is characterized by centralization, in particular in Big Tech's cloud computing centres. Web2 is often linked to walled gardens and a lack of interoperability. It is a possible infrastructure for metaverses, yet those metaverses will have the characteristics of games, not digital economies.

Web3: Denotes the third generation of the internet, which is characterized by decentralization and distribution. Web3 is built on blockchain technology and allows for the ownership and economic exploitation of assets, identity and data.

Whales: Investors that own more than 1 per cent of the circulating supply of a crypto-coin.

Yield aggregator platform: A DeFi protocol that autonomously decides into which crypto-staking opportunities to invest a user's assets. Yields can also be automatically re-invested.

INDEX